BxT 22.00

1911 OHIO DOMINICAN COLLEGE

IN MEMORY OF

LIBRARY

1216 SUNBURY RD.
COLUMBUS, OHIO

SR. RACHEL HOOPER, O.S.F.

PEIRCE'S PHILOSOPHY
OF RELIGION

Peirce Studies
Number 5

Kenneth Laine Ketner, general editor
Institute for Studies in Pragmaticism
Texas Tech University
Lubbock, Texas

PEIRCE'S PHILOSOPHY OF RELIGION

MICHAEL L. RAPOSA

INDIANA UNIVERSITY PRESS
Bloomington and Indianapolis

Manufactured in the United States of America

Library of Congress Cataloging-in-Publication Data
Raposa, Michael L.
Peirce's philosophy of religion.
(Peirce studies; no. 5)
Bibliography: p.
Includes index.
1. Peirce, Charles S. (Charles Sanders), 1839–1914—
Contributions in philosophy of religion. 2. Religion—
Philosophy—History. I. Title. II. Series.
B945.P44R36 1989   200'.1   88–46016
ISBN 0–253–34833–1

1 2 3 4 5 93 92 91 90 89

CONTENTS

For Mary Ellen

PREFACE

The first time I presented my interpretation of Peirce's Neglected Argument in a public lecture, a member of the audience, a prominent American philosophical theologian whose previous encounters with me had always been cordial, remarked that it was the sort of argument (Peirce's, but by the law of association, I suppose, my own as well) that he had always suspected *ought* to remain neglected. The purpose of this book is to refute that remark. Whether or not I succeed in convincing the reader, I am confident that the remark, indeed, is false. It is not wise to neglect anything that Peirce had to say, some scholars would argue, *even* when he was talking about religion; I suggest that Peirce should be ignored *least of all* in those instances. His religious ideas should receive serious attention not only because they have typically been most neglected but also because they are so firmly embedded in the foundations of his thought.

Peirce, both by choice and through circumstance, lived and worked in the partial seclusion of the Pocono Mountains for more than twenty years before his death in 1914. In contrast, I have had the good fortune, while writing this book, to have been surrounded and supported constantly by family, friends, colleagues, and mentors. I am grateful to all of these individuals, too numerous to mention here. Several of them have played an especially important role in the development of this project.

Stephen Dunning, Vincent Potter, and James Ross all reviewed my manuscript at various stages in its evolution, raising insightful questions, supplying dozens of suggestions for improvement. I suspect that this book could be better than it is had I acted on more of those suggestions; but because I pursued many of them, I know that the analysis here has been much improved.

Kenneth Ketner has served as editor, adviser, and critic for this project. I am especially grateful for his patience and for the thoughtfulness and vigor of his arguments.

I have learned more about Peirce's thought from Murray Murphey than from anyone else. Nor could I have had a better teacher; his own commentaries on Peirce's philosophy are the finest that have been produced. His careful readings of my manuscript over the last several years have generated sound criticism, much insight, good sense.

My children, Daniel and Elizabeth, demonstrated very little interest in this book, consistently distracted me from the writing of it, and so helped me to maintain some perspective on it (while filling my life with an unspeakable joy).

To my wife, Mary Ellen, who has sustained, encouraged, advised, and endured me throughout the entire process, I gratefully, lovingly dedicate this book.

A NOTE ON REFERENCES

Full references to works by authors other than Peirce are supplied in the notes at the end of the text. A bibliography is included also.

It will be necessary to refer to a number of different sources for Peirce's published and unpublished writings. These are identified below, along with abbreviations to refer to these writings parenthetically. Where quotations appear in the text without such citation, it is usually because the same word or phrase has been already identified a number of times.

CP   *Collected Papers of Charles Sanders Peirce,* ed. C. Hartshorne, P. Weiss, and A. Burks (Cambridge: Harvard University Press, 1935, 1958). References by volume and paragraph number: read "*CP* 5.119" as volume 5, paragraph 119.

MS   *The Charles S. Peirce Papers* microfilm edition (Harvard University Library, Photographic Service, 1966). References employ the numbering system for manuscripts (*MS#*) developed by R. S. Robin in his *Annotated Catalogue of the Papers of Charles S. Peirce* (Amherst: University of Massachusetts Press, 1967), as supplemented by Robin in "The Peirce Papers: A Supplementary Catalogue," *Transactions of the Charles S. Peirce Society* 7 (1971): 37–57. "MS 325:3" indicates Robin's catalogue manuscript number 325, page 3.

W   *Writings of Charles S. Peirce: A Chronological Edition,* ed. M. Fisch et al., three volumes now completed (Bloomington: Indiana University Press, 1982–). References are abbreviated as "*W*" followed by volume and page numbers.

NEM   *The New Elements of Mathematics,* ed. C. Eisele, four volumes in five (The Hague: Mouton, 1976). References are abbreviated as "*NEM*" followed by volume and page numbers.

HP   *Historical Perspectives on Peirce's Logic of Science,* ed. C. Eisele, two volumes (The Hague: Mouton, 1985). References are abbreviated as "*HP*" followed by volume and page numbers.

N   *Charles S. Peirce: Contributions to* The Nation, ed. K.L. Ketner and J.E. Cook, three volumes plus index volume (Lubbock: Texas Tech University Press, 1975–79). References are abbreviated as "*N*" followed by volume and page numbers.

PW   *Semiotic and Significs: The Correspondence between Charles S. Peirce and Victoria Lady Welby,* ed. C. Hardwick (Bloomington: Indiana University

Press, 1977). References are abbreviated as "*PW*" followed by page numbers.

Peirce's Philosophy
of Religion

INTRODUCTION

Published in 1908, only six years before his death, Peirce's essay "A Neglected Argument for the Reality of God" (*CP* 6.452–91) represents both the maturest form of his thought and one of the very few extended treatments of a religious topic produced by him during a lifetime of philosophizing. In it, he argued that a vague belief in God is instinctive, the natural result of free meditation upon the nature of the universe. Peirce suggested that the idea of God is virtually irresistible when it genuinely arises out of such meditation; once affirmed, it operates within the consciousness of the believer as a powerful ideal of thought and conduct. He proceeded to delineate the "logic" of these claims, linking such a method of acquiring belief to a general theory of inquiry.

Peirce described this essay as the "poor sketch" of an argument; he intended it to function as a "table of contents" for a complete account of religion, on the basis of which others might be able to "guess" what he had to say. I propose to fill in some of the details of that sketch, to suggest the sort of text that Peirce might have written, given the table of contents that he provided. This project requires some "guesswork," but those guesses are both educated ones and fewer in number than one might expect. This is the case because, as I attempt to illustrate, Peirce's reflections on religious topics are continuous with, even integral to, his work in semiotic, metaphysics, and the normative sciences; consequently, Peirce himself, in other writings, supplied much of the "text" for the Neglected Argument.

One of the goals of this project, then, is to refute the claim of the editors of Peirce's *Collected Papers* that his religious writings have "rather tenuous connections with the rest of the system" and are primarily of "sociological or biographical" rather than of "a fundamental systematic interest."[1] Indeed, I contend that Peirce succeeded in sketching much more than a narrowly-conceived argument for God's reality. Filling in the details of his outline necessarily involves reconstructing his entire philosophy of religion. In the process of executing that task, not only Peirce's conception of God but also his perspective on such issues as the problem of evil, religion and science, miracles, immortality, human freedom, the Christian Church, religious language, and the religious character of esthetic experience will be explored and illustrated.

Among philosophers, interest in Peirce's thought has increased continuously during the last several decades. More recently, literary and communications specialists have become enthusiastic about Peirce's highly innovative theory of signification. Consequently, his contributions in such areas as logic, semiotic, and the philosophy of science are now well-recognized and often discussed. Nonetheless, relatively little attention has been paid to Peirce's religious thought, nor have his writings exercised any considerable influence over theologians or scholars working in the field of religious studies.[2] In part, this is because Peirce's writings on explicitly religious topics are scattered and few in number, especially when compared with his tremendous output in other areas. Their number, however, is by no means an index of their significance. Furthermore, Peirce's philosophy as a whole seems to have been shaped and informed by certain religious beliefs and ideas; his philosophy will be vulnerable to misinterpretation, then, until these ideas have been rendered explicit, their function and importance ascertained.

Those few scholars who have dealt with Peirce as a religious thinker have tended to focus on a specific aspect of his philosophy, such as his idea of God, or to treat the Neglected Argument in isolation from the vast but enormously valuable body of material that must be placed under consideration if that argument is to be rendered fully accessible. The results have yielded some key insights but also produced some unbalanced interpretations of Peirce's religious thought.[3] My purpose here is to give a systematic account of his philosophy of religion. I attend to the historical figures and factors that shaped Peirce's thinking only insofar as it is crucial for achieving basic exegetical goals. Moreover, my assessment of the contemporary relevance of Peirce's thought is largely confined to some brief remarks appearing in the conclusion. The Neglected Argument supplies much of the agenda for this project, but the direct explication and interpretation of that essay represents only the culmination of my task. The main body of this work consists of five chapters, pursuing five separate but intimately related lines of inquiry.

The relationship between religion and science from Peirce's point of view is the focus of chapter one. I begin by briefly characterizing his basic religious perspective and concerns. This involves an analysis of Peirce's prescription for "a religion of science," including his portrayal of the scientific community as a model for the Christian Church. Next, I explore his indebtedness to Duns Scotus and medieval thought; Peirce's contention that the spirit of scholastic realism is identical with the spirit of modern science should be interpreted as a theologically significant claim. The chapter concludes with some remarks concerning Peirce's treatment of the topic of miracles, especially his response to the Humean critique of miracles.

The second chapter underscores the religious character and significance of Peirce's objective idealism. It begins with a brief review of his defense of that doctrine and then presents his formulation of the "law of mind." At this point, it becomes appropriate to examine Peirce's "synechism," his mathematical and metaphysical reflections on the concept of continuity. It is also important to determine the extent to which his claims about the "Absolute Mind" can be properly construed as "God-talk." Such a determination presupposes some understanding of Peirce's development of the logic of vagueness and of his defense of anthropomorphic religious language.

The discussion turns next to Peirce's evolutionary cosmology. The laws that govern the growth of mind, he argued, are the same principles that the scientist discovers to be operative in natural evolutionary processes. Significantly, he believed that these principles could be articulated in religious terms. Furthermore, understanding the "logic" of evolution is a prerequisite for dealing with the problem of evil. This third chapter unravels some of the basic themes of Peirce's social ethic. Here, a central task is to provide a careful interpretation of his essay on "Evolutionary Love" (*CP* 6.287–317).

Both that essay and the Neglected Argument become fully intelligible, however, only when perceived against the background of Peirce's inquiries in the normative sciences, particularly his discussion of esthetics. Chapter four pursues his analysis of esthetic values and experience. Peirce's claims about the nature of inquiry, the role played by doubt and belief in that process, and the instinctiveness of certain beliefs are considered. His emphasis on the primacy of esthetics among the normative sciences is assessed, along with the implications of his identification of the *summum bonum* as a religious ideal. This discussion sheds light on what Peirce had to say not only about human values but also about immortality and the freedom of the will.

Drawing on the cumulative results of the preceding investigations, I then attempt to fill out Peirce's "poor sketch." Chapter five supplies some general comments about Peirce's theory of signs in order to facilitate the explication of his vision of the world as God's "argument," God's "great poem." These preliminary reflections will lend substance to my contention that the Neglected Argument is itself an exercise in "theological semiotic," a label that I attach to Peirce's distinctive theological method and theory of religious knowledge.[4] This chapter embodies a detailed analysis of "Musement," the central concept in the argument for God's reality. I consider that concept in relation to (1) Schiller's *Spieltrieb*, (2) Peirce's phenomenology and idealistic cosmology, (3) the theory of abduction, (4) Peirce's semiotic, and (5) his remarks about the nature and purpose of prayer. Such considerations serve to clarify the role that this notion is designed to play in Peirce's argument while underscoring the continuity of that argument with virtually all that he wrote and thought.

A brief concluding chapter summarizes my observations about the relationship between Peirce's religious ideas and his treatment of other topics. It also argues that some of these ideas might constitute an important resource that can be brought to bear on various problems in the philosophy of religion, especially the problem of religious knowledge.

The apparent diversity of Peirce's writings belies their essential unity, the architectonic, even organic quality of his philosophy. This represents, for Peirce's readers, a significant challenge. In interpreting one aspect of his thought, it sometimes becomes necessary to invoke certain principles and notions articulated at various other points in his system. In fact, interpreters of Peirce must deal with their subject's own willingness, even eagerness, to connect the most disparate of arguments and ideas. Peirce's religious insights can and do appear anywhere, in mathematical and scientific papers as well as in his strictly philosophical writings. This is partially because he "thought with his pen," but he also discovered important relations where others have perceived only discontinuity. It is not surprising, then, that the argument for God's reality embodies some of Peirce's most interesting comments about the logic of inquiry; nor is this irrelevant to the project of determining whether or not that argument fulfills the purpose for which it was designed.

Consequently, one who chooses to write about Peirce is confronted immediately with certain organizational difficulties. The discussion embedded in any given chapter, in order to be fully intelligible, presupposes all of the rest. Some concepts early on introduced rather vaguely later receive a fuller explication. Certain notions, usually those with which Peirce scholars will be already familiar, are not fully explicated here. To have done so would have necessitated writing not one but many volumes.

In a sense, Peirce's religious ideas are less adequately conceived as constituting a part of his thought than as supplying an illuminating perspective on the whole of it. Indeed, they are among those guiding purposes by means of which "the whole calls out its parts."[5] I do not pretend to offer a comprehensive interpretation of the nature and development of Peirce's philosophy; nonetheless, as I have already suggested, the explication of his religious ideas has broad implications for Peirce scholarship in general. I am also convinced that these ideas are of enormous relevance to contemporary discussions in the philosophy of religion. Admittedly, the drawing out of those implications and the demonstration of that sort of relevance are projects that can only be initiated here. If my portrayal of Peirce as a religious thinker is clear and convincing however, I am confident that it will facilitate our understanding not only of his philosophy but also of its enduring significance.

I

SCIENTIFIC THEISM

I

Charles Peirce was both his father's son and the intellectual child of his age. Despite his enormous creative energy and the startling originality of much of what he wrote, Peirce's thought was profoundly shaped by his complex inheritance. Nowhere is this fact more clearly evidenced than in the exploration of Peirce's religious ideas, where both his general perspective and basic concerns reveal, upon examination, their special genealogy.

While Charles did not inherit Benjamin Peirce's Unitarian convictions, he did acquire his father's perception of the natural world as the manifestation of a divine ideality. When he described the universe in a 1903 lecture as a "symbol of God's purpose," God's "great poem" (*CP*5.119), Charles echoed Benjamin's sentiments articulated several decades earlier. The latter claimed that

> the universe is a book written for man's reading. If it were destitute of strict logical connection, it would fail of its purpose and be unintelligible. The luminous order of the pages and the successive introduction of strange and new truths are marvelously adapted to the development and expansion of the created intellect. It is a glorious manifestation of the all-pervading affection and the fostering care of divine wisdom.[1]

Noteworthy here is the contention that the "book of nature" is one that the human mind is especially equipped to read and interpret. The divine ideas are not shrouded in mystical darkness; rather, they are incarnate in the various laws and principles that govern natural processes. The elder Peirce was radiantly optimistic about the accessibility of the divine wisdom.

> There is everywhere in Nature a voice audible to human ears, and a speech intelligible to human understanding. It is the truth of science, the beauty of poetry, the logic of philosophy, and the faith of religion. Ignorance cannot hide it, nor deformity degrade it, nor superstition corrupt it, nor skepticism conceal it. It vibrates in every soul.[2]

Such a world-view supplies the background against which Benjamin Peirce's depiction of scientific inquiry as a religious vocation becomes comprehensible. It is the scientist, after all, whose special task involves the discovery of the intrinsic intelligibility of natural phenomena. This intelligibility is grounded in the laws that govern natural objects and events; it transcends the "subjective ideality" that is frequently attributed to nature as the result of "human fancy"[3] and bears witness to the effective presence of a Divine Mind, with whom the scientist, if not blinded by "irreverence," is actively able to commune. Guided by Christian revelation and thus affirming God as Creator of the world, such a scientist is able to avoid "an impoverished and powerless pantheism" while coming to recognize in the process of inquiry that "the observed ideality is the divine thought, and the book of Nature is the divine record."[4]

It was in much this same spirit that Charles later defined the purpose of theoretical science as "simply and solely the knowledge of God's truth" (*CP* 1.239; see also *MS* 325:3). Even as a young man, he attached a special religious significance to the investigations of the scientist; for example, in his 1863 Cambridge High School reunion lecture, he prophesied that "God's wisdom and mercy" as revealed in nature, now "poetically divined shall be scientifically known" (*W* 1:114). It is clear that neither Benjamin nor Charles intended such remarks to function as unqualified descriptions of modern scientific work or of the spirit with which it is imbued; rather, they both reacted against the narrow and mechanical necessitarianism that they perceived to be a dominant force shaping such work. In doing so they prescribed a scientific world-view predicated on the notion that the universe displays all of the essential characteristics of a living mind.

Some of the seeds of Charles Peirce's mature, full-blown objective idealism can already be detected, then, in his father's lectures on the philosophy of science. Similarly, other themes and perspectives that would emerge and take shape in the former's life-long speculations can be traced back to certain elements in Benjamin's thought. This is not to suggest that all of these notions originated with the elder Peirce; they were ingredients of the intellectual environment that nurtured both father and son. Clearly, however, the relationship between the two was an especially powerful one, and it was rooted in and sustained by an ongoing intellectual conversation that had a profound impact on Charles as a boy and young man, regardless of the extent to which he was later to develop and transform, or altogether abandon, his father's arguments and ideas.

To be sure, Charles's metaphysical idealism must be carefully distinguished from his father's dualistic theory of the world as a pre-established harmony of matter and mind;[5] nonetheless, the latter's emphasis on the mind-like quality of the physical universe clearly supplied a creative impetus for his son's

reflections. Likewise, the nebular theory that Benjamin defended and explicated in theological terms can quite reasonably be construed as the forerunner
of Charles's own evolutionary cosmology.[6] This theory "embraces a complete
ideal history of the inorganic world," tracing its evolution from a monotonous
void to the "unity of complete organization." Here, evolution is described as
the "mode" in which God is present in the world and as "the manifestation of
his paternity."[7] In the course of Benjamin's lectures, there are even remarks
that appear to anticipate his son's theory of "agapism" or evolutionary love[8]
(although Henry James, Sr.'s *Substance and Shadow* probably exercised a more
direct influence on Charles in this regard). Furthermore, the notion that the
real nature of this evolving universe is one that the human mind is especially
adapted to comprehend emerges again, albeit significantly developed, in
Charles's theory of instinctive beliefs. Finally, Benjamin asserted that God's
"dwelling is not where the law of continuity is broken" and that the Deity's
"universal plan is apparent to every mind which yields itself to logical induction,"[9] contentions that, however vaguely, resonate with Charles's later
"synechism."

Even if these lines of influence between father and son can be traced with
some confidence, they illustrate only one aspect of the latter's intellectual
heritage. For if he shared with his father a perspective that imbued scientific
inquiry with a special religious significance, Charles nevertheless lived and
wrote at a time when the relationship between science and theology had
become severely strained; for some, irreconcilably so.[10] The factors that
produced this intellectual state of affairs are sufficiently complex that their
explication here is not possible. But clearly the publication of Darwin's *Origin
of Species* in 1859 was the crucial event in an historical development that
supplied part of the background and context for Peirce's scientific theism.

Following in the wake of the disturbances created by the German "higher
criticism" and by Hume's critique both of miracles and of the philosophical
arguments for God's existence, Darwin's work precipitated a severe religious
crisis (one that was clearly not confined to the theological intelligentsia).[11] In
the first place, it threatened to undermine the orthodox theological anthro-
pology, the Christian view of human beings. The continuity between human
and other animal species, characteristic of the Darwinian scheme, seemed to
conflict sharply with the Judaeo-Christian notion of persons as a special creation, given dominion by God over other living things. Furthermore, the chaotic
and violent picture implicit in Darwin's theory of evolution, designed around
his two principles of fortuitous variation and natural selection, was not congenial to a religious mind-set nurtured by the orderly principles of Newtonian
physics. What sort of Deity would create the kind of world that Darwin
described?

Peirce was obviously sensitive to the conflict between religion and science that the Darwinian controversy both exhibited and helped to engender. And he did not try to explain away the difficulty or simply deny its reality. Indeed, it is a conflict that he, as a man of science with deep religious convictions, clearly experienced personally. In fact, Peirce responded positively and creatively to Darwin's theory in a manner that is of no small theological interest. The principle of fortuitous variation, interpreted in the light of Peirce's category of Firstness, became one of the shaping influences on his "tychism" or doctrine of objective chance. This doctrine, although balanced by other perspectives, is a fundamental ingredient of his cosmology. On the other hand, Peirce rejected the primacy of natural selection (the "gospel of greed") in favor of his agapistic theory of evolution, for reasons that might at first seem to be more precisely religious (and specifically Christian) than scientific (*CP* 6.295).[12] Peirce's religious and scientific concerns cannot be neatly separated from one another, however. He was fully aware of the problematic nature of the relationship between them; but, in general, he construed that relationship in such a fashion that the essence or "spirit" of religion and that of science are not in opposition.[13] Existing tensions and apparent conflicts are the symptoms not of a fundamental incommensurability but of various human frailties, prejudices, and misconceptions.

For example, he explained how a difficulty arises when science is rooted in a false philosophy, with scientists relying upon erroneous and excessively narrow premises or methods in conducting their inquiries (see *CP* 6.553ff.; also *MS* 865:1 and *MS* 866:1ff.). More frequently, however, Peirce's critique was directed against religious institutions, not against the faith that sustains or ought to sustain them but against the political concerns and tactics of clergymen and theologians (*CP* 6.3; see also *MS* 865). Looking consistently to the past, and frightened by the unsettling effects of scientific innovation, such individuals formulated creeds with the sole purpose of "cutting somebody off from the Church." Peirce was not attacking creedal affirmations per se, but rather those so narrowly formulated that they precluded genuine community by excluding certain individuals for mistaken and trivial reasons. In fact, he argued, the post-Darwinian "agnostics," by opposing with their "economics" the "principle of love," may yet make necessary the defense of *this* principle in a creed, resulting in "a great spiritualization of religion" (*MS* 865).

It is this sort of "narrowness," among both scientists and religious persons, that seems in general to constitute Peirce's basic object of concern. By contrast, in his own definitions of science and religion, he struggled to avoid any notion that might restrict or prematurely circumscribe the domain of each. Science is not so much a body of "systematized knowledge" as it is a *method* of inquiry.

But since even that method is the *product* of inquiry, the essence of science must be identified with that "spirit, which is determined not to rest with existing opinions, but to press on to the real truth of nature" (*CP* 6.428).

> And what is religion? In each individual it is a sort of sentiment, or obscure perception, a deep recognition of something in the circumambient All, which, if he strives to express it, will clothe itself in forms more or less extravagant, more or less accidental, but ever acknowledging the first and the last, the A and Ω, as well as a relation to that Absolute of the individual's self, as a relative being. But religion cannot reside in its totality in a single individual. Like every species of reality, it is essentially a social, a public affair. It is the idea of a whole Church, welding all its members together in one organic, systemic perception of the Glory of the Highest—an idea having a growth from generation to generation and claiming a supremacy in the determination of all conduct, private and public. (*CP* 6.429)

This statement embodies a number of interesting claims. First, Peirce argued that religion is a matter of "sentiment" or "perception," hinting at the role that instinct plays in the religious life, and anticipating the experiential starting-point that he adopted in his Neglected Argument. Second, he identified religion with an *idea* and with the *growth* of that idea, not thereby from his perspective reducing it to something abstract and lifeless but rather affirming the power that it is able to exercise over the lives of men and women. For Peirce clearly regarded ideas less as the product of human intellection than as the most significant feature of the environment within which persons "live and move and have their being" (see *MS* 439). Finally, Peirce here emphasized the importance of a church, a move that on first inspection might surprise readers, given Peirce's frequent attacks on the institutional aspects of religion, its timid clergymen and theologians, and its rigid and negatively motivated creeds. If one focused exclusively on such remarks, one might have expected a more romantic vision of a "church-less" faith. Peirce did not identify a historically specific or actual church in the passage above, however. He was himself an Episcopalian with a rather loose affiliation with that community,[14] and he clearly perceived in the Christian faith the essential ingredients for the development of an ideal community. Nonetheless, it seems safest to regard the "church" that he refers to here as precisely that, an ideal that must be nurtured and gradually actualized.

> Man's highest developments are social; and religion, though it begins in a seminal, individual inspiration, only comes to full flower in a great church coextensive with a civilization. This is true of every religion, but supereminently so of the religion of love. Its ideal is that the whole world shall be united in the bond of a common love of God accomplished by each man's loving his neighbor.

> Without a church, the religion of love can have but a rudimentary existence; and
> a narrow, little exclusive church is almost worse than none. A great catholic
> church is wanted. (*CP* 6.443)

Within the broad context of Peirce's thought as a whole, such assertions make
perfect sense. His "synechistic" emphasis on the real connectedness of all
things could by itself have led him to adopt this sort of perspective. But Peirce
did not expound on this ideal of a genuine community only in his religious
writings. At least for a significant portion of his philosophical career, Peirce
defined "Truth" as that which the scientific *community of inquirers* will discover
to be the case "in the long run."[15] In the discussion below of Peirce's admira-
tion for the scholastics, this emphasis on the importance of collaboration and
intersubjectivity as essential ingredients of the scientific method will again be
noted. One might easily suspect, then, that Peirce's religious ideal of "a great
catholic church" was influenced by those of his experiences as a scientist that
reinforced the necessity of cooperative effort in research, experiences that
shaped his understanding of the nature of truth. Against the background of
the sketch that is being supplied here of Peirce's scientific theism, one might
even be inclined to conflate or identify the two communities; in their commitment to the truth, to the whole of reality, scientists and genuinely religious
persons could be understood as perfectly united.

There is ample evidence to support such a correlation. For example, in his
correspondence with Lady Welby, Peirce explicitly identified the "man of
science" as one who truly has "Faith in God" (*PW* 75). Elsewhere, he claimed
that "the *raison d'être* of a church is to confer upon men a life broader than
their narrow personalities, a life rooted in the very truth of being. To do that
it must be based upon and refer to a definite and public experience" (*CP* 6.451).
Without the alteration of any significant details, this statement could function
for Peirce as a definition of the scientific community. Of course, such a claim
does not constitute a description of what actually obtains; it is a prescription
for an ideal state of affairs, a "religion of science." Here it must be admitted
that, from Peirce's point of view, the religious community, the Christian
Church, would need to undergo a most dramatic transformation in order for
such a state of affairs to be realized. Most important, the members of that
community would have to abandon the notion that science represents for the
religious believer a rival system of truths, grounded not in divine revelation but
in the puny resources of the created intellect, and thus best ignored or, perhaps,
refuted. For Peirce's prescription is based on the presupposition that the truth
is *one*, a fact that he felt the wise man of faith clearly will be able to perceive.

> While adhering to the essence of religion, and so far as possible to the church,
> which is all but essential, say, penessential to it, he will cast aside the religious

timidity that is forever prompting the church to recoil from the paths into which the Governor of history is leading the minds of men, a cowardice that has stood through the ages as the landmark and limit of her little faith, and will gladly go forward, sure that truth is not split into two warring doctrines, and that any change that knowledge can work in his faith can only affect its expressions, but not the deep mystery expressed. (*CP* 6.432)

This point of view is noteworthy in several respects. In the first place, it underscores the observation, already recorded, that Peirce shared his father's confidence in the ability of human reason, if properly exercised, to acquire religious knowledge. For both men, such knowledge does not represent a result achieved independently of the effects of revelation; rather, that revelation is perceived as an ongoing process, the divine ideas being embedded in a "text" that is continuously being written, and one that the community of interpreters can only gradually decipher. Nevertheless, it will become clear that Peirce was not altogether sanguine about the extent to which, in the foreseeable future, this process would result in any clear understanding of God's nature and purposes. We can hope for a "glimpse" of those purposes; but Peirce's optimism, remarkable in itself, seems subdued when compared, for example, to Hegelian assertions about the attainability of "absolute knowledge."

A second observation concerns the general nature of the role played by Peirce's religious ideas in his thinking. Clearly those ideas had a shaping influence not only on his conception of science but also, as will be illustrated here, on his metaphysics, his cosmology, and his theory of value. But the influence was mutual, and Peirce's religious ideas were transformed by his commitments and discoveries in other areas. He was of course genuinely interested in scientific developments as such, whatever their religious implications. Furthermore, he thought it altogether reasonable that certain religious beliefs should be revised or even discarded as a result of new scientific discoveries (*CP* 6.216). Benjamin Peirce worked and wrote within the framework supplied by Unitarianism throughout his life, but Charles's religious perspective is more difficult to label. He clung to "the essence of religion," to its "deep mystery," but not to any particular expression or articulation of it, while also adhering "so far as possible to the church." At the same time, his perspective was informed by and adapted to his ideals as a scientist. Thus he sought to develop and to advocate for persons of faith a distinctive vision and set of attitudes, rooted in his double optimism that "God's truth" is one and that it is indeed accessible to a community of open and inquiring minds.

Such a state of mind may properly be called a religion of science. . . . It is a religion, so true to itself, that it becomes animated by the scientific spirit, confident that all the conquests of science will be triumphs of its own, and accepting all the results of science as scientific men themselves accept them, as steps toward the truth, which may for a time appear to be in conflict with other truths, but which in such cases merely await adjustments which time is sure to effect. (*CP* 6.433)

This was the sort of strategy, then, that Peirce pursued in responding to the crisis that Darwin, Hume, and the German critics, among others, had engendered. But this sketch of Peirce's general perspective and of his immediate intellectual milieu is painfully inadequate, and it is not rendered less so by the awareness that he was a devoted historian of ideas who drew upon resources far removed from his own day and age in constructing his philosophical system. The scholastic realists, Duns Scotus in particular, supplied Peirce with some of the most important of these resources, and it is Peirce's commitment to realism that sustains both Peirce's philosophy of science and his theism while establishing a link between them. It is, of course, a well-recognized fact that Peirce was a realist because he contended that science and the scientific method demanded it. That his position on this issue might have been religiously motivated as well has been less clearly perceived.

II

Peirce was influenced by the scholastics in a variety of ways, some of them easy to detect and others probably still largely unappreciated. The extent to which, for example, Peirce's reading of medieval philosophy provided the first great creative impetus for the development of his logic has been well documented.[16] Here, the discussion must be focused on issues that will eventually prove to have a religious significance. In addition to (1) Peirce's defense of realism, these include (2) his appropriation of the Scotist notion of *haecceity*, (3) his reflections on final causality, (4) his employment of the argument that ideas can exist in the mind *habitualiter*, and (5) his theory of abstraction. All of these topics will be broached at this point, some of them to be developed more thoroughly in subsequent chapters.

The faithfulness with which Peirce represented certain medieval insights, especially those of Duns Scotus, is not at issue here.[17] Rather, the task is to isolate and interpret those elements in Peirce's thought for which he claimed an indebtedness to the scholastics, and then to assess the role that they played in supporting his conception of science. It will not be an entirely separate project to demonstrate the religious significance of these ideas since, as the sketch above of Peirce's world-view already indicates, his account of the nature and purpose of science can be translated into religious terms.

Whatever the precise nature of Peirce's indebtedness to Duns Scotus, he was obviously quite willing to admit to the fact of it. Furthermore, in doing so he clearly indicated the source of Scotism's attractiveness for him.

> The works of Duns Scotus have strongly influenced me. If his logic and metaphysics, not slavishly worshipped, but torn from its medievalism, be adapted to modern culture, under continual wholesome reminders of nominalistic criticisms, I am convinced that it will go far toward supplying the philosophy which is best to harmonize with physical science. But other conceptions have to be drawn from the history of science and from mathematics. (*CP* 1.6)

This statement is interesting, not least of all for the series of qualifications that it embodies. Scotism was adopted by Peirce as a generally valid position; but, he argued, it must be critically assessed, "updated," and blended with notions and perspectives drawn from other systems of thought. Some of the details of this process of appropriation will have to be spelled out here because they illuminate Peirce's basic concerns; first, more needs to be said in general terms about his positive appraisal of medieval thought.

Oddly enough, one of the characteristics that Peirce admired in the scholastics was their tendency to emphasize the significance of "authority"; in this respect, he suggested, they more closely resemble modern scientists than modern philosophers (*CP* 1.30–32). Peirce's praise here was carefully qualified, and he would never advocate appealing either exclusively or primarily to authority as a method for "fixing belief" (see *CP* 5.379–81). It is their attentiveness to the opinions of others, past and present, their eagerness to come to a "catholic agreement" on problematic issues, that links the scholastics with the modern scientist and distinguishes both from contemporary philosophers, who "have what seems an absurd disregard for others' opinions" (*CP* 1.32). The medieval devotion to authority is excessive by modern standards, but was appropriate for such a comparatively "uneducated" culture; and it contrasts favorably with the attitudes cultivated by those "intellectual monads" on the contemporary scene who develop metaphysical systems like so many new fashions (*CP* 1.32). Here again is an indication of the prominent role that the concept of community plays both in Peirce's philosophy of science and in his religious thinking.

The medieval scholastic and the modern scientist share in addition a disdain for grandiose theorizing and a passion for thoroughness, for painstaking attention to the details of inquiry (*CP* 1.33). Of course, there was nothing modest about Peirce's own theoretical ambitions; but the contention here is that all theoretical assertions must be empirically grounded and testable. This is a plea for the exercise of scientific method in philosophy and not a condemnation of theory as such. It is the tirelessness with which the schoolmen sought to test general propositions that further links them, in "spirit," with the scientist (*CP* 1.34); whatever the limitations of their technique, theirs was truly a "laboratory consciousness."

In contrast, from the nominalistic point of view the whole project of scientific explanation is rendered meaningless. This perspective reduces general propositions or laws to descriptions of regularities; prediction and verification are precluded here by the nominalistic explanations that "merely restate the fact to be explained under another aspect" or "add only something from which no definite consequences can be deduced" (*CP* 6.273). The realist, on the other hand, affirms that universals or "general principles are really operative in nature" (*CP* 5.101). The task of the scientist is to formulate these principles as hypotheses, deduce their implications, and then test these against the actual results of observation and experiment. Consequently, Peirce's defense of scholasticism was grounded in his conviction "that science has always been at heart realistic and always must be so" (*CP* 1.20).

First and foremost, then, Peirce was attracted to the scholastic philosophers because of their realistic position on the issue of universals. Since modern science entails such a realistic perspective, Peirce contended, a modified scholasticism qualifies as the philosophy best suited for the contemporary world. Unfortunately, from his point of view, nominalism has dominated and pervaded Western thinking ever since the demise of the great medieval systems in the fourteenth century.[18] As a "wholesome" or purifying critique of scholastic realism, the nominalistic arguments might have had a certain valuable function (see *CP* 1.6, 4.35); the misfortune is that this perspective became so well entrenched that philosophers from Ockham to Kant and beyond have been caught in its strangle-hold (*CP* 1.17ff.). One might argue without exaggeration that the struggle to loosen that grip, to expose the fallacies inherent in nominalism and thus to defend the cause of logical realism, supplied Peirce's intellectual career with its fundamental purpose, its guiding rationale (at least from that point in time when he firmly embraced realism as the only tenable philosophical stance).

While labeling himself as both a Scotist and a scholastic realist, however, Peirce clearly found the medieval systems to be in need of serious repair. He regarded the scholastics as great allies in his battle for the cause of realism but at the same time complained that even Duns Scotus "inclines too much towards nominalism" (*CP* 1.560). More specifically, he argued that "Duns Scotus is too nominalistic when he says that universals are contracted to the mode of individuality in singulars, meaning, as he does, by singulars, ordinary existing things" (*CP* 8.208). In addition, Peirce distinguished his own perspective from the moderate position of Duns Scotus and others by referring to himself as an "extreme realist" (*CP* 5.77, 5.470).

It should be possible to illuminate Peirce's remarks by reading them against the background provided by F. E. Abbot's *Scientific Theism*, a work that Peirce both consistently praised and identified as articulating his own basic point of view (for example, *CP* 1.20, 4.1, 4.50, 5.423).[19] Abbot argued for a doctrine that he called both "Relationism" and "Scientific Realism." This doctrine "teaches that universals, or genera and species are . . . objective relations of resemblance among objectively existing things."[20] Furthermore, this principle of the "Objectivity of Relations" affirms that "the relations of things are absolutely inseparable from the things themselves."[21]

> It shows that Moderate Realism was right in upholding the objectivity of univer- sals, but wrong in making them inherent in individuals *as individuals* (in re) rather than in individuals *as groups* (inter res). Relations do not inhere in the related terms taken singly, but do inhere in all the terms taken collectively.[22]

These remarks about moderate realism resemble Peirce's criticism of Duns Scotus. Abbot also affirmed that the essence of a thing is "the only proper and real object of scientific cognition," a statement with which both Peirce and Duns Scotus would be in agreement. Abbot's treatment of essences does not appear to be typically "scholastic," however; rather, he felt that that tradition had to be appropriated creatively, its ideas "translated" into the language and the conceptual framework of nineteenth-century scientific inquiry.

> Translating the Moderate Realism of Aristotle into the more accurate language of Relationism, and not forgetting to correct its capital error of making the universal inhere in each individual as an individual (in re) rather than in all the individuals as a group (inter res), the meaning of his doctrine is that science is concerned with the general relations of things rather than with the things themselves—with general laws rather than with the peculiarities or accidents of individual objects.[23]

Whatever the precise source of Abbot's insights, Peirce's dissatisfaction with Duns Scotus's realism is, in many ways, a consequence of certain discoveries that he made concerning the logic of relatives.[24] Peirce came to conclude that the medieval position was basically sound, but that the scholastics were unable to develop their ideas in a satisfactory manner, essentially because their logical equipment was defective. For example, the medieval logicians were able to deal with propositions that involve monadic predicates (such as "—— is hard"), but not with those that involve relational predicates (such as "—— is a lover of——" or "—— gave —— to ——") (*CP* 3.464ff.). Consequently, they were able to talk about specific "classes" or "collections" of things, each class being comprised of all of the subjects bearing a particular monadic predicate. This also allowed them to say something about the relation of similarity (for example, the sharing of a "common nature") that exists between the members of a given class. Useful to a certain point, but for Peirce this type of logical analysis simply did not go far enough.

> The ordinary logic has a great deal to say about genera and species, or in our nineteenth century dialect, about classes. Now, a class is a set of objects comprising all that stand to one another in a particular relation of similarity. But where ordinary logic talks of classes the logic of relations talks of systems. A system is a set of objects comprising all that stand to one another in a group of connected relations. Induction according to ordinary logic rises from the contemplation of a sample of a class to that of the whole class; but according to the logic of relatives, it rises from the contemplation of the fragment of a system to the envisagement of a complete system. (*CP* 4.5)

The logic of relatives provides a means for analyzing relationships other than that of the resemblance of a certain object to the various members of its class. Peirce was much more interested in the way in which laws govern the interactions between objects within a meaningful process. The analysis of such a process or "system" involves the use of dyadic and triadic predicates. But Peirce seemed to have regarded monadic predicates as themselves being relatives of a degenerate sort, and he treated classes as being degenerate forms of systems (*CP* 3.454).[25] To claim, for example, that "*X* is hard" is to do more than simply ascribe a particular quality to *X*; rather, it is to affirm that under certain specifiable conditions *X* will tend to behave in a certain specifiable manner. "Hardness" is to be regarded then as a dispositional property, and a real "habit" or law must govern the behavior of those objects within which it inheres. If a monadic predicate did not represent a degenerate relative in this sense, then it would necessarily correspond to pure "Firstness," a simple quality or pure possibility that could be completely actualized in any individual reaction-event (that is, in any "Second"). In a universe manifesting only Firstness and Secondness, devoid of generality and thus of intelligibility, it might be appropriate to speak of such a non-relational monadic predicate. But there are, for Peirce, no "pure" Firsts or Seconds. Even when one is confronted with nothing more than the case of an individual object enduring through time, real *continuity* is involved and the properties that inhere in such an object are themselves "general" (*CP* 1.411ff., 1.427). Here, the relationship between a thing and its properties can only be defined by a real habit, a "would-be" operating within the actual world of objects and events.

It should be clear then that modern logical theory (much of it, of course, developed by Peirce himself) supplied Peirce with some of the most crucial elements of his metaphysics. He moves quickly and frequently from his study of relatives to the analysis of various types of generality. Once again, Peirce perceives the scholastic definition of generality—"Generale est quod natum aptum est dici de multis"—as standing in need of drastic revision (*CP* 5.102). Such a notion represents only "a very degenerate sort of generality" (*CP* 5.103).

> Take any two possible objects that might be called suns and, however much alike they may be, any multitude whatsoever of intermediate suns are alternatively possible, and therefore as before these intermediate possible suns transcend all multitude. In short, the idea of a general involves the idea of possible variations which no multitude of existing things could exhaust, but would leave between any two not merely many possibilities, but possibilities beyond all multitude. (*CP* 5.103)

Peirce's criticism of Duns Scotus begins now to come into sharper focus. Abbot's formula, "universalia inter res," is intended (at least from Peirce's perspective) to emphasize the fact that between any two actually existing members of a class or fragments of a system there is real continuity ("possibilities beyond all multitude"). By locating the contracted universal within singular existing things, Duns Scotus might be able to explain the type of generality that characterizes a collection of objects having some quality in common. Peirce contended, however, that in the process of doing so, the universal becomes correlated with the Firstness of pure qualitative possibility. Such qualities can be perfectly actualized or "exhausted" by their subjects precisely because they are "indifferent" to singularity or universality. (A quality is what it is regardless of anything else [*CP* 1.424–46]. Equinity is just equinity.[26]) According to Peirce, Scotus's analysis never moves beyond this extremely degenerate form of generality, and so it fails to account for an infinite number of real possibilities, that is, for the real and continuous relationship that exists between any two members of a class, between an object at any one instant and its successive actualizations in time, between the interacting fragments of a system.

The ability to characterize this last type of relationship was especially important for Peirce. "*X* gives *Y* to *Z*" is general not simply because the relational predicate ("—— gives —— to ——") can be applied to many different sets of ordered triads, but rather, because it ranges over the members of any given triad.[27] Here Peirce's concern is with a type of relationship that is very different from the "sameness" that defines the medieval genera and species. The interest in classes of givers, gifts, and recipients has been superseded by an interest in the *system* that encompasses the giver, the gift, and the recipient, and in the laws or habits of behavior that govern their interaction. In all types of relationships, however, even in relationships of resemblance, a real continuity exists between relata, and predicates must be universalized or "projected" in order to range over the infinite number of possibilities, actualized and unactualized, that make up the continuum.[28]

These features of Peirce's "adaptation" of Scotist realism will become increasingly relevant as the details of his doctrine of synechism and its relationship to his objective idealism are subsequently unfolded. At this point, it must be re-emphasized that, for Peirce, the laws or habits of behavior that define the relationships between natural objects and govern natural processes and events are real, and for his concept of "reality" Peirce was, by his own admission, clearly indebted to Duns Scotus.[29] The reality of such laws is a necessary presupposition of all scientific inquiry; that presupposition alone can effectively ground the validity of the inductively based predictions of the scientist. Furthermore, to observe that this concept of reality also figured prominently in Peirce's religious thinking (for example, in the Neglected Argument) is not to abandon the topic of his scientific realism but rather to establish a theological perspective on it.[30] For the very laws that the scientist is bound to affirm as real are the products of a divine mind, the living symbols of a divine purpose (*CP* 5.107). Consequently, nominalism must be regarded as undermining the basic principles not only of science but of theism as well.

> Although nominalism is not credited with any extraordinarily lofty appreciation of the powers of the human soul, yet it attributes to it a power of originating a kind of ideas the like of which Omnipotence has failed to create as real objects, and those general conceptions which men will never cease to consider the glory of the human intellect must, according to any consistent nominalism, be entirely wanting in the mind of Deity. Leibniz, the modern nominalist *par excellence*, will not admit that God has the faculty of reason; and it seems impossible to avoid that conclusion upon nominalistic principles. (*CP* 5.62)

It is the nominalist who, in Benjamin Peirce's terms, attributes to nature only a "subjective ideality," locating the exclusive source of all general conceptions in the human intellect. But for Charles, as for his father, the laws of nature are real and are really intelligible independently of what any human mind or collection of minds may conceive them to be. These laws can be regarded as "ideas" only because the universe itself is of the nature of a Mind, a vast representamen or argument "working out its conclusions in living realities" (*CP* 5.119). The nominalist, however, would make the human mind the author rather than the reader and interpreter of the "book of nature." Nominalistic principles render scientific inquiry farcical, Peirce contended, by dissolving the reality of those general laws that it is the task of the scientist to *discover*. If the world's generality, its intelligibility, is solely the product of human intellection, then the fundamental purpose of theoretical science cannot be, as Peirce had stipulated, to acquire knowledge of "God's truth." Clearly Peirce's theism, in addition to and as an ingredient of his philosophy of science, supplied an important incentive in his battle for the cause of realism.

The nominalistic denial of real generality amounts to a denial of real continuity since, on Peirce's account, *all* relations are continua embodying an inexhaustible number of real possibilities. The theological implications of this denial, from Peirce's perspective, will be clarified in the next chapter. But it is important to note that he regarded nominalism as entailing finitism.[31] In order for the concept of infinity to be employed meaningfully and consistently, in science, in mathematics, or in theology, realistic premises must first be accepted. The nominalists affirm the reality of the actual, what actually was, is, and will be; but they fail to recognize the significance of Thirdness, of the real laws that govern what *would be* the case if specific circumstances were to obtain, whether or not they do obtain in fact. Consequently, the nominalistic perspective is blind to the infinite number of possibilities that *really connect* actual objects and events. Their world-view can accommodate only a finite God who created and governs only the universe of the actual. Once again, for Peirce, this is a God who has been stripped of the faculty of reason; and he makes it quite clear, in critical comments directed against the nominalistic pragmatism of James and Schiller, that a finite God is no God at all.[32]

Given the nature of his criticism of Duns Scotus, some remarks must be addressed to Peirce's analysis of individuality. Although he eventually appropriated the Scotist notion of *haecceity*, Peirce employed that notion somewhat creatively and within the context supplied by his own synechistic philosophy. For Peirce, "the haecceity itself is . . . general" while individual reaction-events "remain irreducibly Seconds";[33] that is to say, individuality is a relative rather than an absolute category. All individuals manifest a certain element of continuity, and thus of generality; they are determined as being individuals by a specific law or habit that both accounts for their identity as "single logical individuals" and constitutes them as a "continuity of reactions" (*CP* 3.613). To borrow a term from Peirce's logic of relatives, it is most useful to speak not of individuals but of individual "systems." An absolute individual would be a brute reaction-event devoid of intelligibility. A "single logic individual," since it endures through time, is of a continuous nature. Its behavior is governed by a habit that causes it both to endure (as a "continuity of reactions") and continuously to manifest certain essential properties and modes of activity. So Duns Scotus's single existing things are, for Peirce, systems of meaningful relations, general in nature, and defined by specific laws or habits.

It is not quite correct then to argue, as some scholars have,[34] that Peirce denied the existence of individuals; rather, he conceived of individuals in a peculiar fashion, as entities continuous in themselves and embedded within continua of higher dimensionalities.[35] And this conception is of great importance for understanding Peirce's religious thought. When he championed the ideals that ought to sustain both religious and scientific communities and attacked the individualism that he perceived to be infecting his own nineteenth-century cultural and social milieu, when he opposed his doctrine of evolutionary love to the individualistic "gospel of greed," Peirce was drawing ultimately not simply on ethical but on metaphysical principles. Whether or not he successfully derived ethical norms from metaphysical presuppositions in this fashion is a question that will have to be addressed if the overall coherence of Peirce's religious perspective is to be evaluated. But it is clear that he felt that his synechism underscored in a radical way the significance of human relationships, and elevated far above individual needs and values the health and the ideals of the community. Persons and things are bound, related, connected to one another in fact; selfish individualism represented for Peirce, then, the result not only of a moral failing but also of a metaphysical blindness.

Scholars have sought to distinguish Peirce's position from that of Duns Scotus by noting the extent to which he emphasized the continuity among rather than the separate integrity of individual things or substances.[36] Some have even questioned whether or not Peirce's philosophy can accommodate the medieval notion of substance at all. Again, the task here is not to assess the faithfulness and accuracy with which Peirce incorporated Scotist notions into his system. Clearly, he felt that the discoveries of the modern physical sciences warranted his talking about substances as a "continuity of reactions." It is true, however, that Peirce described the laws that govern the behavior of such substances as being, at least in some sense, effectively general in nature. Duns Scotus, on the other hand, would have wanted to analyze the behavior and operations of a thing primarily in terms of the form that inheres in the matter of that thing.[37] Insofar as the universal "in re" has any causal efficacy, for Duns Scotus, it operates as an intrinsic formal cause, within substance. But Peirce criticized this "contraction" of the general to the individual existing thing, choosing instead to explicate the "idea" or law that governs the behavior of a thing and determines it to be of a specific kind in terms of *final* causality. Now it is true that Aristotle and the scholastics admitted that, in many cases, the final and formal causes of a thing are indistinguishable.[38] There nonetheless does appear to be an important difference in perspective between Peirce and Duns Scotus on this issue. Peirce seemed to prefer to emphasize the causal efficacy of the "universalia ante rem" rather than the "universalia in re," to move from the "idea" or intelligibility of the system to the behavior of its fragments. So he defined natural classes and kinds in terms of final causation because "final causation is that kind of causation whereby the whole calls out its parts" (*CP* 1.220). And natural kinds of things on any level are themselves the fragments of a more comprehensive system.

Of course, most of the scholastics, including Duns Scotus, did emphasize the ultimate primacy of final causality as the "cause of causes."[39] Here again, perhaps, Peirce's position is not only "scholastic" but also "extreme." As will become clear in the third chapter, his evolutionary cosmology as well as his metaphysics rest heavily upon the operation of final causes. This fact will prove to be theologically interesting since universals "ante rem," as the final causes of natural things, are typically identified by the scholastics with thoughts in the mind of God. There is certainly no reason to suspect that Peirce rejected this identification. His tendency to explicate natural phenomena in terms of final causation, then, can be correlated with his tendency, already observed, to emphasize the efficacy and the visibility of the divine ideality and purpose in nature.

If God's purpose in nature is readily visible, however, it is not always readily perceived, a fact that Peirce himself did not fail to recognize (see, for example, *CP* 6.437). While a detailed analysis of Peirce's theory of religious knowledge must be delayed until certain preliminary issues have been addressed, that discussion can be anticipated here with a few general remarks about his philosophy of mind. Very early in his career, Peirce formulated a theory of unconscious ideas, arguing that universal propositions are not derived from experience but are innate.[40] These include the idea of an infinite God, who cannot be positively known, but can nevertheless have a direct influence on the human mind. Although this early neo-Kantian position was problematic in a number of ways and eventually rejected by Peirce, the theory of unconscious ideas survived in a modified form in his later theory of instinctive beliefs. A major impetus in the development of Peirce's thinking about this topic was supplied by his encounter with the Scotist notion that ideas can exist in the mind *habitualiter*.

> A notion is in the mind *actualiter* when it is actually conceived; it is in the mind *habitualiter* when it can directly produce a conception. It is by virtue of mental association (we moderns would say) that things are in the mind *habitualiter*. In the Aristotelian philosophy, the intellect is regarded as being to the soul what the eye is to the body. The mind perceives likenesses and other relations in the objects of sense, and thus just as sense affords sensible images of things, so the intellect affords intelligible images of them. It is as such a *species intelligibilis* that Scotus supposes that a conception exists which is in the mind *habitualiter . . .* independent of *consciousness*. (*CP* 8.18)

Universals or general conceptions exist in the mind *habitualiter*; while "independent of consciousness," these habits of thought can, by operating as laws of mental association, "directly produce a conception" (*CP* 8.18). It is in this capacity that they play a vital role in inference, where not only the general ideas that serve as major premises or "rules" but the rules of inference themselves often exist and function as implicit mental habits. For example, in hypothetical or "abductive" inferences, a perceived "*X*," bearing a certain configuration of characteristics, might be identified as a specific *kind* of thing by virtue of the operation of a habitual "rule" of thought (the class-concept for things of that kind). Of course, it may be possible to formulate and articulate such a rule explicitly; but it is not necessary that that be the case, and, Peirce suggested, it is often *not* the case with some of our most trustworthy and significant inferences, for example, that which concludes that God is real. It will prove to be important, in interpreting Peirce's Neglected Argument, to determine the precise role that instinctive beliefs or habits of thought play in that argument, their nature and source, and the extent to which they can be explicitly formulated as premises, if at all. At this point it is instructive simply to trace this sort of reasoning back to and connect it with Peirce's early theory of unconscious ideas, noting again that it was by means of such ideas, he argued, that the direct experience of or communication with God is possible.

The choice of abductive inference as an example above was not an arbitrary one; understanding Peirce's theory of abduction is one of the keys to making sense out of his concept of "Musement." Now Peirce indicated quite clearly that Boole's *Laws of Thought* and Book Two of Aristotle's *Prior Analytics* (*CP* 7.249) provided the basic inspirations for his notion of abduction.[41] It remains unclear, however, precisely what sort of impact Duns Scotus's theory of abstraction had on his thinking about this topic.[42] Peirce vigorously defended the significance of abstraction in mathematical and scientific reasoning against what he perceived to be the "timid" criticisms of nominalists (*CP* 1.383, 3.509); at one point, he went so far as to identify abstractions as "the very warp of reason" (*CP* 4.531). In particular, it is "hypostatic abstraction," as Peirce conceived it, that seems to be closely related to abduction.

> That wonderful operation of hypostatic abstraction by which we seem to create *entia rationis* that are, nevertheless, sometimes real, furnishes us the means of turning predicates from being signs that we think or think *through*, into being subjects thought of. We thus think of the thought-sign itself, making it the object of another thought-sign. (*CP* 4.549)

Quite simply, hypostatic abstraction, or "subjectification" (*CP* 2.428), is the process whereby predicates are converted into subjects, so that from considering that "honey is sweet," for example, one proceeds to contemplate "sweetness" itself as a logical subject, capable in its own right of bearing additional predicates. Peirce analyzed this logical operation in terms of the medieval notions of both abstraction and supposition, linked it with the process of forming a hypothesis, and indicated that it is the mode of reasoning by means of which "new information" is acquired (*CP* 2.364, 3.509). Now this sort of analysis clearly resembles his account of abductive inference. The purpose of abduction is, after all, to formulate explanations of surprising phenomena; and frequently, Peirce claimed, explaining a thing will require the utilization of a general conception produced by "abstracting" a given quality or aspect of the thing in question and positing it as a reality, capable in itself of having real effects. Of course, not all abstractions refer to realities; but those real laws, effective in nature, that Peirce insisted are the primary objects of scientific cognition can only be grasped via some process of abstraction. Indeed, to generalize or abstract an aspect of some thing can amount to linking that thing, as a "fragment," to a comprehensive law or system of relations. It is in this fashion that isolated phenomena are rendered intelligible, or, more accurately from Peirce's point of view, that their real intelligibility is ascertained. And it is in this fashion that Peirce will develop his objective idealism and his cosmology, moving from part to whole, from fragment to system, proceeding towards ever more comprehensive systems of relations. It is in contemplating the teleology of this process that Peirce's religious ideas enter the picture. The final cause that defines and governs the most comprehensive of all systems, the universe, will be the ultimate source of intelligibility. In a sense, Peirce's "Humble Argument" is a meditation on that final cause.[43] Moreover, in his cosmological speculations, he tried to illuminate that universal teleology with insights drawn from the Gospel of John.

III

The manner in which Peirce sought, in general terms, to harmonize basic scientific and religious conceptions has already been observed. Now his assessment of certain philosophical claims concerning the authenticity of *miracles* will supply a particular illustration of this general strategy while underscoring some of the essential features of Peirce's scientific theism.

It is not immediately obvious that a discussion of miracles should be even relevant to, never mind illuminate, Peirce's conception of science. Nor is it clear that the scientist, as scientist, has anything meaningful to say about the topic of miracles. Indeed, Peirce himself stipulated that "Science no more denies that there are miracles and mysteries than it asserts them" (*CP* 7.601; see also 1.90). The reasoning that underlies such a claim draws its force from the "sui generis" character of miracles, from the conventional notion that they are marvelous and isolated occurrences, "impenetrable mysteries"; for the scientist is concerned not with isolated facts but with the general laws that render specific facts intelligible, and, far from acquiescing in the mysterious, it is the fundamental "postulate" or "hope" of the scientist "that *any given fact* to which our attention may be directed shall turn out to be intelligible" (*CP* 7.601). If the miraculous is equivalent to the unintelligible, then it surely falls altogether outside of the realm of scientific inquiry.

To argue that a particular alleged miracle cannot be scientifically evaluated, however, is not to deny that the *possibility* of such events can be assessed in the light of a given scientific conception of the world. In point of fact, Peirce did supply some suggestions about what sort of general perspective scientists might adopt vis-à-vis miracles, despite his insisting on the inability of scientists to pass judgment on the authenticity of the claims made about specific occurrences. These suggestions are not developed in Peirce's writings; but his brief remarks about miracles can be considerably expanded if certain notions and arguments, implied there but formulated elsewhere, are drawn upon to fill in some missing details. Very much of what Peirce said in other contexts about "tychism" and the laws of nature, for example, is immediately relevant to the present discussion. Before such relevance can be demonstrated, it is necessary to examine Peirce's only extended treatment of the topic of miracles, a critical review of some of Hume's contentions. He summarized those contentions in the following manner:

> Hume's argument against miracles is substantially based upon the assumption that we ought to judge of testimony by balancing the likelihood that the witnesses tell the truth against the likelihood that no such event as that to which they testify ever took place. It is true that Hume gives a metaphysical definition of a miracle based upon the definition of Aquinas. But his argument in no way turns upon that. The definition he virtually *uses* is that a miracle is something the like of which has never been known to happen. He has completely mistaken the nature of the true logic of abduction. (*CP* 6.537)

Of course, Hume's arguments are not designed to rule out miracles per se, but only to show that the reasons for affirming that any particular miracle took place fail to be compelling, indeed, that they are considerably weaker than those that could be enlisted in support of a skeptical position. Peirce was quick to observe that Hume was not, in fact, making any sort of metaphysical claim here; rather, he was evaluating certain *hypotheses* about the historical *testimony* concerning various miracles.[44] So the issue of what qualities ought most especially to recommend a hypothesis for consideration is one that Peirce felt it is legitimate to raise in this context; and it is his position on that issue that supplied the rationale for his contention that Hume has "completely mistaken the nature of the true logic of abduction." In addition, Hume obscured the issue by supplying a metaphysical definition of "miracle" that differs from the sense of the word as he employed it in his argument. It is moreover Peirce's discussion of the definition that Hume gave but did not use that creates the background against which his own scientific account of miracles can be brought into focus.

That discussion is one that Peirce himself struggled to avoid on this occasion, precisely because of his negative opinion about its relevance to Hume's basic argument. Samuel P. Langley, then the secretary of the Smithsonian Institution, had in 1901 commissioned Peirce to produce a manuscript about the idea of "laws of nature" as that idea had evolved since the time of Hume and under the influence of his critique of miracles. If for no other reasons than financial ones, this is an assignment that Peirce must have desperately wanted to fulfill. Nevertheless, he resisted doing so in the exact manner prescribed, first indicating his preference for the "*logical* question about Hume's argument against miracles and not the *metaphysical* question of law,"[45] and finally, when he felt that he had failed to communicate his point, asserting explicitly that "*Hume's argument has nothing to do with the Laws of Nature.*"[46] Eventually, Peirce produced several drafts of a paper for Langley, treating both topics while continuing to deny any essential link between them. Langley had difficulties with all of the versions, and Peirce could not live with Langley's editorial recommendations; consequently, the essay was never published.[47]

There is certainly a great deal of validity in Peirce's claim that Hume's argument is "not properly an argument against miracles, in general, but only against *historical* miracles," so that it was directed "against those miracles which did *not* form a part of our perceptual data, but were only hypotheses to account for the testimony of documents."[48] At the same time, it is not perfectly clear that Peirce's objections to Hume's critique do not involve certain metaphysical presuppositions; that is, from Peirce's point of view, even Hume's discussion of miracles is somewhat infected by his nominalism. But this contention needs to be clarified by a closer examination of Peirce's objections.

Both Hume and the nineteenth-century German biblical scholars (*CP* 6.536) based their critique of miracles on the assessment and balancing of "likelihoods." This sort of procedure, Peirce observed, was a popular method of legal argument at the time when Hume was writing (*MS* 869:27). Peirce regarded the very notion of "likelihood," however, as "the most deceptive thing in the world, being nothing but the conformity of a proposition to our preconceived ideas" (*CP* 2.101; see also *MS* 872:26v). Consequently, it is never a wise strategy to entertain or reject a hypothesis solely or even primarily on the basis of its likelihood. Explanatory power, testability, refutability, and economic considerations are all appropriate criteria to which the reasoner can appeal in the process of abduction. But that its truth appears "likely" to the reasoner is a fact about a hypothesis that should not carry more weight than it can logically bear. Of course, psychologically speaking, one is frequently tempted to embrace or discard a notion for precisely this reason, but that temptation ought vigorously to be resisted. While Peirce did not pursue this sort of reflection at great length here, it is important to note that it does have theological implications extending beyond the discussion of miracles; indeed, the logic of the Neglected Argument is intelligible only insofar as the factors that can be legitimately claimed to recommend a hypothesis have been clearly identified.

Now Peirce regarded the concept of likelihood as "deceptive" not least of all because it is so frequently conflated with that of "probability," in which case "it does more harm than the yellow fever ever did" (CP 2.101). The difference between the two concepts, while obscured in the writings of Hume and the "higher critics," is for Peirce of the utmost significance.

> An objective probability is the ratio of frequency of a specific to a generic event *in the ordinary course of experience.* Of a fact *per se* it is absurd to speak of objective probability. All that is attainable are subjective probabilities, or likelihoods, which express nothing but the conformity of a new suggestion to our prepossessions: and these are the source of most of the errors into which man falls, and of all the worst of them. (CP 2.777)

Peirce objected, in the first place, to the manner in which Hume calculated probabilities, since his talk of "balancing" suggests that the values ascribed to specific pieces of evidence ought to be added or subtracted, rather than, as the correct rules of probability stipulate, multiplied or divided. More significantly, however, Hume falsely categorized the evidence itself. He labeled a hypothesis as probable or improbable based on the extent to which it appears likely or unlikely to be true, given past experiences. But for Peirce

> Past experience is no "evidence" for future experience, because it is quite conceivable that the arrangement of the universe should change. Nor is there any sense in speaking of the "evidence" of any single event; for "evidence" only shows how often a certain *kind* of event occurs.[49]

Since "it is quite conceivable that the arrangement of the universe should change," probability is to be regarded as a "relative" category; that is to say, the value of a probability describes a statistical *relationship* between a specific *kind* of event and certain generic circumstances, a ratio of the number of occurrences of that event under those circumstances to the total number of instances where the circumstances obtain (whether the event occurs or not). This technical notion of "evidence," Peirce contended, is the one that Hume's argument requires in order to succeed. All that he is able to supply there, however, are claims about the *likelihood* that certain miracles actually occurred and that the testimony supporting them is true; but these claims tell one nothing about probability or the *objective relationship* between events. In fact, the only relationship that is illuminated by them is a "subjective" one: the correspondence (or lack of it) of a hypothesized event to one's preconception of what is "likely" to have occurred.

Note that even Peirce's language here is similar to that employed in his (and his father's) direct and explicit critiques of nominalism. The contrasting of "objective probabilities" with "subjective likelihoods" is a reminder that Peirce identified Hume as a prominent figure among those philosophers who attribute to nature only a "subjective ideality." Furthermore, his insistence that the calculation of a probability defines a *relationship* between types of events is a realistic rejoinder to Hume's treatment of the *individual* instances of an induction as independent arguments. That is to say, the assumption underlying Hume's critique is that single instances drawn from past experience "can logically be 'balanced' against one another, as if they were independent 'evidences.'"[50] The frequency with which stones fall to the earth makes the future occurrence of just such an event "likely"; but for Hume there is no real relationship between these occurrences, each separately constituting an evidential support for the claim about what is or is not likely. "One stone's falling has no real connection with another's fall."[51] This way of thinking is very far removed from Peirce's understanding of probability, which includes the supposition that to evaluate something as "probable" is to ascribe to it a certain "would-be," "to say that it has a property, quite analogous to any *habit* that a man might have" (*CP* 2.664). A habit, of course, is not a monadic predicate but a relational concept correlating the behavior of a thing with those specific factors or circumstances that tend to occasion or elicit such behavior.

Peirce's metaphysical biases emerged, then, even in his criticism of the Humean strategy of balancing likelihoods. The basic purpose of that criticism, however, is to show that Hume's argument about miracles fails. The isolatedness of miracles does not really furnish a valid argument against their reality (*CP* 6.514). At the same time, Peirce admitted, "it effectively prevents our having sufficient evidence of them" (*CP* 6.514). This is the case, once again, because "evidence" cannot be supplied by a single event but rather consists in a relationship between kinds of events. An isolated surprising occurrence, precisely because of its surprising quality, is not the sort of thing that one regards as likely to take place. But its isolated character precludes any determination of its probability, in Peirce's sense of that word; and the assessment of evidence is identical to the process of evaluating probabilities. So Peirce concluded that, on the basis of the evidence alone, one should neither pronounce against the biblical miracle claims nor affirm their validity, "unless the general divinity of the Christian religion be assumed" (*CP* 6.514, 6.538, 6.544).

This conclusion is nothing more than a form of Peirce's contention, cited above, that the scientist is in a position neither to affirm nor to deny the reality of miracles. At most, then, from the perspective of the student of Peirce's religious thought, he may have succeeded here in (1) undermining certain strong negative claims about miracles, and (2) taking, in the process, some "passing shots" at various nominalistic assumptions. And while neither of these accomplishments should be regarded as insignificant, they do not represent the positive and distinctive philosophical treatment of miracles for which Peirce's writings supply at least the outline. To locate some of the essential features of that outline, one must focus attention on those sections of his essay where Peirce discussed Hume's *definition* rather than his critique of miracles.

While Hume's argument assumes nothing more than that "a miracle is something the like of which has never been known to happen," he explicitly defined a miracle as "a violation of a law of nature" (*CP* 6.537–39). Since Peirce regarded the laws of nature as signifiers of the divine purpose, it is conceivable that such a definition, without qualification, made him somewhat uncomfortable. Peirce's God is the source of the world's rationality, its intelligibility, and not primarily a "miracle-maker." Likewise, the scientist is the interpreter of God's "great poem," but can make no decisive pronouncements about miracles. How is Peirce to respond to such a definition?

As already indicated, he preferred to avoid doing so, at least in the form that Hume's discussion seemed to require. But not all of Peirce's reasons for this preference can be conflated with his direct and most immediate response that this definition differs from the one that Hume's argument actually presupposes. In addition, he noted that Hume's definition, the statement of which he borrowed from Aquinas (*CP* 6.537, 6.541ff.), is not one that has been operative throughout the history of Christian theology (so that even Aquinas, along with Augustine and Bishop Butler, were identified by Peirce as thinkers who did not understand miracles in this fashion![52]). The fathers of the church, for example, regarded a miracle as "nothing more than a great wonder" (*CP* 6.540). Consequently, Hume supplied a definition that neither actually grounds his argument nor is itself grounded historically in the Christian tradition.

Furthermore, Peirce was apparently convinced that this definition, if conceived of in any way resembling the manner in which Aquinas construed it, was not only immune to but itself radically undermined Hume's critique of miracles. Peirce's discussion suggests four basic lines of reasoning here.

(1) The scholastic notion of a "law of nature" (or, more appropriately, of the "order of nature"—*CP* 6.542), while representing a reality even more "inviolable" than that of the modern conception, nonetheless conflicts sharply with the nominalistic ("Ockhamistic") principles that inform Hume's strategy of

calculating likelihoods. This sort of realistic rejoinder to Hume has been characterized above. It needs only to be recalled and emphasized at this point how close to the heart of Peirce's scientific theism such an objection lies. The debate about miracles constitutes one of several religiously significant contexts within which his opposition to nominalism manifests itself.

(2) The fact that human knowledge of the universe is limited lends plausibility to the hypothesis that "miracles," appearing to be in conflict with the laws of nature, are *actually* in harmony with the natural order of events. That harmony would be visible from a broader or "higher" perspective. Reasoning in this fashion, Augustine was able to claim "that it is only the order of nature so far as we can penetrate it that can be violated by a miracle."[53] Peirce reminded the reader, however, that Hume was certainly well aware of the efficacy of this sort of argument (indeed, he himself employed a version of it in order to refute the theological arguments from "design," in his *Dialogues Concerning Natural Religion*). All the more reason, Peirce contended, to assume that this metaphysical definition cannot be the focus of Hume's discussion. At the same time, Peirce himself was inclined to adopt something very much like the Augustinian position. He postulated, on one occasion, that what could appear "miraculous" from a certain perspective might, in the long run, be explicable as the manifestation of a specific "would-be" or "habit" (*CP* 2.667); that is, what might seem to be a law-defying phenomenon could, in fact, be the manifestation of some unknown and thus unformulated law of nature. Even more illuminating in this regard are certain of Peirce's cosmological reflections, summarized immediately below, but to be examined more thoroughly in chapter three.

(3) The crucial ingredient of Peirce's cosmology, for the purposes of this discussion, is his doctrine of "tychism." The upshot of that doctrine is that there are, in reality, "deviations from the regular uniformities of the world" (*CP* 6.512). Furthermore, the very laws of nature, if not robbed of their ideality and their evolutionary character, presuppose such deviations.

> For if there are any "laws" of nature, they must be supposed to be supremely reasonable. Now the supreme reasonableness of a "law" will consist in its advancing a rational purpose in every particular case. Here, if there is really a need of an apparently exceptional phenomenon, it will not be contrary to real analogies, but on the contrary required by them, that that apparently exceptional phenomenon should occur. On the surface of it, at any rate, this view creates no objection to Hume's real argument; but it clearly does show that to look upon the order of nature as being of the nature of a "law" is to adopt a view which is really favorable to miracles, rather than the reverse. (*CP* 6.547)

All law is the result of evolution and thus imperfect (*CP* 6.91). Hume's definition is problematic for the believer in miracles only if he or she subscribes to that sort of mechanical necessitarianism against which Peirce so vigorously rebelled. Mechanical law can account for neither variety nor growth in the universe (*CP* 6.58ff.); but both are accommodated by the notion that laws are analogous to ideas in the mind, that they constitute "a reasonableness energizing in the world."[54] Peirce found incomprehensible the assumption made by certain individuals that, if God exists, "he has bound himself with wooden rigidity to a formula of their discovery and devising" (*MS* 842:G125). Law describes no mere uniformity, nor is it to be reduced to the status of a subjective generalization. In point of fact, Peirce insisted, the reality of objective chance must be posited in order to "make room" for a valid principle of generalization, the habit-taking tendency (*CP* 6.63). Chance is a "catalyst" involved in the production of higher levels of uniformity (*MS* 875). So chance begets law; continuity presupposes spontaneity; synechism entails tychism.

These claims should be intelligible if construed against the background of the sketch already supplied of Peirce's scientific theism. But his talk about the ideality of law needs to be explicated within the context of his objective idealism; likewise, tychism is an essential ingredient of Peirce's evolutionary cosmology. Discussions of those topics below (chapters two and three) will supply further evidence for some hypotheses that at least can be articulated here. Abduction, for Peirce, is the mode of inference that generates hypothetical explanations, the cognitive process by means of which new ideas are formulated and entertained.[55] Now, whatever its precise theological status, the Absolute or Universal Mind, in some sense, "thinks" the laws of nature. That kind of thinking presupposes an objective phenomenon analogous to hypothetical reasoning and characterized by its spontaneous or "sporting" quality; it constitutes the source both of variety in the universe and of the growth of ideas as objective habits. This is a cosmology, then, that not only accommodates but presupposes "miraculous" occurrences. Furthermore, in a very real and perhaps theologically decisive sense, the "Muser" in Peirce's Neglected Argument imitates or is modeled on that objective phenomenon, the cosmic "Musing" of the Absolute Mind.

(4) If it seems frivolous to introduce the topic of hypothetical inference into the discussion at this point, one should recall that Peirce was most interested in correcting Hume's misconceptions about "the nature of the true logic of abduction." Moreover, such a "correction" should prove relevant to the task of the Neglected Argument, which, despite the metaphysical and cosmological themes that pervade it, turns essentially on certain claims made about the logic of inquiry. In fact, Peirce never really believed that logic and metaphysics could be divorced; his initial effort to suppress the discussion of metaphysical issues in the essay on Hume was quickly abandoned.

What is not abandoned is Peirce's preoccupation with the true nature of abduction; he returned to that theme in the final pages of the essay. Had Hume taken the scholastic notion of a "law of nature" seriously, Peirce suggested, he would have been forced to admit that experience is not the primary or exclusive source of our knowledge. For by the "order of nature,"

> the scholastic realists had understood something like thought, or reasonableness, really active in shaping the phenomena of the cosmos. But to grant that there is such an energizing reasonableness is to give some hope that the inborn light of man's reason may contribute something to knowledge.[56]

Exactly why does the realistic conception of law ground such a "hope"? For Peirce, a law's reality transcends the actuality of any finite collection of experienced instances. The "leap" from perceiving such individual instances to grasping the objective generality of law presupposes the process of abduction, an inference whose validity further experience only serves to confirm or disconfirm. Consequently, "not only is our knowledge not exclusively derived from experience, but every item of science came originally from conjecture, which has only been pruned down by experience."[57]

This is not to deny that Peirce himself was an empiricist of sorts, for whom "all that we can anyway know relates to experience" (*CP* 6.492). But for Peirce *all* experience is *interpreted* experience; our knowledge is the end-result of such interpretation and thus distinct from that which is simply "given" in experience. Even if one's knowledge is *about* the objects of experience, it is nevertheless "underdetermined" by one's actual encounters with such objects. It is always "related" to experience, but not empirically "derived."[58]

Hume's position, since he began with and confined himself to knowledge empirically *derived*, is wedded to nominalistic assumptions. Peirce not only rejected such assumptions but defended an extreme form of realism, his doctrine of synechism. So one is likely to locate meaningful clues about the nature of the connection between law as "energizing reasonableness" and the "inborn light of man's reason" in Peirce's discussion of this doctrine of real connectedness or "continuity." For Peirce clearly insisted, even here, that his notion of "reasonableness . . . includes *Continuity*, of which, indeed, Generality is but a cruder form."[59] Furthermore, he contended that to label laws as "reasonable" is to affirm that they are of "such a nature as inevitably to realize themselves." This process of "realization" is evolutionary in character and one of its by-products, Peirce hypothesized, is the natural "instinct" that informs human "conjectures." In a remarkable way, then, Peirce's attempt to correct certain Humean misconceptions about the logic of inquiry resulted in his invoking, however vaguely, many of his basic philosophical notions and principles: scholastic realism, objective idealism, tychism, synechism, his evolutionary cosmology, and the notion of a "guessing" instinct. Most especially, it is the tychastic aspect of evolution, the creative role of chance in the development of objective ideas, that renders intelligible, for Peirce, the idea of a "miracle"; that idea, properly understood, Peirce concluded, "is in remarkable consonance with the higher teachings of modern science" (*CP* 6.547).

II

THE ABSOLUTE MIND

I

In 1892, at the end of his *Monist* article on "The Law of Mind," Peirce declared that his synechistic philosophy "carries along with it the following doctrines":

> first, a logical realism of the most pronounced type; second, objective idealism; third, tychism, with its consequent thoroughgoing evolutionism. We also notice that the doctrine presents no hindrances to spiritual influences, such as some philosophies are felt to do. (*CP* 6.163)

This claim has helped to structure the present analysis. For just as Peirce's realism was the focus of concern in the first chapter, and his evolutionary theory will supply the subject matter for the third, most immediately, attention must be directed to his objective idealism. And the thread that unifies all of these investigations is the underlying hypothesis that Peirce's philosophy not only "presents no hindrances to spiritual influences," but actually provides a system of intelligibility for his utterances about religious matters. The doctrine of synechism is a source of evidence in support of that hypothesis, the key to understanding many of those utterances. Before the hermeneutical value of Peirce's reflections on the concept of continuity can be fully realized, however, some sense must be made out of his contention that all of reality is of the nature of living mind.

Peirce's argument in defense of his objective idealism might prove somewhat disappointing for the philosopher who expects an a priori demonstration or "deduction" of its validity. After all, his metaphysics and cosmology are rather clearly and extensively linked to idealistic presuppositions. Of course, it may be that their very significance as presuppositions lends sufficient plausibility, for Peirce, to these idealistic notions; they play a vital explanatory role. His religious thinking, not least of all, is rendered coherent by such notions. In this respect, materialism, like nominalism, is simply too "expensive" a hypothesis from Peirce's perspective.

The form of Peirce's argument was, in fact, abductive; his objective was to discern which hypothesis, among several proposed for consideration, had the most explanatory power. These hypotheses are about the ultimate nature of the universe (*CP* 6.24), the true relationship between mind and matter (*CP* 6.272ff.). Peirce identified three candidates: (1) a dualism of mind and matter, or any account that includes both elements as fundamental ingredients of the cosmos, (2) materialism, and (3) objective idealism. He eliminated the first from consideration by applying the logical maxim of Ockham's razor, "that not more independent elements are to be supposed than necessary" (*CP* 6.24). But the materialistic hypothesis is not quite so readily dismissed. Like nominalism, it is recommended by its "simplicity," and Peirce admitted that it cannot be "absolutely refuted" (*CP* 6.274). Its weakness, however, is that "it requires us to suppose that a certain kind of mechanism will feel, which would be a hypothesis absolutely irreducible to reason" (*CP* 6.24). Materialism must be rejected, that is, because it cannot account for the property of feeling, a property that Peirce contended was not deducible from the laws of mechanics (*CP* 6.264). Whatever the dependence of consciousness or feeling upon the body, mental phenomena cannot be governed completely by "blind mechanical law."

> The fact that our knowledge of the future is of so different a kind from our knowledge of the past seems to be hopelessly in conflict with materialism; since the laws of mechanics, as they are now understood, make the dynamical relation of the past to the future exactly the same as that of the future to the past. (*CP* 6.274)

Peirce was evoking the image of a deterministic "system of forces," wherein particles behave in such a fashion that knowledge of their positions and velocities at any given instant allows one to calculate both their previous and subsequent positions and velocities by applying the same laws of mechanics. Within such a system, there is no way to account for the spontaneity of feeling, for living consciousness. If these laws that govern matter are the only laws that there are, then the properties of mind seem to be inexplicable.

Since the dualistic hypothesis has already been eliminated, at least provisionally, only one option remains to be explored. The laws to which material objects are bound might themselves be derivable from or constitute specifications of the law of mind. Indeed, Peirce argued that matter is "habit-bound" mind; its special properties can be accounted for in terms of the same principles that govern mental phenomena. This is the hypothesis of objective idealism.

> We ought to suppose a continuity between the characters of mind and matter, so that matter would be nothing but mind that had such indurated habits as to

cause it to act with a peculiarly high degree of mechanical regularity, or routine. . . . This hypothesis might be called materialistic, since it attributes to mind one of the recognized properties of matter, extension, and attributes to all matter an excessively low degree of feeling, together with a certain power of taking habits. But it differs essentially from materialism, in that, instead of supposing mind to be governed by blind mechanical law, it supposes the one original law to be the recognized law of mind, the law of association, of which the laws of matter are regarded as mere special results. (*CP* 6.277)

This passage goes some distance, perhaps, towards clarifying Peirce's abductive insight regarding the truth of objective idealism. It is a hypothesis that, after all, "might be called materialistic." Far from embodying any sort of outrageous denial of the reality of the material world, this doctrine claims to account for the properties, behavior, and interactions of objects, while identifying them as species of mind. Now it need not be assumed that human consciousness supplies the paradigmatic exemplification of the law of mind. Matter is mind only in the very special sense that Peirce stipulated; and it is mind so "indurated" or habit-bound that it can hardly be expected to resemble closely other types of mental phenomena. The crucial fact for Peirce was that materialism fails to account for such phenomena, while his idealism supplied a world-view within which matter and its properties can be fully accommodated.

A few historical observations ought to be made here. In the first place, Peirce rejected a materialism that presupposed the laws of mechanics "as they are now understood." These were the laws of Newtonian physics, and Peirce felt that they were thoroughly inadequate for the purpose of explaining the fact of feeling. Of course, his attack on necessitarianism and defense of the doctrine of tychism suggest that Peirce himself was dissatisfied with the classical physics. Twentieth-century developments in quantum theory might have supplied him with significant resources for his purposes;[1] but the result would not automatically have undermined Peirce's objective idealism. He was not committed to the claim that physics would never be able to account for the phenomenon of mind, but only to the contention that it must fail as long as it is bound to the conception of law as blind, mechanical, and necessary (see *CP* 6.265). In the case of material objects such laws do, in fact, display a mechanical regularity. Matter is the limit case of mind, however, mind frozen by habit, and even there the regularity is not perfect or absolute.

A second observation pertains not to the history of science but to the history of philosophy. That is, however idiosyncratic Peirce's metaphysical views might seem to the contemporary reader, objective idealism is a doctrine that, in the nineteenth and early twentieth centuries, was certainly not lacking in proponents.[2] Josiah Royce looms large among this group as a powerful force within the American intellectual milieu, and his relationship to Peirce was a

significant one for both men.[3] In general, the post-Kantian idealistic systems
of Hegel, Schelling, and others had made a significant impact not only in
Europe but, through the mediation of the New England Transcendentalists
and the St. Louis school, in the United States as well. Of course, Peirce was a
highly original thinker, a fact that might explain his peculiar formulation of
the doctrine; but one hardly needed, in the latter half of the nineteenth
century, to apologize for being an objective idealist.

All of this having been said, the most powerful sort of rationale for Peirce's
idealism remains one that is internal to his thought; there, the law of mind
emerges as a fundamental premise, a "leading principle" governing his arguments. His religious concerns, not least of all, motivated this particular
metaphysical stance; the ideality of nature is, after all, divine in origin. Consequently, Peirce's statement and explication of the law of mind deserve some
careful consideration.

What does this law stipulate?

> that ideas tend to spread continuously and to affect certain others which stand
> to them in a peculiar relation of affectibility. In this spreading they lose intensity,
> and especially the power of affecting others, but gain generality and become
> welded with other ideas. (CP 6.104)

All of reality was mind for Peirce; thought and being are "synonymous" (see
MS 931:Q.6). The stuff of mind is feeling, ideas being nothing other than
continua of living feeling (CP 6.138, 6.150). Such ideas themselves "tend to
spread" becoming continuously connected or "welded" to one another. While
their "intrinsic quality" as feeling remains unchanged in this process, the
intensity of that feeling diminishes. So generality is gained at the expense of
vitality; a general idea "calls up" a great many others that are associated with it
in the mind, but it lacks the liveliness and force that it possessed in its original
simplicity (CP 6.136). This is the process of habit formation, the growth of
reasonableness, mitigating but nonetheless rooted in the immediate and spontaneous play of living feeling.

Ideas become affected by one another in a number of ways. That "peculiar
relation of affectibility" may be, according to Peirce, one of resemblance,
contiguity, or causality (see CP 5.307). Whatever its precise nature in any given
case, all such relationships are continuous, so that general ideas form "systems."
The crucial presupposition here is that "an idea can only be affected by an idea
in continuous connection with it" (CP 6.158). Peirce insisted that this is the
minimal requirement for any communication between minds. And his claim
takes on religious significance when it is inspected against the backdrop of his
remarks about personality.[4]

As indicated above, Peirce's notion of mind cannot simply be conflated with any conventional understanding of the nature of human consciousness. A mind is not "something shut up in a skull" (*MS* 881:95v). Likewise, personality need not be regarded as a uniquely human phenomenon. Nevertheless it is a "particular phenomenon," only one possible manifestation of the law of mind (*CP* 6.155). Peirce explained that personality consists in "some kind of coordination or connection of ideas"; it is a general idea or continuum of feeling that, while apprehended in any given instant as "immediate self-consciousness," endures in time (*CP* 6.155). This temporal aspect of personality is essential to Peirce's admittedly vague account. Indeed, personality was ascribed only to those general ideas that display a "teleological harmony" among the simpler, coordinated ideas that they embrace; and such purposiveness manifests itself over a period of time. Even more, they must display a "developmental teleology," that is, purposiveness without a specific "predeterminate" objective (*CP* 6.156).

It is, once again, the mistake of necessitarianism that Peirce was anxious to avoid. Here that error would consist in the identification of "teleology" with the "mechanical" pursuit of explicit ends, "the mere carrying out of predetermined purposes" (*CP* 6.156–57). For personality is, most essentially, a phenomenon that is characterized by "life" and "growth," a general idea "determinative of acts in the future to an extent to which it is not now conscious" (*CP* 6.156). It is mind organized around specific ideals and purposes, ideals not permanently fixed but themselves constantly evolving. Such a conception of personality, Peirce suggested, is quite relevant to the "philosophy of religion."

> A genuine evolutionary philosophy, that is, one that makes the principle of growth a primordial element of the universe, is so far from being antagonistic to the idea of a personal creator that it is really inseparable from that idea; while a necessitarian religion is in an altogether false position and is destined to become disintegrated. But a pseudo-evolutionism which enthrones mechanical law above the principle of growth is at once scientifically unsatisfactory, as giving no possible hint of how the universe has come about, and hostile to all hopes of personal relations to God. (*CP* 6.157)

Within the immediate context of the *Monist* essay cited above, such comments remain a bit opaque, and they certainly will need to be unpacked and explored here. That task must be delayed, however, since it will require a general examination of Peirce's evolutionary cosmology and of the other papers in the *Monist* series (1891–93). Suffice it to say at this point that Peirce considered materialism to be an inadequate hypothesis for *both* scientific and theological reasons. Rather, the cosmos is ideal in nature, evolving and purposive. Construed as an extraordinarily complex general idea, the universe may appropriately be regarded as a vast personality, an Absolute Mind, living and growing. Whether deity or "sub-deity" (this, too, is a complicated issue that must eventually be addressed), this universal mind was clearly a religiously significant reality in Peirce's world-view. And in "The Law of Mind" he seemed willing enough to identify it as "God," a word that elsewhere he appreciated for its vagueness (*CP* 6.494). But what, on this account, does it mean to have "personal relations with God?"

Peirce's discussion at the end of this essay embodies certain claims that lie close to the heart of his theory of religious knowledge. Recall that communication can occur only where there is a continuity between minds and between the ideas that they comprise. Indeed, one's recognition of another's personality occurs by means "to some extent identical with" those involved in one's consciousness of oneself (*CP* 6.160). Yet Peirce's synechistic metaphysics yielded the conclusion that all of reality is both ideal and continuous; this conclusion, upon reflection, underscores a potential "difficulty."

> In considering personality, that philosophy is forced to accept the doctrine of a personal God; but in considering communication, it cannot but admit that if there is a personal God, we must have a direct perception of that person and indeed be in personal communication with him. Now, if that be the case, the question arises how it is possible that the existence of this being should ever have been doubted by anybody. The only answer that I can at present make is that facts that stand before our face and eyes and stare us in the face are far from being, in all cases, the ones most easily discerned. That has been remarked from time immemorial. (*CP* 6. 162)

God and persons are continuously "connected" one to another, as Mind to mind, as Idea standing to idea in a "relation of affectability" (*CP* 6.104). Consequently, religious knowledge is not only possible in principle but the conditions that make it possible, according to the basic tenets of Peirce's synechism, do obtain in fact. So Peirce should be challenged to account somehow for the conspicuous lack of such knowledge, for the epistemic "blindness" that seems to afflict so many minds unable to recognize a reality with which they are directly confronted. Now it is true that he never responded to that challenge in a straightforward and systematic fashion; the "answer" that Peirce supplied above is an assertion, not an explanation. But respond he did; in a sense the entire Neglected Argument, and in particular the prescribed activity of Musement, can be interpreted as a proposed "remedy" for this blindness. Of course, much more needs to be said here before such an interpretation will become comprehensible. For example, "synechism" has been used thus far as the label for a doctrine only very vaguely defined. Yet it is important to understand why Peirce was so devoted to his mathematical and philosophical meditations on the concept of continuity. It should not be difficult to show that his motivation, once again, was at least partially religious in character.

II

> Hitherto the uses of the principle of continuity have been quite restricted. . . .
>
> For me, on the contrary, upon the first assault of the enemy, when pressed for the explanation of any fact, I lock myself up in my castle of impregnable logic and squirt out melted continuity upon the heads of my besiegers below.
>
> I do not merely use it subjectively as a way of looking at things, but objectively put it forward to account for all interaction between mind and body, mind and mind, body and body. (*MS* 949)

It should already be quite obvious that Peirce's employment of the principle of continuity was anything but "restricted." The law of mind represents one metaphysical permutation of that principle. And Peirce's scholastic realism qualifies as "extreme" to the extent that it is synechistic. Likewise, his talk about evolution presupposed that all of reality is continuous. In each instance, too, synechism is the key to understanding the religious dimension of Peirce's thought. Out of this stuff of "melted continuity," he both fashioned his conception of God and defended the vagueness of that conception. The relationship between God and the world, between God and persons is also continuous, and upon this metaphysical insight Peirce erected his theory of religious knowledge and developed an account of the nature and purpose of prayer. Love was described as a power that establishes real continuity in bringing about the growth of reasonableness and the creation of genuine community. Finally, to speculate meaningfully about the prospect of human immortality is to conjecture that death fails to represent an absolute discontinuity, a total rupture in the living continuum of feeling that comprises the personality.

Since so many of his religious utterances claimed this principle as their warrant, it deserves to be carefully explicated. Yet it is not at all clear that Peirce was ever satisfied with his formulation of the doctrine of synechism;[5] and to that task he devoted decades of serious reflection. What follows here, then, must be regarded as the sketch of a sketch, designed to cull from his account its essential ingredients and to trace out their religious implications.

How did Peirce define synechism? He identified it as "that tendency of philosophical thought which insists upon the idea of continuity as of prime importance in philosophy and, in particular, upon the necessity of hypotheses involving true continuity" (*CP* 6.169).

The last phrase is essential to Peirce's definition; in fact, he regarded synechism primarily as "a regulative principle of logic, prescribing what sort of hypothesis is fit to be entertained and examined" (*CP* 6.173). Nominalists and other types of philosophical villains persist in attempting to understand phenomena by analyzing them in terms of their "ultimate parts," entities that are themselves inexplicable. Peirce insisted, however, that "inexplicabilities are not to be considered as possible explanations" (*CP* 6.173). To "explain" is to state the general law or principle that governs a particular phenomenon; it is to locate some "fragment" within an appropriate system of relationships. All such systems comprise real continua, continuity being nothing other than "relational generality" (*CP* 6.190). So a "fit" hypothesis will involve "true continuity," because that is the "form under which alone anything can be understood" (*CP* 6.173).

Now a "true continuum is something whose possibilities of determination no multitude of individuals can exhaust" (*CP* 6.170). The implication here is that not all notions of continuity are to be regarded as adequate. What, then, constitutes a "false," or to use Peirce's preferred designation, a "pseudo-continuum"? The answer to this question is a mathematical one, but it has for Peirce both a metaphysical and a religious significance.

Consider again Peirce's critique of the scholastic notion of generality. There, as well, he had contended that a truly general relationship involves the notion of continuity, of "possible variations which no multitude of existing things could exhaust"; rather, between any two possibilities, there must be "possibilities beyond all multitude" (*CP* 5.103). Recall that this critique was inspired by certain discoveries that Peirce had made in his study of the logic of relatives. It is indeed with such logical commitments and concerns in mind that Peirce first tackled the mathematical problem of the continuum.[6] But if logic served to introduce Peirce to the problem, it was in the realm of metaphysics that he believed its solution would have its most far-reaching implications; in particular, Peirce was eager to develop, using both logical and mathematical resources, a cogent metaphysical theory of the nature of real possibility. The availability of such a theory would prove to be essential to the task of describing the relationship between the Absolute Mind and all that actually exists. These remarks, however, anticipate the end of a story that has just begun to unfold.

It was under the influence of Cantor and, ultimately, in opposition to his views that Peirce's thinking about continuity evolved.[7] He eventually came to regard Cantor's set-theoretic approach to the problem of the continuum as inadequate and the solution that it yielded as ingenious but false (see *CP* 6.121). Cantor had described the continuum as a collection of infinite multitude, more precisely, as a collection equal in multitude to that of the set of real numbers.[8] So the geometrical continuum could be construed as a collection or set of ordered *points*, infinite in number, but each a discrete entity or individual. Clearly, this is a proposal that Peirce could not endorse. For he understood a true continuum to embrace "possibilities of determination" beyond all multitude. That is to say, Peirce came to reject the notion that the continuum was a collection at all, regardless of its multitude. But how, exactly, did he arrive at this conclusion?

The mathematical line of reasoning that Peirce pursued here can be accurately traced, although it must constantly be remembered that his interest in the problem of the continuum was never *purely* mathematical. Like Cantor, Peirce carefully investigated the properties of collections of various multitudes. First, those with a finite number of members had to be analyzed and described. For this purpose, Peirce utilized De Morgan's "syllogism of transposed quantity," which has the following form:

> Every Texan kills a Texan;
> Nobody is killed by but one person;
> Hence, every Texan is killed by a Texan. (*CP* 3.288)

This syllogism is true, Peirce noted, only in the case of finite sets, here, for a finite number of Texans; to collections of infinite multitude it does not apply. An essential feature of any finite collection, then, is that no one-to-one correspondence can be established between it and any of its proper subsets; thus defined, finite collections can readily be distinguished from those that are infinite. Peirce still, however, needed to find a way to analyze the various grades of infinity. The key insight that allowed him to proceed with this task constitutes one of Peirce's most significant mathematical discoveries.[9]

If for a collection with n members, the number of its sub-collections is equal to 2^n, he reasoned, then $2^n > n$. That is to say, the power of a given collection is always exceeded by the power of the collection of all of its sub-collections. For example, a set with three members will have 2^3 or eight proper subsets, including the null set. So for the set of numbers $\{1, 2, 3\}$, its subsets are: $\{0\}$, $\{1\}$, $\{2\}$, $\{3\}$, $\{1, 2\}$, $\{1, 3\}$, $\{2, 3\}$ and $\{1, 2, 3\}$. Utilizing this insight, and beginning with the smallest ("denumerable") infinite set (the set of integers), Peirce was able to generate sets of greater and greater multitude. He referred to the set of all real numbers as the "first abnumeral" multitude. Here was a collection of entities that Cantor had identified as having all of the properties of the continuum; for him, the combined set of rational and irrational numbers displays a certain mathematical "completeness." Yet it could not be of the greatest possible multitude, Peirce argued, since the discovery that $2^n > n$ shows that there *cannot* be a greatest possible multitude. Consequently, to define continuity as a collection equal in multitude to that of the set of real numbers is to leave "gaps" in the continuum, producing only a notion of "pseudo-continuity." In fact, one simply cannot "construct" a continuum by collecting and combining *individuals*, no matter how great, how infinitely great, their number.

Peirce noticed that this conclusion is entailed by the Kantian definition of a continuum "as that all of whose parts have parts of the same kind" (*CP* 6.168). But Kant misunderstood his own definition as implying nothing more than the property of infinite divisibility.[10] Rather, Peirce explained, it "implies that a continuous line contains no points. . . . It seems necessary to say that a continuum, where it *is* continuous and unbroken, contains no definite parts; that its parts are created in the act of defining them and the precise definition of them breaks the continuity" (*CP* 6.168). In contrast, the pseudo-continuum of Cantor and Dedekind, of the calculus and theory of functions, "is only a collection of independent points. Breaking grains of sand will only make the sand more broken. It will not weld the grains into unbroken continuity" (*CP* 6.168).

This unbroken or "melted" continuity has, as its mathematical correlate, the notion of the real infinitesimal. Peirce was clearly committed to such a notion and, as such, at odds with the conventional mathematical wisdom of his day.[11] Yet it should be clear that the rationale for his position on this issue, while complex to be sure, was to a great extent extra-mathematical. That is, in addition to functioning as an alternative to the theory of limits within the calculus, the infinitesimal had for Peirce a metaphysical status; it, rather than the discrete individual, comprises the basic "stuff" of a continuous reality.

Now these considerations are intimately related to Peirce's topological investigations, wherein he drew extensively upon the work of Johann B. Listing.[12] To identify a topological space as continuous, Peirce contended, is to assume that it either returns to itself or contains its own limits. If it is "unbroken," it must return to itself. If it has limits, such limits represent a breach of continuity, manifested as "topical singularities"[13] of a lower dimensionality than that of the continuum itself. The limits of a line segment are its end points. The limits of a two-dimensional space can be either points or lines. In the latter case, the topical singularity is itself continuous, but it is a continuum of a lower dimensionality than that of the space that contains it: "so space presents points, lines, surfaces, and solids, each generated by the motion of a place of lower dimensionality and the limit of a place of next higher dimensionality" (*CP* 1.501).

In this fashion, a whole series of continua of varying dimensionalities can be envisaged, embedded within one another, with any continuum of *N* dimensions having as its limit, in the form of a topical singularity, a continuum of not more than *N* - 1 dimensions. Dimensionality, then, is conceived as a topological characteristic of continua; it can be expressed in terms of a numerical value; thus the relation between continua of varying dimensionalities can be mathematically described.

Toward the end of his life, and utilizing some of the insights gleaned from his topological researches, Peirce was busily engaged in the task of developing a descriptive logic of continua, his "existential graphs."[14] He identified the blank surface or "sheet of assertion" upon which such graphs are scribed as "an undeveloped photograph of the facts in the universe," facts that "blend into one another" to form a "continuum" (*CP* 4.512). This two-dimensional sheet, however, represents only the "universe of actual existent facts." Peirce struggled to develop his system of graphs so that he would be able to analyze as well the "universe of possibilities" that embraces but transcends the actual world. This universe itself would constitute a vast continuum of possibilities, and could be represented in three dimensions as "a book of separate sheets, tacked together at points," each sheet signifying a different "universe of discourse" (*CP* 4.512ff., 4.573ff.).

Peirce never satisfactorily completed this modal or "Gamma" system of graphs (*CP* 4.576). But it is clearly from his study of topology and of the theory of transfinite numbers that he borrowed many of the basic principles for its design. To "scribe" a graph on a sheet of assertion is to render the universe represented by that sheet more determinate (*MS* 455:2–3). And, as one page of a "book," that sheet with all of its inscribed graphs itself determines or actualizes a whole array of possibilities. Nevertheless, "possibilities are general, and no multitude can exhaust the narrowest kind of general" (*CP* 4.514); once again, a true continuum must embody "possibilities beyond all multitude" (*CP* 5.103). Notice also that the relationship between the actual and the possible, both within a given universe and between the actual universe and all other possible worlds, is illustrated in this system by the embedding of one continuum within another of a higher dimensionality: lines on a surface, and a two-dimensional surface or sheet within a book of sheets.

Such graphic representations supply a point of contact between Peirce's logic and his objective idealism. This was no coincidence, from Peirce's point of view, since "the logic of the universe is one to which our own aspires" (*CP* 6.189). Moreover, the key to transforming metaphysics into a "definite science," for Peirce, "consists in making our thought diagrammatic and mathematical, by treating generality from the point of view of geometrical continuity, and by experimenting upon the diagram" (*CP* 6.204). Consider, in broadest outline, Peirce's account of the origin and development of the universe. He speculated that the Absolute Mind, before it ever began to "think" specific thoughts, to form those objective habits that we perceive as the laws of nature, must have comprised a vast continuum of vague or "slumbering" feeling. Such feeling would constitute a primitive state of mind, mind in its "Firstness." Now suppose, Peirce suggested, that we utilize a clean blackboard to represent this Mind in some "early stage" of its development.

> This blackboard is a continuum of two dimensions, while that which it stands for is a continuum of some indefinite multitude of dimensions. This blackboard is a continuum of possible points; while that is a continuum of possible dimensions of quality. . . . There are no points on this blackboard. There are no dimensions in that continuum. I draw a chalk line on the board. This discontinuity is one of those brute acts by which alone the original vagueness could have made a step towards definiteness. There is a certain element of continuity in this line. Where did this continuity come from? It is nothing but the original continuity of the blackboard which makes everything upon it continuous. (CP 6.203)

Ideas are habits or continua of feeling; but they derive their continuous character from that original vague potentiality out of which they emerge. They are determinations of that which is itself vague and indeterminate, the actualizations, first random but then generalized, of pure qualitative possibilities. Once again, the relationship between the actual and the possible in Peirce's thought experiment is that of continua of different dimensionalities.[15] Moreover, while the heuristic device being employed here, the geometrical diagram, is a spatial representation, Peirce carefully observed that such continua need not be confined to relations in space and time.[16] Recall that the primordial continuum is one not of possible points but of "possible dimensions of quality" (CP 6.203). In this original condition it is actually dimensionless, but since no number of determinations could exhaust it, this vast ocean of potential embraces possible dimensions of quality "beyond all multitude" (CP 5.103).

Peirce reminded the reader that these cosmological speculations about an initial state of affairs portray a "slumbering" Mind that

> is not of the order of the existing universe, but is merely a Platonic world, of which we are, therefore, to conceive that there are many, both coordinated and subordinated to one another; until finally out of one of these Platonic worlds is differentiated the particular actual universe of existence in which we happen to be. (CP 6.208)

The logical language that Peirce required in order to be able to analyze and talk meaningfully about such a coordinated system of "worlds" was one that he struggled to develop in the form of his Gamma graphs. Since that project was never completed, one is forced to ground an interpretation of his perspective on these matters in those few highly speculative remarks that he did supply. Several conclusions can be drawn with some confidence. As Peirce indicated (above), the Absolute Mind is most properly construed as being co-extensive not merely with the actual universe, but with the "Platonic" world of possibilities from which that universe is determined. Still unanswered here are certain questions about the precise religious status of such a Mind, questions that will be addressed in the final section of this chapter. But it is clear that Peirce's Absolute is a *personal* and *evolving* reality, describable as a *system* of relations (see especially *CP* 6.189–209).

Remember that Peirce wished to extend the traditional logic of "classes" to embrace relations other than that of the similarity of one thing to another. Such relations, if they can be generalized, constitute systems; that is, a system is defined by some general idea that links its fragments into an intelligible pattern. It has already been noted that Peirce was willing to ascribe personality to any general idea that displays a specific kind of purposefulness; and the law of mind stipulates that ideas naturally tend to generalize, to form associations, thus, to "grow" or evolve. So his logical talk about systems can readily be translated into appropriate metaphysical and cosmological terms.

If the Absolute Mind is the whole, how is one to characterize, on this Peircean account, the fragments of the system?[17] The answer to this question should, at this point, appear somewhat familiar. Any given fragment might itself be a continuum, albeit one of a lower dimensionality than that of the system that encompasses it. If it is continuous, it also can be analyzed as a system; if its behavior is governed by ideals or purposes, it too can be regarded as personal. So a system might include any number of subsystems, "each the limit of a reality of the next higher order" (*CP* 1.501), and each an individual personality while also forming a fragment of the greater whole. The Absolute Mind would represent a kind of all-embracing "supersystem," with its habits of thought and feeling constituting the natural laws that regulate all of its coordinated subsystems (see *MS* 289:4ff.). With this sort of picture in mind, Peirce affirmed that "whatever is real is the law of something less real" (*CP* 1.487).

Now there is clearly some relationship between Peirce's conception of the Absolute and that of Hegel and Royce. While an extended comparison of these three thinkers might prove to be quite illuminating, it is only possible to make a few brief observations here.[18] Whatever the validity of his interpretation of Hegel's philosophy, Peirce consistently articulated two criticisms of it. Although obviously sympathetic to Hegel's objective idealism and appreciative of his attempt to develop a truly "objective logic," Peirce judged his idealism and his logic to be too narrowly conceived. More specifically, the objective logic of events "need not be supposed to be of that wooden kind that absolutely constrains a given conclusion. The logic may be that of inductive or hypothetic inference" (*CP* 6.218).

If the Absolute Mind thinks, it must employ the same basic modes of inference that all, including human, minds employ. Peirce indicted Hegel, perhaps a bit unjustly, for identifying the logic of the universe with deduction; that is a necessitarian position, whereby anything that occurs can be shown to be the necessary consequence of certain rational principles or laws. There is no room in such a philosophy for Peirce's tychism, no way to account for variety in the universe or to accommodate the miraculous or chance event; and it supplies no resources for explaining the origin and evolution of the laws of nature as objective "habits." In contrast, Peirce's universal mind formulates hypotheses and performs inductions (see *MS* 439:29ff.). It can be a playful, musing Mind, especially in its primordial state, where it is nothing other than "feeling, sporting here and there in pure arbitrariness" (*CP* 6.33). And it is a Mind that *wills* as well as thinks; but this was the second of Peirce's criticisms.

Most frequently, Peirce tended to express this criticism in the language of his doctrine of categories. Hegel erred in regarding the third category as being the only true one; in particular, he neglected "external secondness," the real world of actions and reactions (see *CP* 1.368). Such brute reaction events are the metaphysical correlates of what, from the perspective of his psychology of the Absolute Mind, Peirce described as acts of volition. Notice that Josiah Royce's philosophical system was considered by Peirce to be perfectly Hegelian in this respect.[19] Royce assumed

> that the reality of whatever really exists consists in the real thing being thought by God. Ordinary people think that things exist by the *will* of God; . . . that it must be some particular kind of divine thought which constitutes reality; and that particular kind of thought must be distinguished by a volitional element. In short, ordinary people make at once the very same criticism that the profoundest students of philosophy have made, namely, that the Hegelian school overlooks the importance of will as an element of thought. (*CP* 8.40)

Peirce was insistent that "no law determines any atom to exist" (see *MS* 898:3–4). Law may determine what can *possibly* exist and how it must behave, but not *that* it exists. Recall that continuity is the perfect form of generality, of Thirdness, of law. A continuum is not comprised of definite parts; it consists not of actual but of possible existents. Moreover, the actuality of these existents must be "determined" by an act of will. So while Peirce was in perfect agreement with Royce and Hegel that all of reality is mind, his objective idealism was distinguished both by his special formulation of the logic or law of mind and by his appraisal of the significance of volition as a fundamental "element of thought" (*CP* 8.40).

The mathematical foundations of Peirce's synechism have now been at least partially exposed here. Nonetheless, Peirce became increasingly concerned about anchoring his metaphysics solely in logical and mathematical arguments. If all of reality is continuous, he reasoned, then one actually ought to be able to perceive that fact. Moreover, if the divine mind is a continuum or "Third," and Thirdness is directly given in experience, then this fact has implications for any talk about religious experience. (See the discussion in chapter five.) It is not surprising, then, that in the latter stages of his philosophical career Peirce was also preoccupied with his phenomenological investigations. It was there that he believed he could establish the material aspect of his basic categories. As Peirce conceived of it, phenomenology "ascertains and studies the kinds of elements universally present in the phenomenon; meaning by the *phenomenon,* whatever is present at any time to the mind in any way" (*CP* 1.186). It was in an analysis of the phenomenon of *time,* most especially, that Peirce hoped to ground his claim that continuity or Thirdness is directly given in perception.

His essay on "The Law of Mind," once again, is an invaluable resource for interpreters of Peirce's synechistic philosophy. There he argued that "we are immediately conscious through an infinitesimal interval of time" (*CP* 6.110). Such an argument must be valid, Peirce contended, if any sort of intelligible account of human memory is to be developed.

> How can a past idea be present? Not vicariously. Then, only by direct perception. In other words, to be present, it must be *ipso facto* present. That is, it cannot be wholly past; it can only be going, infinitesimally past, less past than any assignable past date. We are thus brought to the conclusion that the present is connected with the past by a series of real infinitesimal steps. (*CP* 6.109)

Here is a powerful indication of the metaphysical seriousness with which Peirce regarded the notion of the infinitesimal. Time really is a continuum, so that it is made up not of discrete "instants" or "points" of time but of "moments" of infinitesimal duration (*CP* 6.111; see also *CP* 1.498–99). A past idea, if perfectly discrete and instantaneous, would be completely isolated in the past, and remembering would be impossible. But it is only "going, infinitesimally past" (*CP* 6.109); for Peirce, it is this continuous, infinitesimal duration or interval that one directly perceives when one is conscious of time.

Space is a continuum as well, and "there may be . . . modes of continuous connection between minds other than those of space and time" (*CP* 6.159). So the human mind might be related to the Absolute, as one of its subsystems, in an infinite number of ways. What, precisely, are the theological ramifications of such a hypothesis? At this point, it seems appropriate to assess briefly the religious significance of Peirce's doctrine of synechism. (But this discussion will be selective; the significance of Peirce's synechism for understanding his perspectives on immortality and prayer, for example, will be evaluated within the more appropriate contexts of chapters four and five, respectively.) Such an assessment will temporarily beg the question about the exact nature of the relationship between God and the Absolute; that is, for the time being, Peirce's descriptions of the Absolute Mind will be loosely regarded as "God-talk."

Peirce's general religious perspective has been identified in the first chapter of this book as a form of "scientific theism." Yet the word "theism" alone can be used with varying degrees of vagueness in philosophical and theological discussions. In its vaguest sense, the word distinguishes believers in God from *atheists*; nothing determinate is implied about the shape or content of such belief. Now Peirce was certainly a theist in this sense; he professed belief in God, formulated an argument for the reality of the Deity, and concluded that scientific inquiry itself is undermined by atheistic presuppositions. Yet there is a more technically precise usage of the word "theism." Most typically, the theist is distinguished from both the *deist* and the *pantheist* as one who affirms God as the creator of the world, remaining active and present in creation, but not indentical in being with it. Here again the label seems an appropriate one for Peirce's point of view. (Of course, this usage is still vague enough to permit a great many different forms of theistic belief.)

It is surely safe to conclude that Peirce was *not* a pantheist. He identified pantheism as "essentially unchristian" and as implying "a denial of God's personality."[20] Regardless of whether or not the description of a perspective as "unchristian" had negative connotations for Peirce, he clearly felt "forced to accept the doctrine of a personal God" (*CP* 6.162). More decisively, Peirce, as his father had done, professed a belief in God as creator of the universe (*CP* 6.452), a belief incompatible with the pantheistic notion that the world and the Deity are perfectly identical. So he seems explicitly to have rejected pantheism. But even if he had never done so, it would be possible to determine his opinion about this issue by making certain inferences based upon the principles of his objective idealism.

Far from being identical with the universe, the Absolute Mind infinitely transcends it, just as a continuum is infinitely greater than any number of determined parts of it (see *CP* 6.189–99); indeed, a continuum embraces not just infinitely many parts but rather possible determinations "beyond all multitude" (*CP* 5.103). Likewise, the Absolute Mind encompasses all possible as well as all actual states of affairs. This is divine transcendence with a vengeance; Peirce rejected not only the finitism that nominalism entails but also the Cantorian claim that a true continuum can be construed as an infinite collection of individuals. If the Absolute Mind is an all-embracing continuum, its reality, its enormous potential, must be greater than the combined reality of any number of its actualized parts. It is the whole that "calls out its parts," without ever being reducible to them. (This is the language, recall, that Peirce utilized in his characterization of final causality.)

In the same fashion, Peirce carefully resisted the remote and indifferent God of classical deism. The discussion in the next chapter will ilustrate that, in Peirce's view, God's creative activity is a continuous, ongoing process; his is a loving Deity that remains involved with its creation. Moreover, while Peirce denied that God is immanent in the world (for example, see *MS* 843:3), he should be understood as insisting that God is not *merely* immanent in the world but also transcends it. Such remarks are by no means designed to affirm an absolute discontinuity between the Deity and its creation. Indeed, divine transcendence, on Peirce's model, entails divine immanence; God is not merely "separate" from or "other" than the created universe in the sense that one object might be completely removed from another in physical space. Any such notion of transcendence as implying absolute separateness is simplistic and impoverished.

Consider God's relationship to persons and things in the world as being, in mathematical terms, like that of a line to the particular points that fall on that line.[21] This seems to be the least adequate topological model that one might supply for such a relationship, however. Its chief inadequacy consists in the fact that "points" are absolutely discrete entities, determinate in every respect. In Peirce's world-view, there was no intelligible metaphysical correlate for such a mathematical notion, except perhaps the category of "seconds" or brute reaction-events; but such events, since they are not generalizable, are hardly intelligible. They are mere "blips" on the screen of possible reality; for even if a point is marked on a line but not immediately erased, it endures in time and is, at least in one respect, continuous.

Nonetheless, God's relationship to individuals in the world might be roughly compared to that existing between a continuum and its topical singularities; these singularities may themselves constitute continua while still being determinate with respect to a given dimension of the embracing whole. Without wishing to belabor the mathematical underpinnings of Peirce's thought, such considerations really do illuminate his religious metaphysics. They suggest that Peirce, while definitely not a pantheist, might be properly labeled a *panentheist*, that is, one who views the world as being included in but not exhaustive of the divine reality.[22] Such a view neither undermines the doctrine of creation nor collapses the distinction between God and the universe.[23] Here the topological model can function as a safeguard, precluding any excessively crude form of panentheism. For even if a continuum is to be regarded as somehow "containing" its limits, still, the continuum *as such* "contains no definite parts" (*CP* 6.168). Indeed, the continuum and its singularities are not the same "sorts" of things at all. They are of different dimensionalities or, to put it metaphysically, they occupy different "levels of reality."[24] Once again, the "whole" has properties and a kind of reality that no mere aggregate of parts could ever have (see *CP* 1.220). As a system, it is *essentially* different from, albeit continuous with, its various subsystems.[25]

At the same time, such reflections indicate the special limitations, for these theological purposes, of any topological metaphor. One is easily tempted to imagine the relationship between God and the world in purely spatial terms.

A line drawn on a blackboard is located "within" that two-dimensional space; once determined, it is a "part" of the "whole" that such a space represents (even if no aggregate of such parts can be said to constitute the whole). It might be more useful to conceptualize the relationship between Creator and creation in terms of that which obtains between a law and the "cases" that it governs. Nominalistic claims notwithstanding, no number of such cases, however great, can "exhaust" the reality of a general rule or law. And while a law is quite distinct, on realistic premises, from the collection of actual "instances" that it governs, nevertheless it is intimately related to each instance, defines it, explains it, lends to it something of its own general character, indeed, its own reality.

Herein lies the rationale for Peirce's affirmation of the divine immanence (but not mere immanence) in the world. While infinitely transcending the actual universe, the Absolute Mind must also be really continuous with it. Returning to the mathematical model, a topical singularity must derive its continuous character from the space that contains it. Such singularities represent, in Peirce's religious metaphysics, the actualizations, by divine volition, of certain real possibilities. But what is accomplished through an act of will is given its shape, its form, by Reason; the intelligibility of any existing thing is derived from that general idea or purpose that links it to other fragments of the system, just as the continuity of the line "comes from" that of the blackboard on which it is drawn. Now the Absolute Mind is that one incredibly complex general idea that renders intelligible everything that exists; its reasonableness is "concretized" in the actual universe, even though it continues to embody possible further determinations beyond all multitude.[26] So at one and the same time, this Mind both infinitely transcends and intimately "informs" all things. And at one and the same time, one may be linked by real and continuous relations both to other persons and to God. (Love, Peirce will argue, is the paradigm of such relations.)

It has already been observed in the review above of Peirce's critique of Duns Scotus that he was willing to talk about individuals only in a relative sense. In logic, an individual is "that which is one in number from a particular point of view" (*CP* 3.93); but no logical term is absolutely indivisible or determinate. Likewise, a topical singularity is discontinuous only from a certain "point of view" or in a certain respect. If metaphysics follows logic and topology on this issue, some important religious and ethical conclusions seem to assert themselves. Peirce was not in the least bit reluctant to articulate these conclusions. A true synechist, he warned, must never say

"I am altogether myself, and not at all you." If you embrace synechism, you must abjure this metaphysics of wickedness. In the first place, your neighbors are, in a measure, yourself, and in far greater measure than, without deep studies in psychology, you would believe. Really, the selfhood you like to attribute to yourself is, for the most part, the vulgarest delusion of vanity. In the second place, all men who resemble you and are in analogous circumstances are, in a measure, yourself, though not quite in the same way in which your neighbors are you. (*CP* 7.571)

Both *ideality* and *purposefulness* are constitutive of personality according to Peirce. One of the ways that "neighbors" might be connected with or continuous with one another, then, is by sharing certain ideals or purposes. Together, they would form a kind of social organism, a community that is itself personal, a system of individuals defined by a single general idea. Given Peirce's formulation of the law of mind, one can assume that there would be a natural tendency for such communities to form, since all simple ideas tend to "spread" or generalize, and become associated with one another. Moreover, for Peirce all of this talk has a metaphysical rather than simply a metaphorical force. It is no less accurate to identify a social entity or even the universe itself as personal than it is to so label one's neighbor or oneself. Of course, the greater or more general the reality so identified, the vaguer will be the concept of personality that applies; but the vagueness of the conception in no way undermines its validity.

Peirce's reflections on the nature of both continuity and individuality ought to shed some light on the problem of religious knowledge as well, that disturbing metaphysical blindness that has yet to be clearly diagnosed here. These reflections show that it is true, after all, that human beings are "individuals" in certain respects. To embrace the "gospel of greed" (*CP* 6.294), to pursue the limited ideals of a selfish individualism, is simply to focus exclusively upon those respects in which one can be identified in the singular. It is also to ignore the very real relations, real independently of one's willing them to be real, that connect one with other persons and purposes. Peirce was reluctant, however, to conclude that human wickedness might be the sole factor responsible for obscuring one's religious vision. It just seems to be the case that the facts that "stare us in the face" are not always "easily discerned" (*CP* 6.162). To perceive one's relationship to the divine mind is to locate not those respects in which one is properly an individual but those aspects of oneself and of one's world that are continuous with a greater reality. Indeed, "seeing" God, for Peirce, is a phenomenon analogous to that described by Wittgenstein in his meditations on "aspect-seeing."[27] It appears to require a certain "skill" or habit of perception. Once again it is the Neglected Argument that provides a method for developing such skill, at least the outline of an "instruction manual" for that purpose; and it is Peirce's theory of signs and sign-interpretation, explicated within the context of his synechism, that supplies some of the crucial details of that method. The present discussion can only serve to introduce such hypothetical claims, their full explication to be pursued systematically in chapter five below.

Little more can be said about Peirce's perspective on miracles here. If the laws of nature are habits in the divine mind, as his objective idealism seems to stipulate, they will be nothing other than natural *tendencies*, more or less regular, just as anyone's beliefs might be more or less firm, depending on the quality of the inductive inferences that support them. Habits develop, are strengthened, sometimes are even "broken" or dissolved. General ideas evolve from simpler ones; altogether new ideas arise spontaneously from out of the "musing" of the Absolute Mind. To preclude miracles by regarding the laws of nature as inviolable is to believe in a God who does nothing but perform valid deductions; and this seems, for Peirce, an unnecessary restriction on the divine rationality.

This and any further discussion of Peirce's conception of God must remain problematic, however, until some sense has been made of his remarkable claim that "whether there be an Absolute or not, it is nothing like God" (*MS* 857).

III

Much of Peirce's cautious talk about the Absolute appears within his commentaries on Royce's philosophical system. For example, in a review of *The World and the Individual*, he observed how Royce analyzed the concept of God in terms of Hegel's Absolute Idea. Peirce objected, in striking terms, to the use of the word "God" within the context of this sort of philosophical discourse. "It is a flagrant offence to use this word in philosophy. It is like inviting a man to see the body of his wife dissected. There is also a pretension in it that the philosophy of religion can be religion" (*CP* 8.125). Elsewhere, in a letter to William James dated June 12, 1902, Peirce reported:

> I have been studying Royce's book. The ideas are very beautiful. The logic is most execrable. I don't think it very good taste to stuff it so full of the name of God. The Absolute is strictly speaking only God, in a Pickwickian sense, that is in a sense that has no effect. (*CP* 8.277)

One might attempt to offer a kind of ad hoc biographical interpretation of such remarks. Disillusioned as a young man, even disgusted, by hostile intellectual controversies surrounding religious issues, not only those between theologians and scientists but among the theologians themselves, Peirce early on developed a romantic anti-intellectualism in matters religious. Religion, he was convinced, is primarily an affair of the heart, not of the head, of instinct and common sense rather than of reason; it has nothing to do with the *philosophy* of religion. Now this sort of interpretation would not be entirely false; but it would be inadequate. For underlying Peirce's reaction to Royce's work are some important philosophical concerns, concerns both about the nature of the Deity and about the language used to identify or describe that Deity. Despite the anti-intellectual rhetoric, Peirce himself certainly did not avoid philosophizing about religion. Even in the review of Royce, he qualified his remarks by admitting that "things shocking to right feeling are sometimes necessary in philosophy" (*CP* 8.125). So there is a significant tension in Peirce's thought on this issue.[28] He argued that religion is a matter of feeling, yet he developed an extremely complex religious cosmology and metaphysics. He insisted that the philosopher's Absolute is "nothing like God," but he seemed to treat them as identical on a number of occasions. Yet one should hesitate to conclude that Peirce is simply and rather crudely inconsistent here; some general patterns and tendencies in his thought *can* be characterized, a coherent point of view defined.

Consider again his complaint to James about Royce's book. There the identification of God with the Absolute is not explicitly rejected by Peirce; but the Absolute is God only "in a Pickwickian sense," which he immediately glossed as a "sense that has no effect." Now in this last phrase Peirce clearly invoked his pragmaticist theory of meaning. The most famous and compact statement of that theory appeared in his 1878 article, "How to Make Our Ideas Clear," in the form of the following maxim: "Consider what effects, that might conceivably have practical bearings, we conceive the object of our conception to have. Then our conception of these effects is the whole of our conception of the object" (*CP* 5.402).

Peirce came to regret the apparent ease with which this formulation lent itself to the nominalistic interpretations of James and others, a state of affairs that was considerably worsened by the infelicitous example that Peirce employed to illustrate it (see *CP* 5.403 and 5.453–57, also *CP* 5.4). But he defended it too, underscoring the crucial significance of the word "conceived" in the maxim (*CP* 5.402, note 3, dated 1906). That is, Peirce never intended to identify the meaning of a conception with the *actual* effects of the object of that conception. Meaning is a "would-be," indeed, a continuum of possible effects, the total set of *habits* of conduct engendered by the object of a conception. What is of primary interest here, however, is the fact that meaning, and thus difference in meaning, is construed in terms of *effects* at all. It should be noted that this sort of pragmaticism also pervades the Neglected Argument, where Peirce, in explicating the God-hypothesis, is especially anxious to talk about its possible effects upon the Muser, the love and adoration that it inspires, the modes of conduct that it precipitates.

Peirce's cryptic little remark to James deserves some thoughtful scrutiny then. What is it that renders the concept of the Absolute inefficacious? Peirce neither asked nor responded to such a question in a direct manner, but at least two possible answers can be gleaned from his scattered reflections: (1) it is not sufficiently *vague*, and (2) it is not sufficiently *anthropomorphic*. For, regarding the ultimate cause of the universe, Peirce doubted "that there is any more adequate way of conceiving it than as vaguely like a man" (*CP* 5.536).[29]

Three aspects of Peirce's "logic of vagueness" need to be discussed at this point.[30] First, Peirce's understanding of what constitutes the vagueness of a term or sign has to be briefly explored. Second, this talk about vagueness must be connected with his remarks about real continuity, with the doctrine of synechism. Finally, the consequences of a sign's vagueness for its interpretation should be identified, the typical effects of that vagueness upon an interpreter ascertained.

In what does the vagueness of a sign consist? "A sign is objectively *vague*, in so far as, leaving its interpretation more or less indeterminate, it reserves for some other possible sign or experience the function of completing the determination" (*CP* 5.505).

If a sign leaves its interpretation indeterminate, but "renders to the interpreter the right of completing the determination for himself" (*CP* 5.505), Peirce understood it to be objectively *general*. So "Man is mortal" is general, because it allows the interpreter to apply its assertion to any man whom he or she chooses (see *CP* 5.447). But no such license is granted to the interpreter of "A man whom I could mention seems to be a little conceited"; such a statement is vague rather than general because, while the answer to the question "which man?" is left to be determined, the "right of further exposition" is granted to the utterer rather than to the interpreter (*CP* 5.447).

Peirce made this same distinction in another way when he explained that

> the *general* might be defined as that to which the principle of excluded middle does not apply. A triangle in general is not isosceles nor equilateral; nor is a triangle in general scalene. The *vague* might be defined as that to which the principle of contradiction does not apply. For it is false neither that an animal (in a vague sense) is male, nor that an animal is female. (*CP* 5.505)

This pair of definitions, however, is less illuminating than the first set, even if somewhat more compact. Return to those initial formulations. There the vagueness of a sign is grounded in the "indeterminacy" of its interpretation. How is this latter notion understood by Peirce? When a character is predicated of a subject both universally and affirmatively, Peirce regarded that subject as being *determinate* with respect to that character; "in all other respects it is *indeterminate*" (*CP* 5.447). This is of course only another version of an argument that Peirce developed in various forms and with great frequency. A logical individual is "one in number from a particular point of view" (*CP* 3.93); (and a topical singularity, even if itself continuous, represents a breach within a continuum of a higher dimensionality.) Determinacy or individuality is, once again, perspectival, a relative rather than an absolute category. Such a perspective having been defined for a given sign, it is vague "in all other respects." That is to say, a sign or term is vague to the extent that it remains logically "divisible," just as "the second Philip of Macedon" can be analyzed into "Philip drunk" and "Philip sober" with respect to "differences in time" (*CP* 3.93). Furthermore, no term is absolutely determinate in meaning, or indivisible. Consequently, every term is necessarily vague to a certain extent.

Vagueness is the quality of a sign; and it can be mitigated to the degree that the interpretation of a sign can be rendered more precise. But signs and their "interpretants" have, for Peirce, similar relationships to the objects of those signs. And such objects, if real, are fragments of a world that has already been depicted here as thoroughly ideal and continuous; they cannot be perfectly determinate "individuals." Moreover, objects "determine" their signs, so that the vagueness of the latter will be, at least partially, a function of the indeterminacy of their objects. It is in this fashion that Peirce's logic of vagueness is linked to his synechistic metaphysics.

Now the divine mind is a vast continuum of the very highest dimensionality. Far from being completely determinate, it embraces an endless number of possible further determinations. It is reasonable for Peirce to have concluded, then, that any sign of that reality ought to be exceedingly and necessarily vague. Yet terms like the "Absolute" carry with them all of the philosophical precision of those systems out of which they were spawned; and here one can err by being *too* precise. In general, Peirce preferred "vernacular locutions" as being best suited for the task of expressing vague ideas (see *MS* 280:5).

> "God" is a vernacular word and, like all such words, but more than almost any, is *vague.* No words are so well understood as vernacular words, in one way; yet they are invariably vague; and of many of them it is true that, let the logician do his best to substitute precise equivalents in their places, still the vernacular words alone, for all their vagueness, answer the principal purposes. This is emphatically the case with the very vague word "God," which is not made less vague by saying that it imports "infinity," etc., since those attributes are at least as vague. (*CP* 6.494)

What, in fact, is the "one way" in which the word "God" is "so well understood"? The answer to this question can be supplied at least in outline here. The meaning of "God" is comprehended in *feeling,* "interpreted in our religious adoration and the consequent effects upon conduct" (*CP* 8.262). For Peirce, in fact, "emotion *is* vague, incomprehensible thought.... That," he explained, "is why the highest truths can only be felt" (*MS* 891; see also *MS* 288:47–49). Of course, thought and feeling are not antipodal phenomena on Peirce's account; recall that vague feeling is the primordial state of mind, out of which specific ideas are determined as habits or continua of feeling. So thought is itself rooted in feeling; and vague but powerful emotion is continuous with the most abstract sort of reflection.

It is instinctive feeling, however, the vaguest of ideas, that functions as the most adequate interpretant for the sign of the reality of God. Moreover, it is the vernacular word "God" that is "best suited," because of its own vagueness as a sign, to produce that sort of interpretant. It has just the right "effect," and one, Peirce argued, that differs considerably from that induced by any philosophical term or expression. So, according to the 1878 maxim, these two conceptions, of God and of the Absolute, must actually differ in meaning.

A certain indubitability also attaches to that vague instinctive idea of the reality signified by the word "God"; that is, it is impossible to doubt the reality of a being so conceived. Of course God's reality is "indubitable" only in a very special sense for Peirce. A belief in God grounded in vital religious experience precludes *genuine* doubt about this reality, that is, anything other than feigned or "paper" doubt.[31] In any event, Peirce argued that this indubitability is necessarily related to the vagueness of the idea. So it, too, is threatened by the rendering precise of the conception of God in the form of some philosophically developed notion of the "Absolute." But this claim is the key element in Peirce's own rather idiosyncratic version of the "ontological proof," and it will be more effectively dealt with at a later point in this inquiry.

Peirce's suggestion that religious language ought ideally to be *anthropomorphic* parallels his remarks about vagueness. In this instance, too, the claim being made is one both about the character of our thought and language and about the nature of the reality being conceived or described. In the first place, Peirce contended, since man's intellect has had to become adapted to his primitive needs and practical experiences, all of our conceptions are to some degree anthropomorphic; one simply "cannot *mean* anything that transcends those limits" (*CP* 5.536; see also *CP* 5.47 and *MS* 290:26). This is a significant claim in itself, but Peirce commenced to argue that the more thoroughly anthropomorphic a notion or hypothesis is, even in science, the more likely it is to be "approximately true." For this reason among others he preferred an "old-fashioned God" to a "modern patent Absolute" (*CP* 5.47, note 1). Once again, God is best conceived as being "vaguely like a man."

This will not be a totally surprising conclusion for one who has taken seriously Peirce's explication of his objective idealism. All that there is, is mind, and the coordination of specific feelings and ideas within a teleological system results in the formation of a personality. Human minds and personalities are manifestations but not paradigms of these phenomena; nonetheless, Peirce felt it reasonable to assume a vague resemblance between them and the divine mind. Of course, to talk in this way about the "mind" of God may seem to be "ludicrously figurative" (*CP* 6.199); but there is simply no better mode of expression available. Moreover, however one chooses to articulate it, the synechist "is forced to accept the doctrine of a personal God" (*CP* 6.162).

Consider now, in light of the above, the following comments, in which Peirce concluded a brief discussion of scholastic realism by invoking the basic premise of his scientific theism.

> Analogy suggests that the laws of nature are ideas or resolutions in the mind of some vast consciousness, who, whether supreme or subordinate, is Deity relatively to us. I do not approve of mixing up Religion and Philosophy; but as a purely philosophical hypothesis, that has the advantage of being supported by analogy. (*CP* 5.107)

Thus far, Peirce's reluctance to equate God with the Absolute has been explained as a concern about language. It is his own peculiar conception of God, to be sure, that intensifies Peirce's suspicion that a certain kind of philosophical vocabulary is totally inappropriate for talking about the Deity. Nevertheless, the issue is primarily terminological; it has been assumed that there is one personal Being in question, for whom various symbols or names have been supplied. The task is to evaluate the appropriateness, the adequacy of each.

Peirce's reference above to a "Deity relatively to us" introduces another possible line of analysis, however. It is grounded in the hypothesis that Peirce understood the relationship between "God" and the "Absolute Mind" to be that of a "supreme" to a "subordinate" being. The one is not the other, that is, the Absolute is "nothing like God" (*MS* 857), but each is real nonetheless. There is a good deal of evidence to support such a hypothesis. Consider again, for example, Peirce's cosmological depiction of a "Platonic world" of infinite possibility (*CP* 6.208). Not only does this world transcend the universe "in which we happen to be," but it itself is conceived to be one of "many, both coordinated and subordinated to one another." What are some of the implications of this sort of cosmic picture?

Peirce was never able to pursue them very far, perhaps because he did not complete the Gamma system of existential graphs. Recall that in that system a "sheet of assertion" represents a single universe of discourse, the scribed graphs on the sheet signifying a "continuum of facts" within that domain. Each sheet is only one of many in a "book" of sheets, "tacked together at points" (*CP* 4.512ff.). Now this book can surely be regarded as the graphic representation of what Peirce metaphysically describes as a Platonic world, transcending but embracing the actual; and so the Absolute Mind might be identified with a single such universe of possibilities. Peirce supposed that there could be many such worlds, however, each the determination of an originally dimensionless reality, each emerging out of but nothing like it. Properly speaking, God must *be* that primordial reality, not one of many, but the creative source of all that exists.[32] But this proposal might seem more plausible in the light of some additional textual evidence.

As early as 1854, for example, in a fragment entitled "Notes on Heaven" (*MS* 891), the young Peirce, referring to God as the creator of the "infinite universe of space," reasoned that the Deity could create another such universe which might bear "no relation whatever to the first." Indeed, Peirce speculated, there could be "10,000 creations" bearing no relations to one another, each governed by an infinite being who is an "angel of God." "Is not our God one of these?" Peirce queried. "Heaven," he concluded by asserting, "is the Kingdom of the God of Gods."

Such youthful ruminations might easily be dismissed as a mere epiphenomenon of Peirce's adolescence. More than half a century later, however, one again discovers him speculating in much the same fashion. In some variant texts of the Neglected Argument (*MS* 843:3ff. and 3vff.), Peirce emphatically denied God's finitude, rejecting the notion that such a being is the "soul of the World" or merely "immanent" in Nature. While most certainly *not* finite, nevertheless,

> the Being of God would not, as far as I can see, necessarily exclude that of a whole race of beings immensely superior to ourselves, such for example, that the whole visible universe might be no more than a nucleolus in a single cell of the body of one of them. (*MS* 843)

The Absolute Mind might well be a member of such a "race of beings," but God *cannot* be merely "one of a genus" (*CP* 8.262). Here again is a radical assertion of the divine transcendence, one that still does not preclude, however, God's being continuous with the created world. And upon closer inspection, it appears not to be altogether unrelated to the argument that Peirce made about religious language. The word "God" is more vague than its philosophical correlate, just as the being of God is more indeterminate than that of the Absolute, the former embracing, above and beyond the latter, any number of "worlds" of undetermined possibilities. In a sense, the metaphysical assertion is the "flip side" of the claim about language. Both together constitute Peirce's rationale for being cautious about using the vernacular and the philosophical terms interchangeably.

In many of his cosmological musings, Peirce conceived of the "universe" (vaguely specified) as a vast personality, which he seems perfectly willing to identify as divine. Of course, one might just assume in those instances that he is treating such a reality as a "Deity relatively to us." It would be misleading to argue, however, that such religious notions were ever systematically explicated by Peirce. Consequently, having analyzed his perspective on this issue, it will be impossible to sort out and neatly organize Peirce's God-talk throughout the remainder of this discussion. Suffice it to say that there is no reason to assume, without serious qualification, that he considered God and the Absolute to be "metaphysically identifiable" realities.[33] His own remarks about a universal or Absolute Mind are religiously meaningful nonetheless.

They are religiously meaningful most especially perhaps because Peirce construed the relationship of the Absolute Mind to God in *semiotic* terms, that is, as the relation between a sign and its object.[34] This is another possible line of analysis, one that does not negate what has been said above but rather contextualizes it in a new way. Peirce supplied some important clues about how such a proposal ought to be articulated, once more in his review of Royce's *The World and the Individual.*

In the "Supplementary Essay" appended to the first volume of that work,[35] Royce attempted to illustrate the relationship between the Absolute Self and all finite selves by employing a map metaphor.

> That is to say, he likens the idea representing the entire life to a map of a country lying upon the ground of that country. Imagine that upon the soil of England, there lies somewhere a perfect map of England, showing every detail, however small. Upon this map, then, will be shown that very ground where the map lies, with the map itself in all its minutest details. There will be a part fully representing its whole, just as the idea is supposed to represent the entire life. On that map will be shown the map itself, and the map of the map will again show a map of itself, and so on endlessly. (*CP* 8.122)

"But each of these successive maps lies well inside the one that it immediately represents," Peirce explained, perhaps, one might add, somewhat like a "nucleolus in a single cell" of a vast cosmic being. Most interesting here however is Peirce's critique of the map metaphor. He complained that "the author recoils, and refuses to admit the continuity, or even the analytic continuity, of the map" (*N* 3:83),[36] an objection the force of which should be readily discernible at this point in the present discussion. More generally, however, "a map wants several of the essential characters of the class of signs to which ideas belong" (*CP* 8.126). The meaning of this objection is the key to achieving a deeper, more complete understanding of Peirce's conception of God and of God's relation to the actual world. It is also one of the keys to interpreting the Neglected Argument, since it is a claim grounded in the basic principles of Peirce's theological semiotic, his poetic of the created universe, principles that inform all of his talk about how God can be experienced and known. It is an objection, then, that must be interpreted with considerable care. But that interpretation may be more readily comprehensible if it is somewhat delayed.

First, recall that Peirce perceived this universe to be an evolving one, drawn to its ultimate objective by a final cause or set of ideals that, once vaguely fathomed, ought also to determine the conduct of human life, to shape human communities. About such matters, it will soon become clear, Peirce had some rather passionate opinions.

III

EVOLUTIONARY LOVE

I

Peirce insisted that the concept of the Absolute functions in metaphysics exactly as it does in geometry. The mathematicians, however, employing more rigorous methods of analysis, have been able to lend to this notion a greater precision than that which characterizes its philosophical usage. He observed, moreover, that the mathematical Absolute is confined to Space, bearing "the same relation to attainable space as the Metaphysical Absolute *ought* to bear to concepts of the Relative" (*MS* L224; also in *NEM* 3:872). Now while such remarks are certainly cryptic, Peirce said enough about this issue to indicate at least in general terms how metaphysicians might proceed to glean from geometry specific insights relevant to their own tasks and agenda. Among the consequences of employing such a procedure, he claimed, is the important discovery that "evolutionism" represents a basic metaphysical option, the one that Peirce himself felt to be most attractive and plausible. What, specifically, are these mathematical insights and what was, in his view, their application in the philosophical realm?

The impact on Peirce's thought both of Cantor's theory of transfinite numbers and of Listing's topology has already been noted. But the remarks cited above appeal for their intelligibility to a different mathematical source, in particular to the work of several individuals who played a prominent role in the development of modern analytical geometry. In 1859, the British mathematician Arthur Cayley had concluded that "the metrical properties of a figure are not the properties of the figure considered *per se* apart from everything else, but its properties when considered in connexion with another figure, viz. the conic termed the Absolute."[1] The argument in support of this claim is complex, but the claim itself can be briefly explicated. On every line extended indefinitely in both directions there are two points at infinity. The assemblage, in a plane, of all points at infinity is a conic section, a curve of the second degree. It is this conic that Cayley identified as the "Absolute"; and his basic contention was that metrical plane geometry could be construed as projective geometry with respect to the absolute conic, so that the metric notions of distance and angle could be reinterpreted in purely projective terms. Cayley's achievement was, in Peirce's evaluation,

> a discovery which has revolutionized our conception of space, and especially of measurement. . . . The "Absolute" is a particular surface—say, a firmament in the midst of the heavens, to which no object from our neighborhood can in any finite time, by any finite speed of motion, be carried, nor from it be removed. And every proposition involving measurement is equivalent, at bottom, to an intersectional property of that surface. This is certainly without exception the most wonderful discovery ever made in analytical geometry. (*NEM* 2:643)

It was a "wonderful discovery" not least of all because it allowed Felix Klein, in 1871, to impose some order on the recently proliferated non-Euclidean geometries while at the same time defining their relationship to the Euclidean system.[2] Klein generalized Cayley's results in order to show that if one proceeds solely on projective principles then the precise nature of the metric can be determined by the choice of the Absolute. In this fashion, one can generate each of the systems of Euclid, Lobatchevsky and Riemann, labeled by Klein as parabolic, hyperbolic, and elliptical geometry, respectively.[3] It is the rationale underlying Klein's particular choice of nomenclature in this instance that needs to be at least vaguely understood if Peirce's metaphysical appropriation of it is to be given a satisfactory explanation.

Assume that, in projective space, two parallel planes intersect at a line at infinity. It is in terms of their relationship to this line that the various conics can be distinguished. Each conic can be obtained as the projection of a circle, so that the resulting curve will intersect the line at infinity in two coincident points, two distinct points, or none at all.[4] There are three basic types of conic in Euclidean geometry, the parabola, the hyperbola, and the ellipse. They supplied Klein with an appropriate terminology for his classification of the various systems of geometry.[5] In the Euclidean or "parabolic" system, every line has only one real point in common with the Absolute. In the "hyperbolic" geometry, there are two real points at which a line meets the Absolute, just as the ordinary hyperbola touches the line at infinity at those two points tangent to its asymptotes. The ordinary ellipse never touches the line at infinity, and so too, in that system that Klein labels as "elliptical," the Absolute is purely imaginary.

Peirce was both quite familiar with and deeply interested in these and similar developments in modern projective and non-Euclidean geometry. His interest was, as always, that of the philosopher as well as the mathematician. That is, while he regarded mathematics as being restricted to the investigation of the world of possibility, with its propositions being purely hypothetical, he held that some of these possibilities might actually obtain in fact (*CP* 1.240–49). In this instance, propositions about the geometrical Absolute, tested against the facts of experience, could prove to have a metaphysical validity, to be applicable not just to the world of space but to all "concepts of the Relative" (*MS* L224). And since Peirce's is a thoroughly religious metaphysics, such propositions should have a theological significance as well.

Peirce, indeed, directly borrowed Klein's terminology and conceptual apparatus while adapting it for his own philosophical purposes. In this fashion he was able to sort out and to classify three basic but conflicting metaphysical world-views. In each case it is a particular conception of the Absolute that plays the crucial and normative role in describing the world, supplying a fixed reference with respect to which the nature and meaning of events are to be ascertained. At the same time, Peirce made clear his preference for one of the three options thus identified.

> The Absolute in metaphysics fulfills the same function as the absolute in geometry. According as we suppose the infinitely distant beginning and end of the universe are *distinct, identical,* or *nonexistent,* we have three kinds of philosophy. What should determine our choice of these? Observed facts. These are all in favor of the first. (*NEM* 4:377)[6]

What are the observed facts that Peirce had in mind? Consider some remarks from another manuscript, quite similar to those recorded immediately above, but providing an additional clue to their interpretation. Once again, he announced that

> all philosophies of the Absolute are of three kinds; for they suppose the absolute first and absolute last, either 1st, to be distinct, or 2nd, to coincide in one, or 3rd, not to exist. The last is Epicureanism, the second is Pessimism, the first is Evolutionism. (*MS* 904; see also *CP* 6.27)

As with Klein, it is the labeling here that is particularly illuminating. What Peirce elsewhere referred to as the "hyperbolic" philosophy (see, for example, *CP* 6.582) is now identified as "Evolutionism." All of the evidence that might be marshalled in support of the claim that the world is really and constantly evolving is evidence "in favor" of that general point of view. Now Peirce himself clearly affirmed the truth of this claim and embraced such a point of view. Remember that tychism, "with its consequent thoroughgoing evolutionism," is one of the doctrines that synechism was said to entail (*CP* 6.163); and the law of mind is really a law governing the *growth* of mind. Likewise Peirce contended that evolutionism is diametrically opposed to nominalism, a strong indication for him of its validity as a general perspective (*MS* 871:11ff.). It is interesting to note, however, that he appealed to religious reasons as often as he did to the "observed facts" when arguing for the superiority of this position over the alternatives. These reasons need to be identified at this point and their impact on Peirce's metaphysical thinking gauged.

The "Elliptic" and "Parabolic" philosophies, Peirce declared, are "irreconcilable with," even "hostile to Spiritualism"; while the "Hyperbolic" philosophy, if it provides no positive support for Spiritualism, is "evidently less unfavorable" than any other "reasonable" system of thought (see *CP* 6.582–85). Moreover, "if you adopt a theistic hypothesis you must either say that God does not think, and therefore, does not *plan*, or else his thought will result in evolution just as surely as the author of a book gives that book a gradual development" (*NEM* 4:140). Once again, nature is a book of divine authorship. And while the plan for that book gradually *unfolds* in time, notice that Peirce avoided claiming that the plan is one that is still being developed, that God's thought in itself is a temporal phenomenon.

So Spiritualism is not precluded by, and theism actually entails, the "hyperbolic" perspective. Even more specifically, evolutionism is, in Peirce's view, the only conception of the universe that is consistent with Christian theology (*CP* 1.362, note 1). For the theologians argue that the universe which has existed from all time "would appear to be in a different condition in the end from what it was in the beginning, the whole spiritual creation having been accomplished, and abiding."[7] Here, Peirce directly alluded to the Christian understanding of God as the Alpha and the Omega, the beginning and the end.[8] Recall that in the hyperbolic geometry, the two points at which a line intersects the Absolute are really distinct. This fact supplied Peirce with a useful and accurate model for his religious cosmology.

> These two points are the absolute first and the absolute last or second, while every measurable point on the line is of the nature of a third. We have seen that the conception of the absolute first eludes every attempt to grasp it; and so in another sense does that of the absolute second; but there is no absolute third, for the third is of its own nature relative, and this is what we are always thinking, even when we aim at the first or second. The starting-point of the universe, God the Creator, is the Absolute First; the terminus of the universe, God completely revealed, is the Absolute Second; every state of the universe at a measureable point of time is the third. (*CP* 1.362; also see *CP* 6.581)

In the Epicurean or elliptical philosophy, the absolute is purely imaginary, the measurable is all that there is, and the universe displays no "definite tendency whence or whither" (*CP* 1.362). Representing a different perspective, the Pessimist believes that, since the two points of the absolute are coincident, the ultimate end of the universe "is nothing but the Nirvana from which it set out" (*CP* 1.362).

> But if your creed is that the whole universe is approaching in the infinitely distant
> future a state having a general character different from that toward which we
> look back in the infinitely distant past, you make the absolute to consist in two
> distinct real points and are an evolutionist. (*CP* 1.362)

The "God" described in this passage is an ideal limit, approachable but unreachable, the absolute reference to which all actual states of affairs are relative, both their source and their ultimate terminus. Perhaps this is the sense in which Peirce felt that it was appropriate to conceive of the Deity as being "remote."[9] There is something potentially misleading about this model, however. It should be remembered that Benjamin Peirce defended the Christian doctrine of creation as a safeguard against what he perceived to be the dangers of pantheism; and for whatever reasons, Charles also consistently embraced such a doctrine, until the end of his life identifying God as Creator. At the same time, he conceived of that creative activity in a particular fashion, not as confined to a single isolated event at the beginning of time but as a continuous and ongoing process (see *CP* 6.505).[10] So however remote the Deity might be, its impact on the created world is direct and persistent.

This fact does not negate the value of the model for Peirce's philosophical purposes. In his hyperbolic cosmology, God is placed, as absolute beginning and end, beyond any measurable point of time. Such a being cannot be regarded as "subject to Time, which is rather one of His creatures" (*CP* 4.67). But this does not preclude the possibility of a positive and continuous relationship between God and creation, although the metaphysical problems engendered by the attempt to define the precise nature of such a relationship are certainly severe enough, and have plagued philosophers for ages.[11] The difficulty is not only in understanding precisely how a time-transcending reality is related to that which changes but also in conceiving of just such a reality. Of course, Peirce denied the validity of anything other than the vaguest of conceptions of God. And he reinforced such a position here, arguing that any attempt to conceptualize the Absolute First or Second must fail. It is always some "third" that forms the object of thought, "even when we aim at the first or second" (*CP* 1.362).

Now on Peirce's account, Thirdness is the category of representation. This passage also embodies then (albeit quite undeveloped here) his claim that the world is a "vast representamen" (see *CP* 5.119); for "every state of the universe" is categorized here as a "Third." Since "this is what we are always thinking," any conception of God must be regarded, in fact, as the conception of a sign of that reality. Furthermore, since a person is "nothing but a symbol involving a general idea" (*CP* 6.270), personality might very well be ascribed to such a representation; indeed, the symbol of God could constitute a cosmic personality. Here is further evidence for the hypothesis that Peirce's God is not identical to the Absolute Mind, that the latter (not restricted to the physical universe but encompassing the worlds of possibility and of real generality as well) is a living symbol of the former.

Of course, on this interpretation, all metaphysical talk about God is rendered problematic; and that is precisely the point of view that Peirce came to embrace. In these remarks, written more than a decade before his criticism of Royce on this score, Peirce himself appeared to identify God with the Absolute. Yet this Absolute-as-Deity is inconceivable, so that all metaphysical and cosmological discourse can have God as its object "only in a Pickwickian sense." Rather, if God *as Creator* and God *as completely revealed* are conceived to be infinitely distant states *of the universe*, its origin as a Platonic world of possibility, its terminus as fully concrete reasonableness, then they are most properly regarded as being symbols of the Deity.[12] If for some particular philosophical purpose the significance of the difference between the real object and its symbol is negligible, the two might easily become conflated within one's discourse, a tendency that Peirce himself obviously displayed in some of his writings. Nevertheless, he was concerned that the distinction not be altogether obliterated, the metaphysically conceived Absolute not be equated with the God encountered in living religious experience.

In any event, Peirce's remarks here indicate that he perceived God, however vaguely, to be both the *Creator* of the world and its ultimate *Ideal.* And Peirce came with increasing confidence to affirm the reality and the real efficacy of ideals.[13] Moreover, just as the choice of the Absolute determines the metric in geometry, one's metaphysical portrayal of the divine ideal provides a standard for the assessment of phenomena, for the measurement of their status within a teleological system. Unlike their mathematical counterparts, however, metaphysical hypotheses must endure the test of experience in the long run. In this instance, speculation about the true nature of the absolute ideal must be supported by data gleaned from the investigation of actual evolutionary processes. Of course, Peirce willingly engaged in this sort of speculation, but the discussion of his conclusions must be delayed until his account of the creation of the world has been examined. First things first.

In his maturest reflections, Peirce understood God to be the "creator of all three Universes of Experience" (*CP* 6.452), including the universe of "mere Ideas"; "*all reality* is due to the creative power of God" (*CP* 6.505). This is an important claim because it affirms that God, rather than simply actualizing certain possibilities, in point of fact, *creates* those very possibilities.[14] Furthermore, they are created ex nihilo. For it is out of the continuum of vague, undetermined, and undifferentiated potentiality that this "Platonic" world of forms evolves; and that original indeterminacy is, for Peirce, "the germinal nothing," a "pure zero" (*CP* 6.217). It is "prior to every first."

How, then, did the universe come into being? Peirce employed as a general principle the claim that

> all the evolution we know of proceeds from the vague to the definite. The indeterminate future becomes the irrevocable past. In Spencer's phrase, the undifferentiated differentiates itself. The homogeneous puts on heterogeneity. However it may be in special cases, then, we must suppose that as a rule the continuum has been derived from a more general continuum, a continuum of higher generality. (*CP* 6.191)

This is, by now, a familiar theme in Peirce's metaphysical story. But its precise cosmological application in this instance needs to be carefully underscored. Note that the evolutionary process that is being described at this stage results in the determination not of the existing universe but of the world of Platonic forms (see *CP* 6.192–95, and 6.208). This is a world of sense-qualities, of "slumbering" feeling, of definite possibilities emerging spontaneously from out of that indefinite potentiality that is itself "prior to every first" (*CP* 6.217). It is the emergence of just such a world that marks, on Peirce's account, the first day of creation, albeit one that occurs "before" time was (see *CP* 6.200). In 1890, Peirce had supplied the following description of this primordial event and its immediate aftermath.

> Our conceptions of the first stages of development, before time yet existed, must be as vague and figurative as the expressions of the first chapter of Genesis. Out of the womb of indeterminacy we must say that there would have been something, by the principle of Firstness, which we may call a flash. Then by the principle of habit there would have been a second flash. Though time would not yet have been, this second flash was in some sense after the first, because resulting from it. Then there would have come other successions ever more and more closely connected, the habits and the tendency to take them ever strengthening themselves, until the events would have been bound together in something like a continuous flow. (*CP* 1.412)

Here Peirce insisted not only on the appropriateness but indeed on the necessity of an account of creation similar to that supplied by religious tradition; that is, it "must be as vague and figurative as the expressions of the first chapter of Genesis" (*CP* 1.412). Again, one simply ought not to be more precise than a given subject matter allows. When he returned to this topic eight years later, Peirce was even willing to admit that such cosmological speculations might actually be translated into an explicitly religious language.[15]

The general indefinite potentiality became limited and heterogeneous. Those who express the idea to themselves by saying that the Divine Creator determined so and so may be incautiously clothing the idea in a *garb* that is open to criticism, but it is, after all, substantially the only philosophical answer to the problem. (*CP* 6.199)

One theologically problematic aspect of this sort of talk ought immediately to be explored. If the vast potentiality that constitutes the vital source of everything that exists is not to be confused with that which is *merely* possible in the logical sense, then it must have been *necessary* that the world be created. For the potential that never actualizes itself "remains a completely idle and do-nothing potentiality" (*CP* 6.219), a lifeless abstraction rather than an active power.[16] Yet this argument would seem to entail the conclusion that God had no choice but to create the world, a conclusion that conflicts sharply with orthodox theistic claims concerning God's freedom and the gratuitous character of the creation event.

Peirce's cosmological meditations, however, seem rather consistently to reinforce rather than conflict with his religious notions. Furthermore, those notions tend to be compatible with classical western theism, albeit often articulated in somewhat unconventional ways. For example, his argument that the potential *must* determine itself runs parallel to his contention that creative activity is "an inseparable attribute of God" (*CP* 6.506). Peirce was convinced, moreover, that he could make this kind of a claim without threatening the divine freedom. Indeed, the original undetermined potentiality is nothing other than "boundless freedom" (*CP* 6.217). And "nothing *necessarily* results from the Nothing of boundless freedom" (*CP* 6.219). There is no immediate paradox here; the necessity that Peirce rejected is a Hegelian necessity, one that is characteristic of deduction. Rather, he affirmed that the creative event is of the nature of a hypothetic inference (see *CP* 6.220); in the latter, *no specific conclusion* is entailed. To put it cosmologically, from out of that vague potentiality, something had to be determined, but no *specific* thing or state of affairs resulted *necessarily. That* God creates is a necessary fact, but the appropriate answer to the question "*what* must God create?" is "nothing in particular" (*CP* 6.218). Peirce's God is a free being who is nonetheless a Creator not by accident but in essence.

This account still raises more questions than it answers, however. Granted that God creates the universe from "Nothing," was Peirce also suggesting that the Deity is to be identified with that very nothingness, that vast ocean of undifferentiated potential that is the ultimate source of all that comes into being? His vague speculations would seem to warrant an affirmative answer to this question; and Peirce was quite obviously sensitive to the fact that such an explanation of the creation of the world will likely be considered by some to be theologically problematic.[17] It is an account, he warned, that "must not interfere with or be interfered with by any religious belief," religion being an entirely "practical matter" (*CP* 6.216). At the same time, he argued that "it is a damnable absurdity indeed to say that one thing is true in theology and another in science." So his warning embodies a methodological prescription for both scientists and theologians; the claims embedded in a truly scientific cosmology cannot, in the final analysis, be theologically irrelevant.

Peirce, in fact, never abandoned his own scientific theism, and his characterization of the primordial nothingness has powerful religious, even quasi-mystical undertones. It is unlimited possibility, boundless freedom, potential being without lack, vital and creative. It is "nothing" in the sense that it is "no thing," "no individual thing, no compulsion, outward nor inward, no law" (*CP* 6.217). In this sense, to say that the Deity determines itself and that God creates the world ex nihilo is to say one and the same thing. (See also *CP* 6.490.)

This is the language of a negative theology, its object an incomprehensible reality that can be known only in the vagueness of thought-as-feeling, a reality that is less adequately construed as the Absolute First than as being "prior to every first" (*CP* 6.217). Of course, Peirce did not rule out positive assertions about God altogether. But such utterances must themselves either remain vague or run the risk of self-contradiction. In a sense, the logic of vagueness functions within Peirce's religious thought much as the doctrine of analogy does for Aquinas, although Peirce clearly never pursued the religious implications of his philosophy of language with anything even remotely resembling the latter's systematic thoroughness. It is because signs are not perfectly "discrete" or determinate in meaning that they are necessarily vague. Similarly, analogy of meaning implies some *continuity* between same term occurrences; *mere* equivocation results when there is no such continuity of meaning between same words used in different contexts. This suggests the possibility of some application of the logic of vagueness to the problem of analogy. Characters predicated both of God and of beings in the world are to be applied to the Deity only vaguely; once again, it is legitimate to conceive of God as being "vaguely like a man," with the understanding that no determinate sense of the word "man" is signified by such a claim.

Furthermore, positive talk about God, even if it avoids self-contradiction, is probably best understood as actually being descriptive of one who is "a Deity relatively to us" (*CP* 5.107), a reality that is itself the determination of, and thus relative to, that mysterious, primordial, potential Being. Of course, as Peirce himself noted, we only "wildly gabble about such things" (*CP* 6.509), and his own "gabbling" is likely to support several possible interpretations of its meaning. The cosmological picture that he is painting becomes clearer, however, its images more definite and well-illuminated, the further one moves within his narrative away from this dark myth of the beginning. Out of that vast nothing-ness, an infinite world of definite possibilities emerges, and this world also evolves; this Mind grows.[18]

II

The logic of the universe was, for Peirce, the law of its development, and that he perceived to be, most essentially, the law of love. It is in the last of his 1891–93 series of *Monist* essays, on "Evolutionary Love," that Peirce explicated his general theory of how the world develops, at the same time supplying for this account a thoroughly religious interpretation. More accurately, religious no-tions and a theological vocabulary are constitutive of that very account; and alternative theories of evolution are rejected, not least of all it seems, because they are *religiously* unsatisfactory. What is implicit in many of Peirce's other writings is made explicit in this paper; his scientific metaphysics is not only shaped by but represents the articulation of his theism.

The stage has already been set for the discussion that is embodied here.[19] The Platonic world of forms, once determined, must be further developed, must emerge into some "theatre of reactions" (*CP* 6.195), the existing universe representing just such a state of affairs. This is the visible universe, its own evolution producing effects that can be sensibly observed. The task of the scientist is not only to record such observations but to seek out the principle or set of principles that will render them fully intelligible. Various theories of evolution have been designed for this purpose. Each of them, Peirce suggested, succeeds in isolating a particular "mode" of evolution. He did not appear to be interested in rejecting any of these theories wholesale but only in subordinat-ing them to a more general principle, incorporating them into an account wherein each will function to illuminate some aspect of the total picture.

Most prominent among these is the Darwinian theory of evolution. On this view, two basic factors underlie all natural processes of development.

> Natural selection, as conceived by Darwin, is a mode of evolution in which the only positive agent of change in the whole passage from moner to man is fortuitous variation. To secure advance in a definite direction chance has to be seconded by some action that shall hinder the propagation of some varieties or stimulate that of others. In natural selection, strictly so called, it is the crowding out of the weak. (*CP* 6.296)

The creative stimulus of chance and the ruthless struggle for existence, operating together, determine the path of evolution. Neither principle is one that Peirce regarded as having originated with Darwin. The latter notion is borrowed from the writings of the nineteenth-century political economists and merely extended by Darwin "to the entire realm of animal and vegetable life" (*CP* 6.293). This was a move that Peirce clearly rejected. His objection was partially grounded in scientific considerations; indeed, "while argued with a wealth of knowledge, a strength of logic, a charm of rhetoric," the soundness of Darwin's position "to a sober mind . . . looks less hopeful now than it did twenty years ago" (*CP* 6.297). Its enormous success in attracting supporters has been, more than anything else, the direct consequence of "its ideas being those toward which the age was favorably disposed" (*CP* 6.297). More fundamentally, it is this very Zeitgeist that Peirce found objectionable, not merely Darwin's application of the principle but the principle itself. Indeed, he wasted very little effort here in refuting Darwin's specific scientific claims. His primary intention was to expose the ideas that lie at the heart of this "greed-philosophy," and to contrast them sharply with the Christian philosophy of love.

As far as Peirce was concerned, the principle of natural selection is neatly articulated in the maxim: "Every individual for himself, and the Devil take the hindmost!" But "Jesus, in his sermon on the Mount, expressed a different opinion" (*CP* 6.293).

> Here, then, is the issue. The Gospel of Christ says that progress comes from every individual merging his individuality in sympathy with his neighbors. On the other side, the conviction of the nineteenth century is that progress takes place by virtue of every individual's striving for himself with all his might and trampling his neighbor under foot whenever he gets a chance to do so. This may accurately be called the Gospel of Greed. (*CP* 6.294)

The reader should probably not be surprised to learn that Jesus was, from Peirce's point of view, a synechist. Individuality, whether within the metaphysical or the moral realm, is always less significant a fact for him than that of the continuity of all things. Yet anyone who has taken too seriously Peirce's characterization of religion as a purely practical matter might very well be surprised by this direct appeal to religious notions within the context of an evaluation of various scientific theories of evolution. Clearly, the gospel of Christ embodied more than a practical moral code for Peirce; it has real explanatory power, representing an attractive alternative to the general perspectives of Darwin, Spencer, and others. Nonetheless, the appropriate contrasts cannot be clearly delineated here until Peirce's analysis of Darwinism has been further unpacked. Recall that natural selection is the form but not the agent of change in Darwin's scheme. The principle of fortuitous variation also figures prominently in his account, and about this issue Peirce had more positive things to say.

This is a principle that, once again, Peirce saw Darwin as creatively employing rather than inventing or discovering. The "idea that chance begets order" had already been exposed and then defended in an especially vigorous way during the decade leading up to the publication of the *Origin of Species* (*CP* 6.297).[20] The statistical method had been applied with great success to problems in both the social and the physical sciences. Most especially, the kinetical theory of gases, developed by Herapath, Maxwell, and others, had clearly illustrated "that fortuitous events may result in a physical law" (*CP* 6.297). This discovery along with the utilitarianism expounded by the political economists helped to forge the intellectual ethos within which Darwin's thinking matured.

Peirce was critical of that ethos, but also quite obviously affected by it. He rejected what he perceived to be its dominant individualism, manifested both in the utilitarian ethic and in a creeping nominalism. But he was deeply impressed by the efficacy of the new statistical method in the sciences, and he worked to refine that method. Peirce's studies convinced him that the notion of *chance* or *fortuitous distribution* is a crucial element in the explanation of the action of non-conservative forces (*CP* 6.74–81). It is in such forces that the power of mind consists, by means of them that an idea achieves its effects. In this respect, Darwin had a positive impact on Peirce's thinking. He successfully extended the principle that "chance begets order" to the biological realm, encouraging Peirce's own highly speculative applications of it in his metaphysical and cosmological arguments; the doctrine of tychism becomes an essential ingredient of Peirce's objective idealism. In those arguments, however, while the primary agent of change is objective chance, the *form* of change is no longer natural selection, but rather, creative love.

Darwin's is not the only theory that Peirce both criticized and appropriated. Directly opposed to *tychastic* evolution is the theory of evolution by mechanical necessity, or *anancasticism*. Hegel and Spencer were among its philosophical proponents; it had numerous representatives in the geological and biological sciences. The latter held "that nothing is due to chance, but that all forms are simple mechanical resultants of the heredity from two parents," a conclusion, Peirce contended, "to which the facts that come under their observation do not point" (*CP* 6.298). His discussion here is quite brief, but it is supplemented by his numerous attacks, in other writings, on all forms of mechanical necessitarianism. The crucial point that needs to be underscored once again is that religious as well as scientific reasons were enlisted in support of his critique; not only are such theories unwarranted by the available data but they also inaccurately portray the Deity as one who is bound by the exigencies of deduction, not free to think new thoughts, and thus not truly a "creator" at all. Such a "pseudo-evolutionism . . . is at once scientifically unsatisfactory, as giving no possible hint of how the universe came about, and hostile to all hopes of personal relations to God" (*CP* 6.157).

At the same time, the doctrine of anancasticism shares with agapasticism a certain teleological perspective, development "tending on the whole to a foreordained perfection" (*CP* 6.305). It is not, to be sure, the sort of teleology that Peirce regarded as being properly characteristic of personality in his essay on "The Law of Mind" (*CP* 6.156–57). Nonetheless, this very element of purposefulness places anancasm, as a mode of evolution, in sharp contrast to pure tychasm, allowing it, like the latter, to be represented as a "degenerate" form of agapasm.

> Herein, it must be admitted, anancasm shows itself to be in a broad acception a species of agapasm. Some forms of it might easily be mistaken for the genuine agapasm. The Hegelian philosophy is such an anancasticism. With its revelatory religion, with its synechism (however imperfectly set forth), with its "reflection," the whole idea of the theory is superb, almost sublime. Yet, after all, living freedom is practically omitted from its method. (*CP* 6.305)

Peirce's basic complaints about Hegelianism have already been summarized above. But there was a pronounced ambivalence in Peirce's attitude towards that system of thought, so that his critical remarks about Hegel, scattered throughout his writings, oscillate between high praise and severe condemnation. Peirce's negative attitude was at least partially grounded in his religious world view; Hegel's is a philosophy that abolishes "living freedom," not only human but divine freedom. The passage above indicates clearly, however, that Peirce's more positive feelings about Hegel's "theory" were also nourished by his religious beliefs. In accommodating revelatory religion and articulating an imperfect synechism, that theory deserves to be characterized as "superb, almost sublime" (*CP* 6.305). That is to say, Hegel affirmed the truth both of the Christian religion and of the only type of metaphysics with which, in Peirce's view, such a religion is genuinely compatible.

Nevertheless, these "degenerate" theories of evolution reveal only partial truths. The whole truth, or at least a closer approximation to it, is embodied in the principle of *agapism*. This principle, Peirce suggested, achieved its most eloquent expression in the Gospel of John. After all, it was that "ontological gospeller" who "made the One Supreme Being, by whom all things have been made out of nothing, to be cherishing-love" (*CP* 6.287). Here is the foundation for a truly evolutionary philosophy: the double conviction that God is love and "that growth comes only from love" (*CP* 6.289). Regarding the second of these premises, Peirce supplied the following elucidation.

> Suppose, for example, that I have an idea that interests me. It is my creation. It

is my creature; for as shown in last July's *Monist*, it is a little person. I love it; and I will sink myself in perfecting it. It is not by dealing out cold justice to the circle of my ideas that I can make them grow, but by cherishing and tending them as I would the flowers in my garden. The philosophy we draw from John's gospel is that this is the way the mind develops; and as for the cosmos, only so far as it yet is mind, and so has life, is it capable of further evolution. Love, recognizing germs of loveliness in the hateful, gradually warms it into life, and makes it lovely. (*CP* 6.289)

It is precisely this sort of perspective on evolution, Peirce continued, that every careful reader of his essay on "The Law of Mind" will perceive to be entailed by the doctrine of synechism. Indeed, here one encounters again the central argument of that essay, cast now in an explicitly religious form. In fact, it is an argument that is developed in all of the papers of that *Monist* series. Consider, briefly, the fourth of these, "Man's Glassy Essence," to which Peirce directed the reader with his reference to "last July's" issue (*CP* 6.289). More specifically, he invoked the claim embedded there that "a person is only a particular kind of general idea, . . . nothing more than a symbol involving a general idea" (*CP* 6.270).[21] It was hardly a revolutionary claim when it appeared at that point, given what Peirce had already written about the nature of personality. But his general strategy is clear. He broadened considerably the notion of personality to embrace a wide range of phenomena, human, non-human, and trans-human. As a consequence, it now became appropriate for him to argue that "there should be something like personal consciousness in bodies of men who are in intimate and intensely sympathetic communion" (*CP* 6.271).

> *Esprit de corps*, national sentiment, sympathy, are no mere metaphors. None of us can fully realize what the minds of corporations are, any more than one of my brain cells can know what the whole brain is thinking. But the law of mind clearly points to the existence of such personalities, and there are many ordinary observations which . . . give evidence of the influence of such greater persons upon individuals. (*CP* 6.271)

Perhaps these "greater persons" need not be described in specifically religious terms. Nevertheless, here at the end of the fourth *Monist* article it is the Christian Church that supplied Peirce with an exemplification of such a phenomenon. He concluded with the following personal recollection and commentary.

> When the thirty thousand young people of the society for Christian Endeavor were in New York, there seemed to me to be some mysterious diffusion of sweetness and light. If such a fact is capable of being made out anywhere, it should be in the church. The Christians have always been ready to risk their lives

for the sake of having prayers in common, of getting together and praying simultaneously with great energy, and especially for their common body, for "the whole state of Christ's church militant here in earth," as one of the missals has it. This practice they have been keeping up everywhere, weekly, for many centuries. Surely, a personality ought to have developed in that church, in that "bride of Christ," as they call it, or else there is a strange break in the action of mind, and I shall have to acknowledge my views are much mistaken. (*CP* 6.271)

If the views that Peirce articulated in his final essay are not "much mistaken," love is the creative force responsible for the development of such "personalities," for the growth of mind. It is the primordial and quintessential principle of generalization. Human beings, out of love for one another and through a common devotion to specific goals and ideals, form communities, greater "selves." The paradigm for such behavior, the prototype for such feeble imitations, is the divine love, a love constitutive of God's very being. Moreover, it is a love that must embrace its opposite, since that which God "loves must be defect of love; just as a luminary can light up only that which otherwise would be dark" (*CP* 6.287). Here, under the influence of Swedenborg and Henry James, Sr., Peirce conceived of the divine "agape" as a power that harmonizes discordant elements.[22] Armed with such a conception, he attempted confidently to "resolve" the problem of evil. More immediately, however, this understanding of the nature and dynamics of love has important implications for Peirce's evolutionary cosmology.

Love is creative in at least two senses for Peirce, causing things both to be and to be-in-relation. He made this point, somewhat poetically, when he proposed that "The movement of love is circular, at one and the same impulse projecting creations into independency and drawing them into harmony" (*CP* 6.288).

Ideas spring up spontaneously, spread, become affected by one another, and form general ideas. This is the law of mind. It is also, Peirce contended, the law of love, love constituting not only the creative origin of such ideas but also the gentle force that welds them into harmony. Both the divine *will* and *reason* are exercised in this circular movement of love, since it is only through an act of will that anything can be made to exist, yet the tendency towards generalization is itself the manifestation of law, of reasonableness. So this love that is the source of all new ideas also establishes those relations that connect them one to another, projecting them as individual creations, even while drawing them into sympathetic communion.

In this way, agapasticism, as a theory of evolution, succeeds in accounting for both the elements of *variety* and *growth* in nature. But this fact should not be stated in such a way as to obscure the radical dependence of the latter upon the former. Variety is itself a factor in the process of development. Growth, on

Peirce's account, is not "mere increase" but involves diversification (*MS* 955:36). So evolution is marked both by an increase in variety, or diversification, and an increase in regularity, or the development of law (*CP* 1.174). These tendencies are not in conflict, but rather they represent "one and the same impulse" (*CP* 6.288). That impulse is towards greater heterogeneity; but even as "the homogeneous puts on heterogeneity" (*CP* 6.191), these diverse elements are drawn into harmonious relationship *on another level*, become coordinated within some more general *system* of relations. From this perspective, variety is never mere chaos, the simple disruption of order; it is, most essentially, a necessary catalyst for the growth of reason.

God's creative love, thus described, is to be identified neither with the randomness of pure chance nor the rigidity of mechanical law. Nonetheless, it is a love that is spontaneous and free, the ever vital source of new ideas, so that some of the essential features of tychasticism are preserved in Peirce's theory of evolutionary love. Likewise, it is an ordering love, seeking no simple uniformity or regularity but a general harmony, the continuity of all things. In this fashion, drawing upon theological, even biblical resources, Peirce was able to formulate his hypothesis about how development occurs. Now this scientific theism cuts both ways; for if religious notions are to be regarded as having real explanatory power, then the scientific method must have some bearing on the issue of how, precisely, such notions are to be formulated. Furthermore, apart from the teachings of any "revelatory religion," something like this theory of agapism ought to have been formulated on purely scientific principles. Such an account ought to represent, to the truly scientific intelligence, the best possible construal of the available data.

That is perhaps why Peirce appealed to Lamarck as well as to the Gospel of John in order to make his case for the doctrine of evolutionary love. The former supplies a scientific account that "supersedes" the conflict between those rival proponents of "evolution by sporting" and "evolution by mechanical necessity" (*CP* 6.299). In the Lamarckian scheme of things, at least according to Peirce's interpretation of it, it is the concept of *habit* that is of central importance for explaining the development of natural forms. That is to say, Lamarck's theory of the transmission of acquired characteristics describes a process that "is of the general nature of habit-taking" and, as such, "essentially dissimilar to that of a physical force" (*CP* 6.299). For Peirce regarded habit as a gentle force that nonetheless serves to establish patterns of regularity. It is to be distinguished from that spontaneous "energetic projaculation" by means of which "the new elements of form are first created" (*CP* 6.300).

> Habit, however, forces them to take practical shapes, compatible with the structures they affect, and, in the form of heredity and otherwise, gradually replaces the spontaneous energy that sustains them. Thus, habit plays a double

part; it serves to establish the new features, and also to bring them into harmony with the general morphology and function of the animals and plants to which they belong. (*CP* 6.300)

Here, just in case the reader might fail to recognize in this description of habit's double function the circular movement of love, Peirce himself proceeded to make the connection explicitly. Some clarification is required at this point, however. Habit does not cause things first to be but rather to endure as a continuity of reactions. It establishes them, gradually replacing that "spontaneous energy" out of which they were originally formed. Yet, for Peirce, the divine agape (since God *is* love) is the creative source of *all* that there is, all possibilities, all actualities, all generalities. So this notion of love would appear to be somewhat broader, more comprehensive, than his understanding of the nature and function of habit. The movement of love would seem to originate in and not merely to replace that spontaneous creative energy.

This is a reasonable enough conclusion. God creates the world ex nihilo, but no habit, no law, no Third can cause anything to exist. Moreoever, God is that incomprehensible reality, prior to every first, the ideal limit transcending every actual state of affairs, to whom one would not expect that Peirce's basic categories could be neatly applied. Still, insofar as he attempted to describe the Deity at all, the concept of continuity and the general category of Thirdness were the most adequate tools available for his purpose. This produces a certain tension in Peirce's thought, manifested, for example, in his ambiguous claim that God is the independent Creator of all three "Universes of experience" or "at any rate two of the three" (*CP* 6.483).[23] For despite the divine transcendence, the divine agape seems to share some of the characteristics of any habit or "Third" (at least, "so far as it is manifested in time"—*CP* 6.490). It has a mediating, harmonizing influence. It achieves its effects gradually. It is a gentle force, tolerant of diversity, of the spontaneous or chance event. Finally, it establishes such chance results, orders them, coordinates them into some general pattern formed around some higher purpose.

This last feature, such purposefulness, is essential to Peirce's account. The development of the entire cosmos, all of evolution, represents nothing more than love's teleology, worked out "in living realities" (*CP* 5.119). But how is this teleology to be understood? If the movement of love is "circular" how can the end be different from the beginning? If God is *both* the Absolute First and the Absolute Second, then how, precisely, does Evolutionism differ from Pessimism, the hyperbolic from the parabolic philosophy? Once again, some caution has to be exercised in interpreting Peirce's mathematical metaphors. The two distinct points at which a hyperbola intersects the Absolute represent, in Peirce's scheme, different *states of the universe*. This is not to say that there is more than one Absolute, but rather that the real Absolute, like the geometrical conic, *determines* these two ideal points and thus the path of evolution. It is the universe that "would appear to be in a different condition in the end from what it was in the beginning" (*CP* 1.362). And if the Absolute First and the Absolute Second designate infinitely distant states of this universal mind, then, as indicated above, they are best construed as being determinations of, indeed, representations of the Deity.

Likewise, if the movement of love is circular, that which love moves, its creation, experiences real growth, changes and evolves. This process of growth can only begin at that point when it has already been projected "into independency"; that is the moment of creation, from which all progress towards ultimate harmony or reasonableness can be traced. The gentle forces that guide this progressive motion have been described here, explicated, in terms of the concepts of self-giving love, or agape, and habit. Since they are genuinely purposeful forces, not in a rigid mechanical sense but manifesting a truly "developmental teleology," Peirce could also describe the moving power of evolution in terms of *final causation*. "For evolution is nothing more nor less than the working out of a definite end" (*CP* 1.204).

Final causes bring about a result of a "certain general character" (*CP* 1.211). Since they do not determine any particular result, their efficacy is inevitably linked to the operation of efficient causes. "Law, without force to carry it out, would be a court without a sheriff; and all its dicta would be vaporings" (*CP* 1.212). Law itself is not force in this sense of actual compulsion, so that "final causality cannot be imagined without efficient causality" (*CP* 1.213). Now this is just a new language for expressing one of Peirce's most persistent claims. No law, habit, or idea can cause anything to exist, any *particular* event to occur. A "rule" does *govern* its "cases," however; habit exercises a formal influence, harmonizing and channeling those "energetic projaculations" that do produce specific effects. In theological terms, God's creativity is a matter of *willing* the existence of particular things, as well as of determining, in *thought*, that such results will be of a certain general character or kind.[24]

If this new language embodies no startlingly new ideas, nevertheless, it does serve to place in the foreground one particular aspect of the evolutionary process, its purposefulness, the tendency towards ends. The Lamarckian theory illustrated the manner in which habit establishes new forms. That is precisely what it means to say that the members of a natural class *derive their existence* from an idea or final cause. Peirce was careful to explain the precise meaning of such a claim.

> Do I mean that the idea calls new matter into existence? Certainly not. That would be pure intellectualism, which denies that blind force is an element of experience distinct from rationality, or logical force. I believe that to be a great error . . . . What I mean by the idea's conferring existence upon the individual

members of the class is that it confers upon them the power of working out results in this world, that it confers upon them, that is to say, organic existence, or, in one word, life. (*CP* 1.220)

To be established in this fashion, to possess life in this sense, is both to be a certain *kind* of thing and to pursue those *ends* appropriate for things of that kind. Ideas or final causes define the essence of a living system of relations, determining the manner in which this whole calls out its parts; that is to say, they are laws governing the behavior of the fragments of such a system.[25] These ideas do have a reality of their own, a potential being, a being *in futuro* (*CP* 1.218). But their real power consists in their ability to get themselves thought, to create their own proponents. This is the perspective of objective idealism; ideas are not "locked up" in somebody's skull but constitute the very environment to which human minds must adapt and within which they develop. Thus, Peirce argued,

> you must see that it is a perfectly intelligible opinion that ideas are not all mere creations of this or that mind, but on the contrary have a power of finding or creating their vehicles, and having found them, of conferring upon them the ability to transform the face of the earth. (*CP* 1.217)

Of course, all ideas are the creations of *some* mind; Peirce was rejecting here any purely subjective ideality, the identification of the human intellect as the exclusive source of such notions. He was also emphasizing, in a remarkable way, the degree to which men and women are empowered by ideas to work out results in the world, "to transform the face of the earth." This power *is* purposefulness, conferred when action is directed towards its proper end. Without such direction, while there may be no lack of spontaneous energy, there can be no consistency in behavior, no reasonableness, only "helplessness" and "chaos" (*CP* 1.220). Moreover, reasonableness is not only a characteristic of purposeful activity but the very end to which all such activity is ultimately directed.

How is this last claim to be understood? Persons might form communities as a result of their commitment to any number of ideals. But the growth of reasonableness is the ideal of ideals, the general form that gives all other values their meaning. So much is obvious from Peirce's explication of the law of mind, the law of love. Ideas naturally tend to spread, to generalize; love seeks to harmonize disparate elements, to facilitate the continuous growth of the beloved. Perfect reasonableness, not merely potential but embodied in the actual arrangement of specific facts, is the final goal of cosmic evolution.

Surely such an end, thus described, is exceedingly *general* and *vague.* This does not represent a difficulty for Peirce, however, since on his account no genuinely ultimate ideal could be conceived otherwise (see *CP* 1.205ff.). This state of fully embodied or *concrete reasonableness* is clearly an ultimate ideal, the absolute terminus of evolution, infinitely removed from any present or actual state of affairs. It is "God completely revealed," the full development of the universe as the symbol of the Deity. Such an ideal, Peirce contended, can be approached even if never fully attained, partially realized perhaps in the Christian Church when it achieves a genuine community of love or in the scientific community when its members are sincerely devoted to discovering the truth of nature. It is exemplified in these communities, manifested in the harmony of certain natural forms, represented by the collective artistic genius embodied in the great Gothic cathedrals (see *CP* 6.315). And it is an ideal that ultimately ought to govern all social and political activity, whatever the more immediate ends of such activity might be.

Peirce's social ethic is not only radically communitarian but utopian as well, since individual behavior is to be oriented not only to the good of the existing community but also to that of the ideal community. The formation of the latter is the end to which present activity, when viewed in its proper evolutionary perspective, must be directed. Peircean individuals are responsible for the future, then, in a remarkably tangible way. On synechistic principles, the future is really continuous with the present, and the parameters of any community in which one claims membership are only vaguely defined; they cannot in principle be defined in any perfectly determinate sense. This sort of perspective explains Peirce's impatience not only with utilitarian individualism but with the mutual hostility between scientists and theologians, with the narrowness that typically characterizes religious doctrines and creeds.

Even Peirce's pragmatic maxim needs to be understood within the context of his synechistic evolutionism. As such, it takes on a moral, indeed, a religious significance. Consider Peirce's own commentary on the maxim, written in 1893, some fifteen years after the publication of "How to Make Our Ideas Clear." There Peirce identified his theory of meaning as "an application of the sole principle of logic that was recommended by Jesus; 'Ye may know them by their fruits'" (*CP* 5.402, note 2). But these fruits need to be regarded in a collective sense as "the achievement of the whole people."

> What is it, then, that the whole people is about, what is this civilization that is the outcome of history, but is never completed? We cannot expect to obtain a complete conception of it; but we can see that it is a gradual process, that it involves a realization of ideas in man's consciousness and in his works, and that it takes place by virtue of man's capacity for learning, and by experience continually pouring upon him ideas he has not yet acquired. We may say that it is the process whereby man, with all his miserable littleness, becomes gradually more and more imbued with the Spirit of God, in which Nature and History are rife. (*CP* 5.402, note 2)

It should be clear by now that this sort of use of religious language was intended by Peirce as more than a mere embellishment. Nature's teleology, history's teleology are most perfectly understood when conceived in religious terms. Of course, with regard to the final outcome of world history, we can have no complete conception of it. Surely, however, the goal of evolution can be understood clearly enough to require that one abjure the utilitarian ethic of individualism as not only immoral but illogical. The true logic is the logic of John's Gospel, the logic of synechism.

> When we come to study the great principle of continuity and see how all is fluid and every point directly partakes the being of every other, it will appear that individualism and falsity are one and the same. Meantime, we know that man is not whole as long as he is single, that he is essentially a possible member of society. Especially, one man's experience is nothing, if it stands alone. If he sees what others cannot, we call it hallucination. It is not "my" experience, but "our" experience that has to be thought of; and this "us" has indefinite possibilities. . . .
>
> Individual action is a means and not our end. Individual pleasure is not our end; we are all putting our shoulders to the wheel for an end that none of us can catch more than a glimpse at—that which the generations are working out. But we can see that the development of embodied ideas is what it will consist in. (*CP* 5.402, note 2)

This passage will represent no surprising new claims for anyone who is already familiar with the basic ingredients of Peirce's synechism. Still, several important nuances of his communitarian ethic emerge here into sharper focus. That ethic has now clearly taken on an evolutionary aspect. A genuine community is a living idea, a greater person, and, precisely as such, it experiences real growth. This growth is never mere increase, but rather it involves both continual diversification and the harmonization, one with another, of ever more complex systems of ideas. Moreover, these ideas must not be conceived as idle abstractions; they must be of the kind that get themselves thought, find or create their own vehicles, become embodied in actual, concrete fact.

Such an ethic prescribes no more elaborate code of behavior than the law of love. The divine agape, the "Spirit of God," manifests itself in the natural laws or ideas that govern the development of the universal mind. No human intellect can fully comprehend the divine plan; but one can grasp certain determinate features of it as it unfolds, can catch a "glimpse" or a "fragment of His Thought as it were" (*CP* 6.502). "Warmed into life," responding to this divine initiative, human love too plays a role in the evolutionary process. It is such a love that motivates the scientific search for truth, that underlies the process of artistic creation, that nurtures the development of a philosophical idea, indeed, that affirms and cherishes other persons as the living embodiments of an idea. Ultimately, it is a love directed to the divine ideal, to God, whose own love is the creative source of all possible and actual states of affairs but who "permits" men and women a "share . . . in the work of creation" (*CP* 5.402).

The Christian principle of love supplies for Peirce, then, both a "rule of ethics" and a "universal evolutionary formula" (*CP* 6.441). It is a principle, Peirce was willing to admit, that the Stoics and the Egyptians, the followers of Confucius and of the Buddha clearly "anticipated" (*CP* 6.442). So this insight into the nature, power, and significance of love is hardly an exclusively Christian achievement; nor can the Christians claim to have realized, in some actual community, the full flowering of that insight. Once again, "a great catholic church is wanted" (*CP* 6.443). This ideal or "invisible church" is one that must not only "embrace all Christendom" (*CP* 6.444) but also include within itself anyone whose "sole desire" is "to hasten the chariot wheels of redeeming love" (*CP* 6.448).

Remarks of this sort raise interesting questions about Peirce's perspective on non-Christian cultures; but such questions are not easily resolved. It is difficult, for example, to gauge the impact of eastern religious and philosophical traditions on Peirce's thinking. Some of the classical texts of these traditions must have been accessible to him, and there are references in his work to the teachings of Confucius and the Buddha.[26] In particular, Peirce seemed to have been attracted to the *moral* wisdom of these religious sages. For example, he admired the selflessness and stoic resignation of the Buddha, as evidenced by comments in several of his letters to William James (see *MS* L224). Of course, Peirce died before the history of religions emerged as a vital scholarly discipline, so that his knowledge of these eastern traditions was likely to have been vague, quite incomplete, distorted by western concepts and categories. Peirce himself denied ever having been "stricken with the monstrous mysticism of the East" (*CP* 6.102), an infection that he detected in the writings of Schelling, Emerson, and others. While this denial may have been a bit ironic, it does suggest that a good deal of his knowledge of the east was second-hand (unlike his grasp of medieval materials, for example, which he clearly studied in the Latin originals). And he does seem for the most part to have identified himself as a Christian and to have conceived of Christianity as a highly evolved form of more "primitive" systems of belief (*CP* 6.442), in particular, "a higher development out of Buddhism" (*PW* 78). Most importantly, the *framework* for the majority of Peirce's explicitly religious writings is decisively theistic and Christian (however creatively he formulated his own ideas within that context).

Peirce has not been and is not likely to be remembered primarily as a moral philosopher. He wandered only occasionally into the realm of ethics and his substantive moral claims are of a broad and sweeping character. Moreover, these claims can quite reasonably be regarded as the extensions of his metaphysical point of view. This is not to suggest that Peirce actually conceived of ethics as a science dependent upon metaphysics; indeed, just the opposite is true, since he clearly asserted that metaphysics rests "on phenomenology and on normative science" (*CP* 1.186). Nevertheless, certain of his metaphysical convictions, for example, those about the continuity of all things and about the evolving nature of reality, shaped his thinking about love and community, about how persons ought ideally to think and to behave. His pronouncements about these latter issues have the same general character as those metaphysical principles that inform them. Of course, one might choose to reverse the lines of causal influence; Peirce's own predisposition to embrace a particular religious and moral world view might very well explain the attractiveness to him of certain metaphysical notions.[27] As has been suggested repeatedly throughout this discussion, that seems very much to have been the case. Still, the precise manner in which such a world view is elaborated, the arguments that are employed in order to justify it, reveal this tendency to appeal to the basic metaphysics of synechism as a standard maneuver.

This sort of philosophical move, from metaphysics to morality, is by no means unproblematic. Assuming Peirce can convince the reader that, metaphysically speaking, there are no absolute individuals, it remains unclear whether or not there can be "individuals" in any ethically relevant sense. Peirce did grant, after all, that someone or something can be individuated with respect to a given character, or from a specific point of view. Such a point of view does not negate the fact of continuity, but rather specifies those relations that are to be regarded as significant for a given purpose. For the purposes of the moral agent, one might ask, is every relation to be regarded as significant? In what sorts of relations does genuine community subsist? If the answer to the first question is "yes," then "*A* loves *B*" is no more ethically meaningful a fact than "*A* and *B* both have brown hair." If the answer to the second question is "any sort," then community always already exists. But are these the answers that Peirce himself would supply?

Clearly Peirce considered individualism to be an immoral perspective, not least of all *because* of its falsity. Conversely, nominalism is not only a mistaken but a morally reprehensible point of view; it is the metaphysic of hedonism and of *laissez-faire* practices. So Peirce's ethical claims about the way that persons ought to live seem to be grounded in his arguments about the way the universe really is. At the same time, the creation of a genuine community is a process in which human beings have to participate. It is those relations that ought *ideally* to exist between persons, relations of love and not any already existing "connectedness," that would seem most essentially to be formative of community, to define it as such. And so the principle of synechism, in itself, cannot adequately ground Peirce's communitarian ethic. Evolutionism must be invoked as well, and not just the *fact* of evolution (which Peirce believed synechism to entail anyway) but a particular sort of teleology with a specific terminus, the sort described in Peirce's essay on evolutionary love.

If this is the case, then normative science really is independent of metaphysics; the decision about what ought to be regarded as truly ideal has a certain primacy and cannot be based on synechistic principles alone. How then is such a decision to be made? The kind of choice that Peirce did make, his general perspective on the ultimate end of evolution, has already been sketched here, the thoroughly religious character of that end noted. But *esthetics* is the proper science of that which is ideal or admirable in itself, and so a good deal more has to be said in the next chapter about this topic. It is important to observe, however, that this move from metaphysics to morality is not so unambiguous as it first seemed to be. Peirce did invoke synechism in rejecting the ethics of utilitarianism. Yet his own communitarian love-ethic cannot be so easily established. Some conception of the ultimate ideal must be arrived at by other means, even if it is subsequently elaborated along synechistic principles.

Peirce's version of the ontological argument, it will be shown, involves the contention that the contemplation of a certain ideal will compel one to affirm that such an ideal must be real. It is the great beauty of the *idea* of God, among other factors, that produces in the consciousness of the Muser belief in God's reality. In the Neglected Argument, it will be suggested, phenomenological and normative considerations function as a necessary prelude to the metaphysical claim about God, so that there the logic of Peirce's classification of the sciences remains intact. At the same time, that classification itself suggests another possible perspective on the present discussion. The concept of continuity, while employed creatively in Peirce's synechistic metaphysics, is itself formulated mathematically; moreover, the material aspect of continuity, of Thirdness, he believed to be given in experience, so that it could be ascertained by means of phenomenological inquiry. While he perceived normative science to be independent of metaphysics, it "rests largely on phenomenology and on mathematics" (*CP* 1.186); thus, it is possible, at least in principle, to utilize the concept of continuity in an ethical argument without necessarily invoking certain metaphysical assumptions.

Still, Peirce's critique of individualism, embodied in the passages cited above, did rest on the claim that all things in the universe *really are continuous*. This is neither a mathematical nor a phenomenological proposition; rather, it clearly has a metaphysical status. Of course, Peirce was less than clear about the precise sense in which one science can be said to rest upon another; and his own practice blurs rather than sharpens the distinctions drawn in theory.

Before attending to Peirce's discussion of normative science and to the Neglected Argument proper, one more aspect of his theory of evolution needs to be treated. It is clear that love is a harmonizing force for Peirce, that it serves to bring discordant elements into relation. Love also "projects" its creations "into independency" (*CP* 6.288), however, causing things to be as well as to be of a kind. Peirce insists on the importance of this moment in love's teleology, chides the Hegelians for forgetting that God wills as well as reasons, yet in his moral deliberations this aspect of reality appears insignificant. Actual individuals, who are after all the products of this first movement of love, and individual experiences are hardly relevant features of the evolutionary picture. "One man's experience is nothing," since, in fact, a man is nothing more "than a possible member of society" (*CP* 5.402, note 2).

Such remarks can easily be distorted when taken out of context, but they do hint at a possible weakness, an inadequacy in Peirce's evolutionary ethic. The logic of love supplied Peirce not only with a "universal evolutionary formula" but with a ready "solution" to the problem of evil as well. Peirce's understanding of that problem and the solution that he prescribed need now to be assessed.

III

In many respects, Peirce's perspective on evil represents a quite typical nineteenth-century point of view, especially among evolutionists and the proponents of an absolute idealism. His discussion of this topic resembles the treatments of it given by thinkers as diverse as Emerson, Royce, and Teilhard de Chardin.[28] Peirce himself never made any claim to originality for his solution to the problem of evil. Indeed, he consistently reported that his own argument was, for the most part, borrowed from the writings of Henry James, Sr. Nonetheless, once appropriated, the latter's claims take on distinctively Peircean qualities, become integral components of Peirce's world-view.

What is perhaps most striking about Peirce's comments on this issue is the sense conveyed by them that evil is a problem readily dissolved. Among Peirce's trademarks as a philosopher are the rigor and creativity with which he typically addressed the classical philosophical questions. Old answers to these questions are scrupulously assessed, often rejected or reformulated. But in this instance, Peirce's position can scarcely be said to represent a solution to the problem of evil; it is tantamount to denying that any such problem exists.

Consider the following claims, entirely characteristic of what Peirce had to say about evil. "Whatever is is best" (*MS* 970:11ff.). That which one experiences as being evil or bad in some respect is more than "counterbalanced" by being good in a different way. In point of fact, evil ought to be regarded as one of the "perfections" of the universe (*CP* 6.479). "God delights in evil per se" and "sin" itself is God's own creation (see *MS* 330:4–5 and *MS* 890:1ff.). The Deity inflicts pain as a "warning" to avoid certain harmful feelings and things; as such, the existence of pain "harmonizes beautifully" with the notion that this universe is one whose ends are only gradually unfolding, being "worked out" (*MS* 843:32ff.).

Now the religious significance of these remarks needs to be underscored. Whatever practical difficulties it may represent for others, the reality of evil is only *philosophically* problematic for the theist, in particular, for one who believes in the existence of an omnipotent and benevolent Deity. Peirce was most definitely a theist, albeit one who insisted that God can only be vaguely understood. Several prominent features of his religious metaphysics, however, seem to soften the classical theological dilemma that arises out of the human experience of suffering and evil. Interpreted within that particular metaphysical context, the claims listed above become intelligible. Consider, in turn, Peirce's *synechism*, his *evolutionism*, and the principle of *agapism*. (It should be clear by now, of course, despite their distinctive nuances and emphases, that each of these doctrines represents a variation on the same theme.)

In the first place, evil can have no perfectly separate reality if *all* of reality is continuous. The problem of evil reduces to a matter of aspect-seeing; what appears to be evil from some point of view will, from another perspective, be perceived as continuous with that which is positively good. All suffering and evil are counterbalanced, Peirce argued, within the context of some system of relations sufficiently broad to embrace and to harmonize them with other elements of experience. Viewed as aspects of the most comprehensive or universal system, one should understand them to be "perfections." That is to say, the world is better than it might otherwise be precisely because, within it, such evil is accommodated and overcome. Furthermore, the presence of evil in the world is not fortuitous but divinely ordained; it is a part of God's own dialectical strategy which, once executed, results in the gradual achievement of specific ends, ultimately, the growth of concrete reasonableness.

Here Peirce's evolutionism, linked with his synechism, grounds his solution to the problem of evil. It is somewhat misleading for him to have asserted that "whatever is is best" (*MS* 970). In order to be properly understood, this argument should be temporalized: whatever is *will prove to work out for the best.* Now this fact may not be demonstrably true, given the data supplied by any individual's experience. But it is quite clear that Peirce attached no great significance to the experience of individuals, perceiving them, indeed, *evaluating* them as nothing more than possible members of society. He never really shifted his gaze from the evolutionary "long run," so that, most perfectly expressed, his contention is that whatever is will prove to work out for the best *in the long run.*

This counterbalancing of evil in the universe is the work of love, a divine agape that gradually warms the hateful into life, hatred itself being nothing other than an imperfect form of such love. Peirce formulated these claims in the course of an argument that begins with a meditation on the Gospel of John and proceeds to a consideration of the Swedenborgian perspective of Henry James, Sr.

> Thus, the love that God is, is not a love of which hatred is the contrary; otherwise Satan would be a coordinate power; but it is a love which embraces hatred as an imperfect stage of it, an Anteros—yea, even needs hatred and hatefulness as its object. For self-love is no love; so if God's self is love, that which he loves must be defect of love; just as a luminary can light up only that which otherwise would be dark. Henry James, the Swedenborgian, says: "It is no doubt very tolerable finite or creaturely love to love one's own in another, to love another for his conformity to oneself: but nothing can be in more flagrant contrast with the creative Love, all whose tenderness *ex vi termini* must be reserved only for what intrinsically is most bitterly negative and hostile to itself." (*CP* 6.287)

Thus is disclosed for the problem of evil, Peirce announced, "its everlasting solution." But what, precisely, is the logic of this argument? It appears to be dialectical, in the Hegelian sense; the hateful, while "aufgehoben" in the process, nonetheless constitutes a necessary negative moment in love's creative development. Several explicitly theological concerns emerge here as well, supplementing the metaphysical biases that form the rationale for this set of claims. If such claims are affirmed as true, then the divine omnipotence is preserved (since Satan is no "coordinate power"), God is rescued from a narcissistic self-love, and the presence of evil in a theistic universe is explained.[29]

Notice that, according to Peirce's agapism, that which love draws into harmony is also that which love has projected into independency. It seems that Peirce intended to be understood quite literally when he asserted that God is the creator of sin and "delights" in the hateful. Out of nothing, God has created everything, including that which is evil. What is evil? Anything that is the opposite of love, love's proper object, anything insofar as it persists in its otherness or independency. Individuals *ought not* to conceive themselves or to be conceived apart from those various systems of relations that give them purpose and constitute their reality. Such a conception is the essence of sinfulness, even if it consists in nothing more than an ignorance on the part of some individual of the fact that all things are fragments of a greater whole, a universal mind.[30] But is this the sense, one might ask, in which the words "evil" and "sinful" generally tend to be understood?

One of the weaknesses of Peirce's argument is this very inability to distinguish, within the broad class of individuals, those persons, things, and events that are typically considered to be evil. He insists that "it is man's duty to fight" evil (*CP* 6.479), but exactly how are the battle lines to be drawn? Who is the enemy? Undoubtedly, for Peirce, the enemy is anyone or anything that impedes the growth of concrete reasonableness, that resists the process by means of which individuals are harmonized with one another. Individuality is the locus of evil, then, if it is construed as the terminus rather than as a moment or phase of the circular movement of love. In this respect, an individual preoccupied with his own personal suffering might be no less evil or sinful than that individual who, in his own self-affirmation and lack of concern for others, is responsible for inflicting such suffering. Neither individual succeeds in transcending the "metaphysics of wickedness," each clinging to a notion of selfhood that is nothing but "the vulgarest delusion of vanity" (*CP* 7.571).

If self-love was no-love for Peirce, it is nevertheless the case that selves are proper objects of love. Love, he insisted, is not for abstractions but for persons, for those others who are, in the teachings of Jesus, our neighbors, both in life and in feeling (*MS* 891:1). Even God's love is directed to these finite others, first creating them, establishing them in their independence, then nurturing their growth and coaxing them into fruitful relationships. If this is the case, then any suffering, any pain experienced by the beloved ought to be something that the lover would struggle to mitigate, to eliminate. Peirce argued that, since "Evil is 'that which man ought to fight,' . . . nothing which man cannot put down can be evil" (*MS* 843). Here Peirce invokes the venerable principle that ought implies can; anything that lies beyond one's control is not to be considered evil. But nothing is beyond the control of an omnipotent deity; and there exist in this universe all sorts of natural evils, natural forces that are disruptive of harmony, that are sources of suffering. Why should these evils not be regarded as 'that which God ought to fight'? If God creates the world ex nihilo, why should such evils exist at all?

Peirce could respond to such questions once again by shifting attention to the end of evolution: God not only does combat but actually conquers evil *in the long run.* Indeed, it is precisely as an obstacle to be overcome that God "delights" in that which is evil. But even if a convincing argument could be supplied to validate such a claim, Peirce needed also to indicate precisely what it is that God accomplishes by allowing certain evils to remain temporarily dominant, to exert their disruptive and pain-inducing influence. How is it that the same or superior ends could not have been achieved by means of a different process from which such pain and suffering were altogether absent? Here Peirce seemed only to be able to point to the pedagogical value of human suffering; pain is a "warning" device (*MS* 843:32), serving God's purposes as a means for "detaching us from false dependence on Him" (*MS* 845:38; see *CP* 6.507).

This line of argumentation is rendered more effective, of course, if it is assumed that Peirce was a "process" thinker, for whom God is a being that also grows or develops, a being who is not omnipotent in the classically theistic sense.[31] From this perspective, the answer to the question about why the same ends could not be accomplished by different means is to be given in terms of some talk about *constraints* upon the divine activity. Whatever is is best, quite simply, because God does the best that God can.

Such a characterization of Peirce's position is problematic for a number of reasons. It is at odds with Peirce's own tendency to affirm those divine attributes traditionally ascribed to the Deity by classical theists (*CP* 6.452, 6.508–10).[32] God, he asserted, *is* omnipotent, albeit in a vague sense (*CP* 6.508); and Peirce was so concerned to safeguard this claim that he even speculated that God might "refrain" from knowing much, since God's very "thought is creative" (*CP* 6.508). In fact, for this very same reason, if there are many possible worlds, as Leibnitz suggested, they must all somehow be actual; otherwise, "some limitation upon Omnipotence" seems to be implied (*CP* 6.509). And, again, one of the reasons for insisting that love must "embrace" hatred was the concern that the divine agape not be limited by some coordinate power. Even more consistently, however, Peirce seemed to argue quite clearly for the time-transcending character of the Deity. The *Ens necessarium*, as disembodied spirit or pure mind, "has its being out of time" (*CP* 6.490). Even the vague ascription of purposes to God should not be understood to entail that God literally "grows" (*CP* 6.466).

Peirce's various remarks about the problem of evil, articulated over a long period of time, do not represent a perfectly coherent, tightly argued point of view. But they do reflect, as has already been suggested, his general religious and metaphysical outlook. All of reality is continuous, gradually evolving towards an ideal state, under the gentle but ultimately irresistible influence of a divine love. From a certain limited perspective, evil is a temporary resistance to the growth of reasonableness, an obstacle that must be overcome. From the perspective of the long run, when the cosmic story will have completely unfolded, when the divine work of art will be contemplated as a whole, evil has no distinct reality at all.

Perhaps it is unfair to criticize on philosophical criteria that which Peirce might never have intended as a strictly philosophical solution to the problem of evil. Even so, there are elements of Peirce's own philosophy that seem to stand in tension with his treatment of this issue. Someone or something can be, as the fragment of a greater system, both continuous with that system and yet discontinuous in some respect with regard to a specific dimension of the embracing whole. Such discontinuity or Secondness is a very real aspect of human experience; in fact, it is an irreducible category of experience. Furthermore, it is correlated by Peirce with talk about divine volition, about a God who does not simply contemplate possibilities but causes things actually to be. Even the summum bonum, was, for Peirce, not an ultimate harmony abstractly conceived but a fully *concrete* reasonableness. Once again, it appears that Peirce, in his treatment of evil, is vulnerable to the very same sort of critique that he directed against the Hegelians. This category of Seconds, of actuality, of individuals is posited as real only to be *aufgehoben.* Individuality, like evil, is finally something that is to be overcome. But this conclusion is somewhat at odds with Peirce's portrayal of the Deity as one who has a real interest in persons, having created them, as the very individuals that they are, out of nothing. How would one expect such a Deity to respond, then, to a given individual's experience of tremendous suffering, or to the moral corruption of that individual? All may turn out for the best "in the long run," but how is one to argue that "whatever is is best" for *that* individual?

A more rigorous analysis of Peirce's discussion of evil is precluded by the quite unsystematic character of that discussion. It should be recognized, however, that Peirce's philosophy presented him with certain resources that might have been brought to bear on this issue. Without "explaining" the existence of evil in the world, he might have underscored the problematic nature of inferences, of moral judgments, that are made about a being of an infinitely greater dimensionality than our own.[33] Predicates that might be readily applied to human agents can be applied to God only vaguely if at all. This is not to suggest that by appealing to the necessary vagueness of all God-talk, some positive "solution" to the problem of evil is engendered. Peirce's own reference to a solution is problematic for the very reason that it presupposes that God's purposes can be understood clearly enough to allow one to defend the Deity's moral perfection, to explain the "logic" of the work of creation.

Peirce did not normally speak about God in this fashion. If the solution to the problem of evil is so simple that even an uneducated "tramp" could readily understand it (*CP* 8.263), more generally, God's nature and purposes tend to be inscrutable for Peirce; we can "catch a glimpse" of them, perhaps, but to attempt to describe them is to "wildly gabble." Indeed, God so far transcends any morality one might be able to formulate that the divine perfection ought probably to be regarded as "above all restraint and law," as something "aesthetic" (*CP* 6.510). Known more properly in feeling than in abstract thought, God is revealed to persons, and transforms their habits of conduct, as one who is perfectly *beautiful.* So it is through a consideration of Peirce's esthetics that a deeper understanding of his religious thought can be achieved.

IV

HABITS AND VALUES

I

Some fifteen years before he published his cosmological reflections in the *Monist*, Peirce produced another series of essays upon which his reputation as a philosopher, both during his lifetime and in the first few decades after his death, was largely based. Insofar as he came to be regarded as a champion of the scientific method and of a rigorous empiricism, as the first of the American pragmatists, these essays were taken to be representative of his thought as a whole, at least of that which was of enduring value in his philosophy.[1] Appearing in *Popular Science Monthly* and collectively entitled "Illustrations of the Logic of Science," they were clearly never intended for a strictly academic audience; but they were destined to articulate for philosophers in the first half of the twentieth century a perspective quite congenial to the mind-set that dominated American intellectual circles during that period of time. So "The Fixation of Belief" (*CP* 5.358–87) and "How to Make Our Ideas Clear" (*CP* 5.388–410), prominent among this collection, achieved something of a classical status within the American philosophical canon, at the same time functioning as the lens through which Peirce's work was to be surveyed. As a result, certain important aspects of his thought were obscured, not the least of which were those specifically religious concerns that motivated and shaped so many of his deliberations.[2] At the same time, Peirce's thinking evolved considerably between the late seventies and his death in 1914. These essays cannot be properly regarded, then, as representing either the full breadth or the maturest form of Peirce's philosophical perspective.

Nevertheless, the articles are distinctively Peircean and treat many of those issues with which Peirce was typically concerned. Most especially, they are designed to explicate the nature, purpose, and methods of human inquiry. That account will be briefly examined here and the evolution of Peirce's thinking about such matters quickly traced. This discussion will serve as a necessary prelude to the interpretation of his claims about normative science, and ultimately will illuminate his remarks about the various stages of inquiry in the Neglected Argument.

In "The Fixation of Belief," Peirce distinguished between doubt and belief as two dissimilar states of mind, each characterized by different sensations and each having a radically different effect on human behavior. Doubt is an irritant, "an uneasy and dissatisfied state from which we struggle to free ourselves and pass into a state of belief" (*CP* 5.372). In contrast, the believer experiences feelings of calmness and satisfaction, so that one generally struggles not to avoid this state of mind but tenaciously to maintain it. More importantly, "our beliefs guide our desires and shape our actions" (*CP* 5.371). The influence of Alexander Bain on Peirce's thinking ought to be noted at this point, the former having defined belief "as that upon which a man is prepared to act."[3] To hold a belief is to be convinced that certain kinds of actions or events occurring under a specific set of circumstances will tend to produce certain definite results. Consequently, one is disposed to behave in a particular and appropriate manner under such circumstances.

> Thus, both doubt and belief have positive effects upon us, though very different ones. Belief does not make us act at once, but puts us into such a condition that we shall behave in some certain way when the occasion arises. Doubt has not the least such active effect, but stimulates us to inquiry until it is destroyed. This reminds us of the irritation of a nerve and the reflex actions produced thereby; while for the analogue of belief, in the nervous system, we must look to what are called nervous associations—for example, to that habit of the nerves in consequence of which the smell of a peach will make the mouth water. (*CP* 5.373)

Here, the relationship between belief and action is modeled on a physiological phenomenon, a certain "habit of the nerves." Indeed, beliefs *were* habits for Peirce, as he suggested at an earlier point in this essay. That is, "the feeling of believing is a more or less sure indication of there being established in our nature some habit which will determine our actions" (*CP* 5.371). The actions so determined should be broadly construed so as to include mental acts, that is, inferences, desires, and volitions; beliefs function as habits of thought and feeling, then, as well as of conduct.

Beliefs are constantly tested, however, by new, surprising experiences. The essence of belief is expectation, and when the expectations generated by a given belief are disappointed, doubt arises in the mind of the believer. That is to say, old habits of thought are disrupted when in a specific situation the inferences to which they give rise yield conclusions that fail to describe the actual resulting events. Doubt stimulates inquiry, the sole purpose of which is the dispelling of doubt through the fixation of some new and satisfying belief. So inquiry is an adaptive process, while doubt and belief stand in a constant state of dynamic tension. Consider Peirce's remarks when he returned to this topic in "How to Make Our Ideas Clear."

> And what, then, is belief? It is the demi-cadence which closes a musical phrase in the symphony of our intellectual life. First, it is something that we are aware of; second, it appeases the irritation of doubt; and, third, it involves the establishment in our nature of a rule of action, or, say for short, a *habit*. As it appeases the irritation of doubt, which is the motive for thinking, thought relaxes, and comes to rest for a moment when belief is reached. But, since belief is a rule for action, the application of which involves further doubt and further thought, at the same time that it is a stopping-place, it is also a new starting-place for thought. (*CP* 5.397; see also *CP* 5.417)

It is doubt that both "stimulates us to inquiry" and then maintains that stimulus "until it is destroyed" (*CP* 5.373). But beliefs also should be regarded as playing a certain role, indeed, a normative role in human inquiry; they "influence further thinking" (*CP* 5.397). Since Peirce rejected the Cartesian program of universal, methodological doubt, every investigation must proceed within the context created by a whole stock of beliefs that function, at least initially, as unchallenged assumptions. He regarded as unintelligible the claim that inquiry commences from a point of 'zero-belief.' Some situation must be presupposed, some context or set of conditions established, if questions are even to be formulated properly, relevant experiments devised. Otherwise, talk about doubt and belief must fail to say anything meaningful about human experience. If a given principle is not really doubted, but only doubted as a matter of procedure ("paper doubt"), then that principle is perfectly adequate for philosophical as well as for practical purposes. Peirce was concerned only with "living" beliefs and doubts, that is, with real habits that inform and shape choices and actions, and with doubts that have a genuinely debilitating effect, that actually disrupt habitual responses. In summary,

> we cannot begin with complete doubt. We must begin with all the prejudices which we actually have when we enter upon the study of philosophy. These prejudices are not to be dispelled by a maxim, for they are things which it does not occur to us *can* be questioned. . . . A person may, it is true, in the course of his studies, find reason to doubt what he began by believing; but in that case he doubts because he has a positive reason for it, and not on account of the Cartesian maxim. Let us not pretend to doubt in philosophy what we do not doubt in our hearts. (*CP* 5.265)[4]

These "prejudices" constitute the starting-place for thought; more significantly, they comprise the rules of thought that, unless challenged and undermined, effectively shape the whole process of inquiry. For beliefs can and do function in a significant way as both formal and material leading principles, that is, as both the formal rules of inference and the specific premises that, in conjunction with such rules, yield reasonable conclusions.[5] Even if never explicitly formulated or articulated, beliefs can still have this effect, this habit-function; they elicit or evoke, under the appropriate circumstances, certain associated ideas and feelings. This fact renders problematic Peirce's contention, recorded above, that a belief must be "something that we are aware of." On occasion, Peirce himself seemed flatly to reject such a contention. "A belief need not be conscious," he insisted elsewhere (*CP* 2.148); in fact, since properly conceived as a "habit of mind," it must be "mostly . . . unconscious" (*CP* 5.417). How, if at all, are such apparently contradictory assertions to be harmonized?

Here, the influence on Peirce of Duns Scotus should be recalled, especially the latter's claim that ideas can exist in the mind *habitualiter*.[6] Surely one's belief cannot be regarded as genuine if it has no discernible or conceivable effect on one's behavior. But such an effect is not contingent upon one's having a clear and continuous awareness of what it is that one believes. For example, one's speech and conduct can betray sexist or racist beliefs, even if one is not fully aware of having such beliefs. In like manner, one's belief in God might consist in nothing more than a latent tendency and yet, under the appropriate circumstances, still prove to have significant cognitive and emotional effects.[7] Ideas existing in the mind *habitualiter* are not themselves actually conceived but, nevertheless, they "can directly produce a conception" (*CP* 8.18).

Indeed, a belief, like any habit, is general, a Third, not reducible to or identifiable with any number of actual or conceivable effects. It is a tendency, more or less powerful, an idea, more or less vague, present to consciousness and explicitly conceived only to the extent that it is *determinate*. Of course, once the process of inquiry has been initiated in a certain area, this sort of awareness is likely to become more pronounced, well-defined. Those beliefs that represent the upshot or "stopping-place" (*CP* 5.397) of thought are likely to be the ones that we are aware of, at least perhaps until they become thoroughly habitual or second nature for us (and so less determinate because now more *continuous* with a general system of beliefs). At the same time, inquiry's starting-place will always consist of a complex web of beliefs,[8] mostly vague, many of them at any given point in time altogether unconscious.

The argument that belief need *not* be conscious is one, it should be observed, that is typical of Peirce's later writings.[9] Increasingly he became interested in those vague, instinctive, commonsense beliefs that, while somewhat elusive, nonetheless have an enormous impact both on the progress of science and on everyday practical human affairs. Since the belief in God's reality seems to be of this type, their significance ought not to be underestimated, by theologians as well as scientists. Yet they resist precise definition, so that they can play no explicit role in formal argumentation. For this reason, their very real effect upon the process of inquiry is typically obscured, neglected in the philosophical accounts of that process. How, precisely, did Peirce gauge that effect? Where did he locate the origin of such commonsense beliefs?

The answers that Peirce's writings supply to these questions are most intelligible if interpreted within the context of his scientific theism. Biology and evolutionary theory to a great extent informed his reflections concerning the nature and origin of instinctive beliefs. Other animal species display instinctive patterns of behavior that can be explained as the products of natural selection. Their adaptive utility accounts for the persistence, the survival of those instincts that are transmitted from one generation of organisms to its successors. Human instincts have a comparable adaptive function; it is the need to survive and to prosper within both natural and social environments that engenders the development of specific "commonsense" beliefs, beliefs about the physical universe and about other human beings. Having evolved under the continuous influence of certain forces, the human mind is adapted to their effects, instinctively apprehending those laws that govern such forces. More specifically, human beings are predisposed to discover the truths of "mechanics" and of "psychics," precisely because knowledge of them is necessary for "nutrition" and "reproduction" (*MS* 844:5v; also *CP* 6.418, 6.491). Beliefs acquired as the result of effort or experience can then be passed on from generation to generation, not simply by pedagogical means as learned truths but inherited as natural instincts. Consequently, Peirce's argument rests on certain Lamarckian assumptions about the inheritability of acquired characteristics.

"The mind having been formed under the influence of phenomena obeying certain laws, it naturally happens that the mind becomes habituated to conceptions in harmony with those laws" (*MS* 956). Such conceptions, once again, constitute the starting-place of inquiry. Indeed, our vague natural beliefs about the world make science possible; they are the fertile sources of scientific insight. At the same time they need to be rendered explicit, criticized, corrected, and supplemented in light of the results of rational inquiry. Moreover, as such inquiry proceeds far beyond those phenomena that directly govern the growth of mind, the utility of such instinct dramatically decreases while its fallibility becomes ever more pronounced.

The laws operative in the natural world are themselves, ultimately, ideas in the mind of the Creator (*CP* 5.107). Not only the instinctive belief in God but all such commonsense notions have developed under this continuous divine influence. So instinct is indeed the product of evolution, but evolution itself is nothing other than, in Benjamin Peirce's words, the manifestation of God's "paternity."[10] Notice that in "The Fixation of Belief," however, while certain biological and Darwinian notions lurk visibly in the background (for example, the physiological analogues for doubt and belief, and the portrayal of inquiry as an adaptive process), there is no discernible religious context. It is important to consider, then, some gradual shifts in emphasis that marked the development of Peirce's thinking about the logic of science, at the same time rendering it more congenial to his religious perspective.[11]

The first of these has already been identified here, but needs to be discussed in greater detail. It is exemplified in Peirce's growing willingness to identify his own philosophical position as a species of "critical common-sensism" (*CP* 5.502–37),[12] as such, a position that takes into full account the instinctive basis of human knowledge. Consequently, when Peirce emphasized the importance of natural instinct and sentiment as sources of *religious* knowledge, this should not be regarded as a point of view peculiar to his philosophy of religion; rather, it is characteristic of Peirce's philosophy of science as well, indeed, of his general understanding of the nature and conditions of inquiry. It *is* true, however, that Peirce tended most especially in his religious writings to disparage the potential efficacy of human reason, to exalt common-sense and to suppress the critical moment of reflection. In philosophical terms, he often appeared to be a pronounced fideist on the issue of what faith and reason each contribute to the religious life. Trust the dictates of the "heart" over those of the "head," he counseled; in matters of "vital importance" living experience is to be regarded as more reliable than the abstractions of philosophy.

> If, walking in a garden on a dark night, you were suddenly to hear the voice of your sister crying to you to rescue her from a villain, would you stop to reason out the metaphysical question of whether it were possible for one mind to cause material waves of sound and for another mind to perceive them? If you did, the problem might probably occupy the remainder of your days. In the same way, if a man undergoes any religious experience and hears the call of his Saviour, for him to halt till he has adjusted a philosophical difficulty would seem to be an analogous sort of thing, whether you call it stupid or whether you call it disgusting. If on the other hand, a man has had no religious experience, then any religion not an affectation is as yet impossible for him; and the only worthy course is to wait quietly till such experience comes. No amount of speculation can take the place of experience. (*CP* 1.654)

Now such remarks may have been intended as more than a little bit ironic.[13] Clearly, they were designed to achieve a certain rhetorical effect, and they need not be assumed to conflict directly with the basic tenets of Peirce's scientific theism. While reason can never be a surrogate for commonsense or direct experience, Peirce did not preclude the possibility that a chastened reason might have some role to play in the religious life. It is the scientific community, after all, its members devoted to the discovery of "God's truth," that Peirce selected as a model for the Christian Church.

In any event, Peirce's understanding of the role that instinct plays in general in human life did seem to broaden considerably. As one indication of this fact, observe the manner in which he revised his own writings. For example, having designated the settlement of belief as inquiry's basic objective in the first of his *Popular Science* essays, Peirce proceeded to describe alternative methods for achieving this end (*CP*5.377ff.). Individual "tenacity," or the simple refusal to abandon one's beliefs, institutional "authority," and the criterion of "natural preferences" are all rejected in an argument, the sole purpose of which is to establish the supremacy of a scientific mode of inquiry. Yet in the case of the third method of fixing belief Peirce's rejection was subsequently qualified. In 1877, he was already willing to admit that this appeal to taste or natural preferences is a "more intellectual and respectable" procedure (*CP*5.383) than either of the others. Moreover, in 1910, he supplemented this observation with the inserted prescription that "Indeed, as long as no better method can be applied, it ought to be followed, since it is the expression of instinct which must be the ultimate cause of belief in all cases" (*CP*5.383).

By 1910, and for a variety of reasons,[14] Peirce had become entirely convinced of the epistemological significance of human instinct. It is not simply the case, however, that one ought to appeal to natural preferences when "no better method can be applied," as the statement above suggests. The scientific method itself commences with a process of hypothesis selection within which such natural preferences play a decisive role, and one ever more accentuated in Peirce's thinking. The "Neglected Argument," in fact, represents his maturest perspective on this issue.[15] So the emphasis ought to be placed here on the latter part of this inserted remark, that *"instinct . . . must be the ultimate cause of belief in all cases."* But there is one additional respect in which Peirce's account of human inquiry evolved. For just as the instinctual bases of reasoning became increasingly central to that account, the role of doubt as the stimulus to inquiry gradually diminished.

Perhaps this is a misleading claim. Perhaps it is less a matter of evolution here than of "The Fixation of Belief" representing something of a caricature of Peirce's true position, even in 1877. In "How to Make Our Ideas Clear," he was already criticizing the arguments articulated there, the words used to portray belief and doubt having been "too strong," as if he "had described the phenomena as they appear under a mental microscope" (*CP*5.394). The basic mechanics of his doubt-belief theory of inquiry remained intact, however, undisturbed until new factors began to shape Peirce's thinking at a later point in time. That is to say, Peirce's formulation of the principle of agapism and in general those cosmological issues that represent his main preoccupation in the

Monist essays of the early 1890s all mark the shifting of his attention away from the efficient causes of change to those ideas or final causes that govern all development.[16] Once again, natural selection gives way to love as the basic principle of evolution; so too the irritation of doubt is supplanted by the gentle, attractive power of ideal ends as the key motivator of human reason. Although the law of mind describes what is still a process of habit-formation, it is a process that results in the harmonizing of fortuitous or spontaneous energies through the influence of the higher ideas in some objective Mind. The belief-habits of the inquirer are now described as being molded by the attractive transforming power of those objective habits that constitute the very laws of nature.

Now it is true that as late as 1910, in some unpublished remarks, one discovers Peirce attempting to explain how the principle of natural selection might help to account for even the natural belief in God's reality. That is, since "belief in the Ens necessarium would adapt individuals for eternal life," it can be assumed that "natural selection will act here on earth to the cultivation of this belief" (*MS* 844:6v). But this is a rather strained and strange argument for Peirce to be making so late in his career. It should be clear by now that he considered that principle to be woefully inadequate as an explanation of how evolution occurs. It is not natural selection but the creative power of God's love that ought, from Peirce's viewpoint, to be regarded as the primary factor molding human nature and human instincts. It is not to the exigencies of some future life but to the direct and ongoing encounter between human beings and the divine mind that one should expect him to appeal on this issue.[17]

How can these changes in Peirce's perspective be summarized? It is probably safe to conclude that from his point of view evolution is nothing other than the process of inquiry writ large. Anthropomorphic conceptions had more than a merely metaphorical validity for Peirce. Macrocosm mirrors microcosm; the logic of objective mind is the same logic that ought to govern human reasoning. Evolution is always, then, a "thinking" process, the development of ideas embodied in concrete fact; and human inquiry is itself evolutionary. In the 1870s, under the influence of Darwin and his American disciple, Chauncey Wright, the principle of natural selection supplied Peirce with his best answer to the question about how chance events are organized into patterns of gradual change. Insofar as belief-habits change, it is as a result of the shock of experience, the surprise occurrence that undermines typical expectations, precipitates doubt, and triggers the adaptive response, inquiry.

That picture of evolution was never really a satisfactory one for Peirce, however. As he worked to repair it, his theory of inquiry had to be adjusted in certain relevant respects. Peirce eventually came to regard our abductive insights, those instinctive conjectures about how phenomena are to be explained, as the ultimate source of knowledge, experience functioning now only as an editor, to "prune down" ideas thus acquired;[18] "all science rolls upon presumption" (*CP* 6.422). His reflections on the problem of the continuum very likely helped to inspire this conclusion; a general belief or principle can never be determined inductively, no matter how great the number of observed cases to which such an induction appeals. Beliefs are, with respect to the evidence supplied by such cases, always underdetermined. Of course, in order to be valid, knowledge must still survive the test of experience, and it is still correct to talk about the human organism developing in response to its environment. But vague, instinctive beliefs are now seen to be at least as significant a factor in inquiry as those that we acquire or that we are aware of, and the stimulus of doubt alone cannot account for the *growth* of knowledge, for its teleology; inquiry is too narrowly conceived as an exclusively adaptive process.

Recall that Peirce's thinking about evolution frequently unfolded within an explicitly cosmological framework. Not only was he concerned with how various natural forms and species have developed *in* the world but also he was exercised by the question about how this world mind, this super-system itself evolves. Now the universe as a whole has no environment. So the adjustment or adaptation to environmental changes was useless as an explanation of how development occurs at this most general level.[19] The principle of agapism was formulated to provide just such an explanation; and that account became paradigmatic for Peirce, any genuinely evolutionary process now being regarded as inherently *purposeful.*

It is the realization or embodiment of ideal ends in thought and conduct that gives human life its purpose. Such ends owe their causal efficacy to an innate attractiveness, their great, indeed, irresistible *beauty.* It is precisely because "God's truth" is so exceedingly beautiful, that Peirce's remarks about esthetics took on a religious significance.

II

Most of the time, Peirce identified esthetics, along with logic and ethics, as one of the normative sciences.[20] The goal of inquiry is the fixation of belief; these particular sciences have as their object true beliefs about how one ought to think and to act. Such beliefs are not empty abstractions, of course, but are properly regarded as being habits of thought and conduct. One might argue that all beliefs have a normative function in the sense that they "guide our desires and shape our actions" (*CP* 5.371); but certain among these are specifically about ends or ideals, about how one *ought* to feel, think, or act, those beliefs typically identified as values. Consequently, values are habits, and the normative scientist is preoccupied with the question about what sorts of habits, ideally, an individual should struggle to cultivate.

This particular nuance of Peirce's thinking has already been and must continue to be underscored. Values or ideals have real effects, a certain power "to transform the face of the earth" (*CP* 1.217). They are gentle forces, general ideas that get themselves thought, becoming embodied as habits in those individuals who are first attracted by and then devoted to them. To have values is, on Peirce's account, quite literally to be possessed by them. One's belief-habits bear the imprint of, in fact, are the *fragments* of specific thoughts in the mind of some greater embracing personality. From it they derive their own force and character, just as the line drawn on the blackboard is, in some respects, continuous both with and *because of* that background surface.

Some sense must be made at the outset of Peirce's claim that esthetics, in his scheme of the normative sciences, occupies a position of primacy. The argument in support of that claim will make it clear that he understood logic, ethics, and esthetics to be enterprises bearing more than a family likeness to one another (see *CP* 2.156ff.). The relationship among them is to a certain degree hierarchical, a relationship of dependence, and it reflects the basic structure of Peirce's system of categories. Esthetics is the science of Firstness, but in a highly peculiar sense. How so? One is wise to proceed here, as Peirce himself frequently did, by treating the first last, by beginning instead with logic, defining it within this scheme.

Logic is, in simplest terms, "the theory of deliberate thinking" (*CP* 1.573). This definition had at least three important implications for Peirce. In the first place, a *theory* "directly aims at nothing but knowing," so that logic should never be confused with the various practical arts of reasoning (*CP* 2.1). Secondly, the word "deliberate" suggests self-control; automatic, unconscious, or otherwise uncontrolled inferences fall outside of the purview of logic as science. In the third place, controlled action is action directed to some specific end. Logic is concerned with the sort of thinking "that is controlled with a view to making it conform to a purpose or ideal" (*CP* 1.573). It is in this respect that logic clearly deserves to be classified as a normative science. As such, its ideal is truth, the logically good, and herein consists the special relationship between logic and ethics.

> Logical goodness and badness, which we shall find is simply the distinction of *Truth* and *Falsity* in general, amounts, in the last analysis, to nothing but a peculiar application of the more general distinction of Moral Goodness and Badness, or Righteousness and Wickedness. (*CP* 5.108)

Peirce often described this as a relationship of dependence (for example, in *CP* 5.35, 5.131); logic depends upon ethics in the sense that one must be able to distinguish between moral goodness and badness in general in order to make those specific normative judgments that are peculiar to logical inquiry. In addition, one must be a person of sound character in order to be an effective reasoner; logical skill is directly linked to moral virtue. For instance, success in inductive reasoning, Peirce insisted, requires a certain "habit of probity," as well as "industry," while "in the presumptive choice of hypotheses, still higher virtues are needed—a true elevation of soul" (*CP* 1.576). He concluded,

> If it were true that every fallacy were a sin, logic would be reduced to a branch of moral philosophy. This is not true. But we can perceive that good morals and good reasoning are closely allied; and I suspect that with the further development of ethics this relation will be found to be even more intimate than we can, as yet, prove it to be. (*CP* 1.576)

Interestingly enough, it is in another of the *Popular Science Monthly* papers that this point is most dramatically articulated. Only there, "good morals" are less vaguely characterized; in fact, they are rather explicitly correlated with the traditional Christian virtues. Here, in "The Doctrine of Chances" (*CP* 2.645–68), Peirce is engaged in an analysis of the idea of probability. As the discussion of miracles above has already indicated, it is absurd from Peirce's perspective to talk about the probability of "a fact *per se*" (*CP* 2.777).[21] Since the value of a probability describes a *general relationship* among events, it follows that "in reference to a single case considered in itself, probability can have no meaning" (*CP* 2.652). That relationship is a certain ratio that will be "ultimately fixed," but not by any limited series of inferences, since it represents a "real fact" to be determined only "in the long run" (*CP* 2.650). Indeed, "whatever is truly general refers to the indefinite future; for the past contains only a certain collection of such cases that have occurred" (*CP* 2.148).

Now while death makes the number of any *individual's* risks or probable inferences finite, "the very idea of probability and of reasoning rests on the assumption that this number is indefinitely great" (*CP* 2.654). This fact represents a certain "difficulty," that is, the "mean result" of one's inferences must always remain "uncertain" (*CP* 2.654). Consider, then, Peirce's attempt to resolve this difficulty.

> It seems to me that we are driven to this, that logicality inexorably requires that our interests should *not* be limited. They must not stop at our own fate, but must embrace the whole community. This community, again, must not be limited, but must extend to all races of beings with whom we can come into immediate or mediate intellectual relation. It must reach, however vaguely, beyond this geological epoch, beyond all bounds. He who would not sacrifice his own soul to save the whole world is, as it seems to me, illogical in all his inferences, collectively. Logic is rooted in the social principle. (*CP* 2.654)

"To be logical men should not be selfish" (*CP* 2.654). Here is the ethic of synechism transformed into a logical maxim. But it is also the ethic of agapism. It is my love, my devotion to "an idea that interests me" (*CP* 6.289) that compels me to nurture its growth, to promote its generalization or spreading, thus requiring me to recognize, at the same time, that my "interests should not be limited." Ultimately, then, a sound logic presupposes the love-ethic of the New Testament. And Peirce was prepared to draw this conclusion already in 1878. He claimed to have demonstrated that three "sentiments" must be regarded "as indispensable requirements of logic," specifically, "interest in an indefinite community, recognition of the possibility of this interest being made supreme, and hope in the unlimited continuance of intellectual activity" (*CP* 2.655). These three sentiments, he noticed,

> seem to be pretty much the same as the famous trio of Charity, Faith, and Hope, which, in the estimation of St. Paul, are the finest and greatest of spiritual gifts. Neither Old or New Testament is a textbook of the logic of science, but the latter is certainly the highest existing authority in regard to the dispositions of heart which a man ought to have. (*CP* 2.655)

Of course, according to St. Paul, the greatest of these virtues or "dispositions of heart" is Charity. Correspondingly, it is the interest in an indefinite community that constitutes the highest value in Peirce's normative scheme. This is no merely human community, but one embracing "all races of beings with whom we can come into . . . relation" (*CP* 2.654). That is to say, this interest, this love, must reach "beyond all bounds." Here, quite significantly, one observes Peirce invoking certain religious ideas for the purpose of articulating the ultimate presuppositions of logical inquiry.

Notice that Peirce's description of the science of logic revealed his commitment to a critical common-sensism. This fact is most clearly manifested in the distinction that, following the medieval scholastics, he wants to make between *logica utens* and *logica docens* (*CP* 2.186ff.). The latter is the direct result of scientific study; but prior to any such methodologically formalized study, the reasoner is already in possession of "some general idea of what good reasoning is" (*CP* 2.186). This is his or her *logica utens.* It is comprised of a whole system of opinions, habits of thought that may be regarded either as instinctive or as "due to infantile training and tradition" (*CP* 2.170). It will produce bad inferences more often than good ones, so that it stands in need of constant and rigorous criticism. Nonetheless, it constitutes an essential precondition of the scientific study of logic. It is the foundation of commonsense upon which every *logica docens* must be erected.

One ought to include alongside these fundamental habits of rationality that comprise the starting-place of logical inquiry those specifically moral virtues described above. Return then to the issue of the relationship between logic and ethics. The former is

> a study of the means of attaining the end of thought. It cannot solve that problem until it clearly knows what that end is. Life can have but one end. It is Ethics which defines that end. It is, therefore, impossible to be thoroughly and rationally logical except upon an ethical basis. (*CP* 2.198)

Here ethics is defined as the science of ends, ultimately of that "one end" to which all living and thinking must be directed in the long run. It is not altogether clear, from the immediate context of these remarks, why Peirce assumed that "life can have but one end." He was certainly not making the trivial claim here that every life must end at some one point in time, under certain specific circumstances. He was speaking of the *ideal* end, the ultimate value that ought to govern one's living, and here it is not obvious that the singular is appropriate. In the total hierarchy of one's values, does a single value have to occupy a position of supremacy? It is an interesting question that Peirce never systematically pursued. But perhaps the implicit context for these remarks is supplied by Peirce's talk about natural classes. To be a certain kind of thing is to "derive one's existence" from a specific idea or final cause, to share with all of the other members of that class a certain *end* appropriate for things of that kind (*CP* 1.203–23).[22] Moreover, there is a sense in which all real things are of a single kind, that is, of the nature of mind, so that all must share a single, common end, must display the same sort of teleology, must obey the very same law of mind (see, also, *CP* 1.613).

"*Ethics*," then, "*is the study of what ends of action we are deliberately prepared to adopt*" (*CP* 5.130). As a theoretical discipline also, it must be distinguished from the various practical arts of morality, as well as from "the doctrine of rights and duties" which is "a mere superstructure upon ethics proper" (*CP* 1.577). Furthermore, like the logician, the ethicist is concerned only with conduct that is deliberate or self-controlled. In a certain respect, ethics is the paradigmatic normative science, "because an *end*—the essential object of normative science—is germane to a voluntary act in a primary way in which it is germane to nothing else" (*CP* 5.130). If one's conscious, deliberate inferences are to be classified as voluntary acts, with the logically good being "simply a particular species of the moral good" (*CP* 5.130), then it is hard to resist the conclusion that, on Peirce's account, logic has, indeed, been subsumed into ethics.

This is not an altogether surprising result if one recalls that, on Peircean premises, actions and events in the world ought to display an objective logic comparable to that which governs human reasoning. Indeed, individuals are nothing other than the embodiment of general ideas, their actions, embodied inferences. But the "logic" of individual conduct or of collective behavior within communities defines what are typically regarded as ethically meaningful phenomena, delineates a moral landscape. And since logic has already been limited by Peirce to reasoning that is deliberate and end-directed, the distinction between it and ethics is sufficiently softened or blurred to render intelligible the conclusion recorded above.

If the logician must be able to discern the true from the false, the ethicist's task is to distinguish between *right* and *wrong*, not as categories already at hand, but as conceptions the formulation of which is part of the ethical enterprise itself.[23] Furthermore, just as the determination of truth, of right reasoning, presupposes a broader, ethical inquiry, any judgment about the rightness or wrongness of choices and actions requires a conception of moral goodness that is itself derivative. For

> an ultimate end of action *deliberately* adopted—that is to say, *reasonably* adopted—must be a state of things that *reasonably recommends itself in itself* aside from any ulterior consideration. It must be an *admirable ideal*, having the only kind of goodness that such an ideal *can* have; namely, esthetic goodness. From this point of view the morally good appears as a particular species of the esthetically good. (*CP* 5.130)

Here is one of the many instances where Peirce argued for the primacy of esthetics among the normative sciences. In order to determine the appropriate ends of reasoning, to define ideals of conduct, one must first draw some conclusion about the nature of that which is admirable *per se*, that which "reasonably recommends itself in itself." This will be the ideal of ideals, the summum bonum, and esthetic goodness, Peirce contends, is "the only kind of goodness that such an ideal *can* have" (*CP* 5.130). The morally good will thus be a species of the esthetically good, "specially determined by a peculiar superadded element" (*CP* 5.131), that is, the element of Secondness, of brute actions or volitions. Likewise, the logically good will be a determination of moral goodness, once again by means of "a special superadded element," in this case the element of Thirdness, the category of thought or representation. Now all of this was rather vaguely argued by Peirce, the justification for such claims at times a bit obscure. It *is* clear that he wanted to understand esthetic goodness as a certain quality (Firstness) of thoughts and of actions; indeed, an ideal quality that gets itself embodied to a greater or lesser degree in human thinking and conduct.

How is such a quality to be described? In what does esthetic goodness consist?

> In the light of the doctrine of categories I should say that an object, to be esthetically good, must have a multitude of parts so related to one another as to impart a positive simple immediate quality to their totality; and whatever does this is, in so far, esthetically good, no matter what the particular quality of the

total may be. If that quality be such as to nauseate us, to scare us, or otherwise to disturb us to the point of throwing us out of the mood of esthetic enjoyment, out of the mood of simply contemplating the embodiment of the quality . . . then the object remains none the less esthetically good, although people in our condition are incapacitated from a calm esthetic contemplation of it. (*CP* 5.132)

Of such a "positive simple immediate quality" one can provide no adequate description, precisely because it is a genuine First, that is, because of its very simplicity and immediacy. Peirce did explain here, however, that it is in the relationship among the various parts of a thing that such goodness consists; the esthetic quality of a thing represents the total effect of its constituents, is imparted to it as a result of their inter-relationships. It is a coherentist notion of the beautiful, then, to which Peirce subscribed, one for which he quite plausibly may have been indebted to Emerson and the Transcendentalists.[24] More likely than not, however, the significance of other influences on Peirce's thinking in this regard must be evaluated as subsidiary to that of Friedrich Schiller's *Aesthetische Briefe.* This is a work that by Peirce's own admission had a subtle but powerful impact on his philosophy from the very earliest stages of its development.[25] And Schiller is among that group of thinkers identified by Peirce as having aided him in conceiving the "ultimate purpose" of human life (*CP* 5.402, note 3). Such a purpose or aim he understands to be one that "*would be* pursued under all possible circumstances" (*CP* 5.134). So it must be a general ideal, exceedingly vague because it must be applicable in all situations, governing and thus capable of being embodied in individual actions and events. Yet it can never be exhausted by these instances that it governs (just as no true general can consist in a collection, however multitudinous, of individual cases), so that "its being never can have been completely perfected," but rather, "always must be in a state of incipiency, of growth" (*CP* 1.615).

> Pragmaticism makes thinking to consist in the living inferential metaboly of symbols whose purport lies in conditional general resolutions to act. As for the ultimate purpose of thought, which must be the purpose of everything, it is beyond comprehension; but according to the stage of approach which my thought has made to it . . . it is by the indefinite replication of self-control upon self-control that the *vir* is begotten, and by action, through thought, he grows an esthetic ideal, not for the behoof of his own poor noddle merely, but as the share which God permits him to have in the work of creation. (*CP* 5.402, note 3)

The context for these remarks is another of Peirce's later commentaries on his pragmatic maxim. Once again, his synechism, with its implied evolutionism, supplies the backdrop against which that maxim is to be perceived anew. The esthetic ideal is, of course, concrete reasonableness, the ultimate end of evolution, the embodiment in actual fact of the ideal-as-such, of the reasonable-in-itself. The argument represented here should have a familiar ring to it, then, should clearly recall the discussion in the previous chapter. Several noteworthy features of that argument need to be brought into sharper focus at this point, their peculiar relevance to Peirce's view of esthetics assessed.

Note first that the ultimate "purpose of everything" (*CP*5.402), the summum bonum, constituted for Peirce a religious ideal. Evolution *is* creation; its purpose is God's creative purpose. Insofar as human beings work, each in some fragmentary way, towards the realization of that ideal, they are contributing to its growth, sharing in the work of creation. Of course, they derive from that very ideal their ability to "work out results in this world" (*CP* 1.220). And its power over them consists simply in its positive esthetic quality, its attractiveness or great beauty. Persons share in this great work by serving as the vehicles of an idea that God thinks, an idea that is, in a sense, self-referential, since the ideal end of creation is God's own self-manifestation, God completely revealed.

"Esthetics considers those things whose ends are to embody qualities of feeling" (*CP*5.129). On Peirce's account, the embodiment of a quality is a form of *representation* (*CP*5.138), although one must remember that a sign is general, so that the representative character of a thing is not to be identified exhaustively with the thing itself. Peirce also observed that every representamen, "in some degree," *must* possess and express esthetic goodness (*CP*5.140). But insofar as objects are considered "simply in their presentation" (*CP*5.36), as the embodiment of qualities of feeling, they function specifically as *icons*, analogous to any work of art. Such objects tend to evoke a certain mood, to invite a certain typical response. For example,

> in contemplating a painting, there is a moment when we lose the consciousness that it is not the thing, the distinction of the real and the copy disappears, and it is for the moment a pure dream—not any particular existence, and yet not general. At that moment we are contemplating an *icon*. (*CP*3.362)

Now the universal mind is nothing other than a symbol of the Deity and of the divine purpose, growing in beauty as it evolves, as its ideas shape concrete fact. Yet it is a symbol that clearly has iconic features (see *CP*5.119), features to which one attends whenever one contemplates it simply as the embodiment of a certain quality of reasonableness. Such contemplation should elicit in the individual consciousness a certain feeling response, ideally, a certain *habit* of feeling. Indeed, Peirce concluded, "this vast universe of Nature which we contemplate with such awe is good only to produce a certain quality of feeling" (*CP*1.614). He explained that

> the esthetic quality appears to be the total, unanalyzable impression of a reasonableness that has expressed itself in creation. . . . It is a Firstness that belongs to a Thirdness in its achievement of Secondness. As a matter of opinion,

I believe that Glory shines out in everything like the sun and that any esthetic odiousness is merely our Unfeelingness resulting from obscurations due to our own moral and intellectual aberrations. (*MS* 310:9)

Again, this positive esthetic quality is indescribable or "unanalyzable." It is, in a sense, epiphenomenal, since a thing is beautiful "quite irrespective of any purpose to be so" (*CP* 1.575); that is, the beauty of a thing consists in its internal relations, and not in its serving some ulterior purpose. To use once more the sort of vague and highly figurative religious language that Peirce himself often seemed to prefer, it is a quality that God the Creator effects or expresses within creation, this extraordinary artwork, God's real symbol. And in Peirce's view this is an ongoing creation, a symbol that grows continuously without ever reaching the ideal terminal state of absolute Secondness.

Notice also the reference above (*MS* 310) to certain "obscurations," that blindness to the religious significance of natural phenomena that the Neglected Argument is designed to mitigate. "Moral and intellectual" factors are identified here as causal, their result, an "Unfeelingness," a numbness to the continuous presence and influence of the Deity. Furthermore, it is just this sort of moral and intellectual failing that prevents one, Peirce contended, from "seeing" the obvious solution to the problem of evil.[26] "Glory shines out in everything like the sun"; that which appears to be wicked or evil or "odious" appears as such only to one who lacks the appropriate esthetic (and religious) sensibilities. In order that those sensibilities might be developed or restored, one must create a "mood of esthetic enjoyment," a "mood of simply contemplating the embodiment of the quality" (*CP* 5.132), as if it were a "pure dream" (*CP* 3.362). One must be "born again and become as a little child" in order to "look upon the world with new eyes" (*CP* 1.219). Such is the strategy of Musement.

Here, since the problem, the negative condition, is one of unfeelingness, the solution to the problem will consist in having a certain kind of feeling. But it must not be any mere flash of feeling, a momentary experience; rather, the development of an appropriate sensibility will presuppose a process of habit formation. And "the theory of the deliberate formation of such habits of feeling is what ought to be meant by *esthetics*" (*CP* 1.574). The German philosophers, Peirce noted, explained this process in terms of the "action of the *Spieltrieb*," and his own thinking about esthetics bore the powerful imprint of their analyses. So Schiller's play-impulse became one of the basic models for Peirce's concept of Musement.[27]

Review briefly the results of this inquiry. The normative sciences, in Peirce's view, are concerned with the deliberate formation of certain ideal habits, habits of thought, of conduct, and of feeling. Esthetics is presupposed by the other sciences, because the admirableness or excellence of thought and conduct consists in their embodiment of a certain positive quality. That quality is a First, the precipitate of the harmonious interplay of those more simple, elemental ideas and actions that make up a complex whole or system. It is, in essence, a quality of *reasonableness*, manifested or concretized whenever something functions as the representation of a general purpose. And so "it is a Firstness that belongs to a Thirdness in its achievement of Secondness."

Now every representamen determines another distinct from itself (*CP*5.138), forms part of a "living inferential metaboly of symbols." Such is the nature of the universe, a vast symbol that is itself a complex system of symbols, a cosmic work of art, beautiful to the extent that it displays this quality of reasonableness; and "its leading idea is growth" (see *MS* 843:29f.). Notice that growth is a process of habit formation, while simple Firsts or qualities are nothing other than objectified feeling, so that the universal mind exemplifies the very same sort of deliberate development that esthetics prescribes for individuals. It too is in the business of forming certain habits of feeling.

Values *are* habits; it is through the mediation of habit that some general purpose becomes an ideal *for this particular individual*, guiding her desires and shaping her conduct.[28] Of course, ends can be subjected to criticism and habits can be deliberately established or dissolved, so that this entire process is one that is self-controlled. That is why esthetics is a normative science, a genuine form of inquiry. But it is an inquiry grounded in common-sense, in natural tastes and preferences, in certain vague, instinctive beliefs about ideals, about that which is admirable per se. It will develop as a science, in large measure, to the extent that it is able to utilize creatively these instinctive resources, these vague insights.

Such claims are worth noting here, most especially because Peirce's religious thought represented a general point of view that he will come to label as "esthetic theism" (*MS*L224). Given what has already been said above, it should not be too difficult to guess why he felt such a characterization to be appropriate. The preceding commentary has also initiated the task of linking Peirce's esthetic to its semiotic framework, a task that will be resumed systematically in the next, penultimate chapter. Several other aspects of Peirce's philosophy of religion ought to be examined first, however, and the discussion above has provided the immediate background against which they can be illuminated and made intelligible. Consider, then, Peirce's scattered remarks about human immortality and the freedom of the will.

III

"The doctrine of Immortality which makes men last forever is not so ennobling as its contrary which makes man's interest outrun himself, in time as well as space" (*MS* 339:2). The individual ego, Peirce once opined, is "mere moonshine shimmer upon the soul, which is a vast formless ocean, the same in all men" (*MS* 953:4).[29] Thus it follows that happiness will consist in a "contempt" for the ego and an abiding love for the "community of soul." It appears, then, that the question about human immortality was of very little interest to Peirce, if that question is to be formulated in a certain manner. He entertained it, but felt that its answer was of no great significance. That is, he had no special investment in a positive outcome, in a demonstration that the individual human ego survives beyond death into the indefinite future.

In a sense, the question fails to fit the categories that Peirce's synechistic philosophy supplies. It is difficult to see how it can even be articulated intelligibly within that framework. What is an individual for Peirce? Someone or something that is determinate in a certain respect. But nothing is determinate in every respect; once again, there are no absolute individuals. On this account, persons can most certainly be immortal in some respect, that is, insofar as their interests "outrun" themselves and extend to the indefinite "community of soul."

So did Peirce believe in a future life?

> *Some* kind of future life there can be no doubt of. A man of character leaves an influence living after him. It is living; it is personal. In my opinion, it is quite proper to call that a future life. Jesus so spoke of it when he said he would always be with us. It is in some respects more fit to be made the subject of a promise than any other kind of future life. . . . Beyond that, I simply am content to be in God's hands. If I am in another life it is sure to be most interesting; but I cannot imagine how it is going to be *me*. At the same time, I really don't know anything about it. (*CP* 6.519)

Since individuals are nothing other than possible members of society, a preoccupation with the concerns of this "me" is the silliest of vanities; if extreme, the essence of wickedness. Nevertheless, and granting that Peirce had but a "slight interest in the matter" (*CP* 6.520), what evidence might be elicited in support of the claim that individual human beings survive death, that the "soul" is immortal? Is it not the case that consciousness, that memory depend upon the "mental action of the brain," so that with the death of the material body memory ceases? (*CP* 6.520).

Peirce's answer to the first question was "very little." His answer to the second question was "not necessarily." Consider the latter first. While it is "commonly assumed to be the case" that memory ceases with brain death, Peirce suggests that "the matter is open to some doubt" (*CP* 6.520). For example, we discover that certain faculties are temporarily lost when a part of the brain is damaged. "But after a time they are recovered" (*CP* 6.520). Some other part of the brain has learned to perform these functions. Similarly, something else, and Peirce did not offer a specific candidate here, might assume the memory function once the brain has been destroyed. No absolute dependence of mental action on the brain can be assumed. Still, it is undoubtedly true that upon dying one loses consciousness, "at least for the time being" (*CP* 6.520).

The theological relevance for Christians of these sorts of considerations is limited, Peirce observed, by the fact that Christian doctrine asserts not simply the immortality of the soul but the restoration of the body as well. For this latter claim there can be no proof "except that it was a belief clung to by St. Paul and founded by him upon the resurrection of Jesus" (*CP* 6.520). But even the argument above suggests that consciousness must be embodied in *something*, that as Peirce contends elsewhere (*MS* 298:11) the notion of a soul without a body is an "impossibility" and an "absurdity." It is like the notion of a sign without a sign token; there is nothing *to be* significant. More fundamentally, however, Peirce's suspicion of the claim that the soul is able to act and feel independently of the human body was grounded in his objection to the Cartesian dualism of mind and body that such a claim presupposes (*MS* 878:4). On his account, all that is is mind, so that "embodiment" consists in the representation of a general idea by some more determinate reality.

Return to the first question. Reports about spiritualism and telepathic phenomena are typically enlisted as evidence in support of the belief in immortality.[30] Peirce was not impressed, however, by the status of such evidence. It consists largely in testimony supplied by persons who are not scientifically trained (*MS* 877). This fact constitutes no direct argument against the reality of such phenomena, but it does make it difficult to evaluate the evidence, to form any definite opinions based upon it. Even if one were to grant the validity of "all the ghost stories that ever were told," Peirce asked, "what would they prove?" These ghosts and spirits seem to display a remarkable "stupidity," exhibit "but a remnant of mind," so that if the soul does not die with the body, it must be reduced to a mere "pitiable shade . . . of its former self" (*CP* 6.550).

> Then these spirits and apparitions are so painfully solemn. I fancy that, were I suddenly to find myself liberated from all the trials and responsibilities of this life, my probation over, and my destiny beyond marring or making, I should feel as I do when I find myself on an ocean steamer, and know that for ten days no business can turn up, and nothing can happen. I should regard the situation as a tremendous frolic, should be at the summit of gayety, and should only be too glad to leave the vale of tears behind. Instead of that, these starveling souls come mooning back to their former haunts, to cry over spilled milk. (*CP* 6.550)

This evidence is not likely to reinforce the orthodox Christian view of the afterlife as a beatified state of heavenly bliss. Still, Peirce encouraged the further examination and evaluation of this data by individuals employing careful scientific methods. Like his friend William James, he did not dismiss reports about psychic phenomena out of hand and he considered it entirely appropriate that they should be subjected to careful scientific scrutiny (see *CP* 6.587). In fact, he was unable to discover any direct arguments against spiritualism or telepathy, while his own objective idealism appears to be a hypothesis readily capable of accommodating these phenomena. If matter acts upon matter from a distance, he reasoned, why not mind on mind? (*MS* 880:1ff.). Indeed, on Peirce's synechistic account, even ordinary communication between living persons is to be explained in terms of his fundamental claim about the continuity of mind.

In the final analysis, no definitive answer to the question can be given. Peirce added, however, the following summary of his perspective.

> Those of us who have never met with spirits, or any fact at all analogous to immortality among the things that we know, must be excused if we smile at the doctrine. As far as we see, forms of beauty, of sentiment, and of intelligence are the most evanescent of phenomena. . . . Besides, scientific studies have taught us that human testimony, when not hedged about with elaborate checks, is a weak kind of evidence. In short, the utter unlikeness of an immortal soul to anything we cannot doubt, and the slightness of all the old arguments of its existence, appear to me to have tremendous weight. (*CP* 6.552)

The scientific status of the question aside, even "common-sense," Peirce suggested, is coming to reject the belief that "soul is able to feel and act independently of its animal body" (*CP* 6.577–78). But Peirce's discussion of the issue continues to create the distinct impression that it was his primary intention not to rule out the notion of immortality per se but to undermine the very conceptual framework within which that notion is typically formulated. This framework is the one supplied by "the obsolete Cartesian dualism" (*CP* 6.580). Yet Peirce's objective idealism represents for the philosopher of religion an entirely different context; and within that context it is surely possible to talk about "*some* kind of future life" (*CP* 6.519).

Recognize that such talk is clearly *not* metaphorical for Peirce. To say of the influence that a man's character leaves after him that it is living and personal is to describe it literally and accurately. For that influence consists in certain *habits* of thought and feeling, gentle forces that are purposeful and have the power to shape the conduct of others. Yet persons are nothing other than "bundles of habits."

> Habit tends to coordinate feelings, which are thus brought into the order of Time, into the order of Space. Feelings coordinated in a certain way, to a certain degree, constitute a person; on their being dissociated (as habits do sometimes get broken up), the personality disappears. (*CP* 6.585)

Death is the dissolution of habit. But personality consists in a complex system of inter-related habits, and that system is itself connected as a fragment to some more comprehensive pattern of relations. These habits are generalizing tendencies; such relations are continuous. And so one should be reluctant to pronounce dead anyone whose habits of thought and feeling, whose ideas continue to have an influence in the world. Certain factors by means of which these ideas might have been rendered determinate in specific respects or individualized may have ceased at some point to be operative. Certain habits that formed part of that individual bundle may have completely dissolved (but this occurs, of course, throughout the life of the individual). Nevertheless, if those ideas that once vivified a particular self continue to work out results in the world, becoming embodied in the living thoughts and actions of others, then that self is immortal in the only sense of the word to which Peirce ascribed any significance.

Compare Peirce's semiotic version of this argument about human immortality (W 1:500–501; see MS 359, esp. pp. 19ff.). The unity of personality, he reminded us, is the unity of symbolization; persons are complex symbols, living and growing. Now a "true symbol" is immortal because "it has an interpretant as long as it is true" and thus, since it is identical with its interpretant, it always exists. So a man will be immortal, Peirce concluded, "insofar as he is vivified by the truth."

This argument is rather obscure upon initial inspection. In the first place, a symbol is identical with its interpretant only in the sense that it determines that interpretant-sign as bearing a similar relationship to its object. But that is precisely the point that Peirce wanted to make here. Any person, as a real symbol, is part of a living inferential metaboly of symbols. That person will determine, insofar as she has "influence," the meaning of any number of interpretants. The power to so determine others, however, will be derived from certain general ideals that by virtue of their great beauty get themselves enacted or embodied. That is, a person will have influence, will be immortal, "insofar as he is vivified by the truth" (MS 359).

This ideal becomes *my* ideal, once again, via the mediation of habit. So the achievement of at least some measure of personal immortality will be contingent upon the success of a certain deliberate process of habit formation. And the normative sciences have no other purpose but to guide that process.

It is from this particular perspective that the question about *human freedom* can be linked to the problem of immortality. Some parameters for Peirce's answer to this question have already been defined in previous chapters. His ongoing critique of mechanical necessitarianism, his rejection of Hegel's restriction of objective logic to the deductive mode, his identification of the primordial origin of the universe as boundless freedom are all indications of the sort of position that Peirce was likely to adopt. At the very least, some positive claims about human freedom seem to be entailed by Peirce's tychism. Why should the human will be absolutely determined by natural laws and forces in a way that other objects and phenomena are not?

In fact, the question about the freedom of the will, far from being a single question, is a complex of many; for this and other reasons it is one that is difficult to settle (*CP* 5.403, 5.565). On what particular issue, then, is attention to be focused? How is the question to be simplified? Peirce remarked, in "How to Make Our Ideas Clear," that

> the question of free-will and fate in its simplest form, stripped of verbiage, is something like this: I have done something of which I am ashamed; could I, by an effort of the will, have resisted the temptation, and done otherwise? The philosophical reply is, that this is not a question of fact, but only of the arrangement of facts. (*CP* 5.403)

It is important to determine the precise meaning of this philosophical reply. Peirce explains that the facts can be arranged in such a way as to result in two different conditional propositions (see *CP* 5.339), each serving to exhibit a particular consideration. While the reproachful moralist judges (with regard to whether or not I could have done otherwise) that "if you had tried, you would have done it" (*CP* 5.339), the scientific man, attending to the determining power of the laws of nature, announces that "even if you had tried, you would not have done it" (*CP* 5.339). But in the case of both conditionals the hypothesis is false; in fact, I did *not* try to do otherwise. And "there is no objection to a contradiction in what would result from a false hypothesis" (*CP* 5.403). Here the word "could" in the original formulation of the question is the key to solving the problem; it implies an unexpressed condition, a "state of things that does not actually come to pass" (*CP* 5.339), so that in this instance the *reductio ad absurdum* results in a logically harmless contradiction.

In this fashion, Peirce claimed to have resolved the problem of "free-will and fate in its simplest form" (*CP* 5.339, note 1). Yet it is of interest to the student of Peirce's religious thought that he perceived this question to be "overlaid with many others" (*CP* 5.339, note 1). Moreover, he never intended to suggest that "both sides are equally right"; rather he was willing to argue that "one side denies important facts, and that the other does not" (*CP* 5.403). Notice that the "scientific man" in the example above is a necessitarian who seems to assume "that every event in the physical world depends exclusively on physical antecedents" and, furthermore, "that every act of will is determined by the strongest motive" (*CP* 5.339 and note 1). These were, in Peirce's view, unwarranted assumptions at best and, if his own metaphysical position can be established, demonstrably false. To claim otherwise would be to undermine not only the agenda of the normative sciences, but Peirce's religious perspective as well.

> Self-control seems to be the capacity for rising to an extended view of a practical subject instead of seeing only a temporary urgency. This is the only freedom of which man has any reason to be proud; and it is because love of what is good for all on the whole, which is the widest possible consideration, is the essence of Christianity, that it is said that the service of Christ is perfect freedom. (*CP*5.339, note 1)

In order to be reasonable, an action must be voluntary, behavior must be deliberate or self-controlled. Self-control is not an end in itself, however; deliberate conduct must be deliberate *toward some end.* Here Peirce invoked the summum bonum, the interest in an indefinite community, which constituted for him both the essence of Christianity and a fundamental presupposition of logic. At the same time, it is "perfect freedom," the only sort of freedom that one ought to value.

As early as 1861, Peirce had defined freedom from a religious perspective, stipulating that "that man has a free will who follows God's will" (*MS*891). Now God's purposes are the laws that govern the universe; to serve Christ or to follow God's will is thus to harmonize one's purposes with the world's own teleology, to share in the work of creation, to develop habits of thought and feeling under the influence of and consonant with the habits of objective mind. So one becomes free in the same way that one achieves immortality. The end result is the embodiment of an esthetically pleasing quality, the creation of something beautiful.

> Originality is not an attribute of the *matter* of life, present in the whole only so far as it is present in the smallest parts, but is an affair of *form*, of the way in which parts none of which possess it are joined together. Every action of Napoleon's was such as a treatise on physiology ought to describe. He walked, ate, slept, worked in his study, rode his horse, talked to his fellows, just as every other man does. But he combined those elements into shapes that have not been matched in modern times. (*CP*4.611)

"Those who dispute about Free Will and Necessity" (*CP*4.611) typically fail to perceive that freedom is a formal quality, not to be ascribed to individual actions but consisting in their total resultant effect. The whole calls out its parts. The genuinely free person embodies, symbolizes, concretizes an idea or final cause that both gently determines and empowers that individual. So this ideal source of power is the source of human freedom. But it is accessible only to one who has developed those habits of feeling essential for the recognition of its value, those habits of thought and conduct appropriate for its realization.

V

MUSEMENT

I

Peirce delivered his seven "Lectures on Pragmatism" at Harvard in the spring of 1903 as a guest of the department of philosophy. William James, who played no small role in bringing about this state of affairs, perceived in these lectures "flashes of brilliant light relieved against Cimmerian darkness."[1] But what topics did Peirce *attempt* to illuminate? Here one discovers, in summary form, many of the basic ingredients of his maturest philosophical outlook. Peirce expounded on the normative sciences, explicated the logic of abduction, and described his system of universal categories. Midway through this series of presentations, he offered some reflections on "the reality of Thirdness," and then concluded his fourth lecture with the following set of claims.

> the universe is a vast representamen, a great symbol of God's purpose, working out its conclusions in living realities. Now every symbol must have, organically attached to it, its Indices of Reactions and its Icons of Qualities; and such part as these reactions and these qualities play in an argument that, they of course, play in the universe—that Universe being precisely an argument. (*CP* 5.119)

In order for us to be able to comprehend even a "little bit . . . of this huge demonstration" (*CP* 5.119), we must actually perceive some of these qualities. That is to say, such qualities must be presented *iconically* in the predicates embodied in our perceptual judgments; for icons illustrate the significations of predicate-thoughts, reveal their "logical depth" (*MS* 200:E76f.).[2] Moreover, these judgments serve as the basic premises for each of our own inferences about what the world "means." Finally, some of these must take the form of *esthetic* judgments, since

> The Universe as an argument is necessarily a great work of art, a great poem—for every fine argument is a poem and a symphony—just as every true poem is a sound argument. But let us compare it rather with a painting—with an impressionistic seashore piece—then every Quality in a Premiss is one of the elementary colored particles of the Painting; they are all meant to go together to make up

the intended Quality that belongs to the whole as whole. The total effect is beyond our ken; but we can appreciate in some measure the resultant Quality of parts of the whole. (*CP* 5.119)

The "Cimmerian darkness" in which such remarks seem to be shrouded is at least partially dispelled if they are interpreted against the background of Peirce's esthetic. his vague but consistent characterization of the summum bonum as the embodiment of a quality of reasonableness. Nor should it be forgotten that this universe that grows more reasonable as its argument unfolds is essentially a cosmic Mind; and that Mind both wills the specific actualities that we experience as fact and thinks the very order that is worked out or concretized in these living realities. So the basic principles of Peirce's evolutionary cosmology and objective idealism, once presupposed, lend some intelligibility to his remarks as well.

Finally, however, it is a *semiotic* framework that Peirce invoked here; for the world is described as a representamen, a symbol with iconic and indexical features, and even the partial construal of its meaning will be a matter of sign-interpretation. More specifically, these claims supply the "crude sketch" of a *theological semiotic,*[3] identifying the world as God's great poem, as a symbol of God's purpose. Consequently, its interpretation ought also to be regarded as religiously meaningful.

In one sense, of course, that interpretive activity is nothing other than the process of scientific inquiry, its ultimate purpose, the discovery of God's truth. Indeed, "if we cannot in some measure understand God's mind, all science . . . must be a delusion and a snare" (*CP* 8.168). Yet such inquiry typically takes the form of a highly specialized study (*CP* 6.459) rather than engaging the inquirer in a more general contemplation of the universal artwork as a whole. It is this latter type of contemplation that Peirce prescribed for the Muser. Before exploring the nature, purpose, and effects of Musement, however, review more carefully some of the basic features of this world symbol, its exact relation to the divine reality symbolized.

Peirce's rather cryptic but nonetheless provocative critique of Royce's map metaphor supplies a useful starting point for this line of reflection. Recall that Peirce considered that metaphor to be inadequate in a number of respects, most significantly because "a map wants several characters of the class of signs to which ideas belong" (*CP* 8.126). Now ideas are symbols on Peirce's account, so that Royce can be supposed to have misconstrued their true nature as such. Here Peirce employed one of the fundamental trichotomies in his extensive classification of signs (see *CP* 8.119). An *icon* is a sign that represents something by virtue of some quality that it possesses, by "merely resembling" its object. In contrast, an *index* represents its object by virtue of "being really connected" with it, just as in the case of a "symptom of disease." Finally, there is a third class of signs, or *symbols*, that perform their representative function by virtue of intending to be interpreted as a sign; a particular rule or habit governs their interpretation. "Such for example is any general word, sentence, or book" (*CP* 5.73). How does attending to the general features of symbols illumine the special relationship between individual selves or ideas and the Absolute Mind? What is it precisely that Royce's argument neglects?

On the one hand, Royce "refuses to admit the continuity . . . of the map."[4] On the other hand, even if he were to allow for its continuity, Royce's account fails to distinguish properly between the various finite selves that make up the whole map. Consider now Peirce's own articulation of this complaint.

> It will be observed that if the Selves did form a continuum, each would be distinguished by its own point of Self-consciousness. This would not generally be the same as the point of self-consciousness of an idea within self, since each idea is distinguished by its own exclusive self-consciousness. The systems of delineation must be different. Here we see an inadequacy in the metaphor of the map; for what, more than anything else, makes my ideas mine is that they appeal to me, and are, or tend to become, represented in my general consciousness as representations. (*CP* 8.125)

The "organic aggregate of all the Selves" (*CP* 8.125), represented here as an infinite series of maps, is Royce's conception of the Deity; it embraces all finite selves. Peirce observed that "in the map the boundaries of the selves are somewhat indeterminate," since they can be drawn in any fashion so long as each embraces "no more nor less than a complete map of the whole surface" (*CP* 8.125). Herein lies the chief inadequacy of the map metaphor. For "the boundaries between Selves are not so indeterminate, because all that is in one Self appeals by a continuum of representations to that Self's self-consciousness" (again, *CP* 8.125).

Once again, the darkness threatens to overwhelm Peirce's reader. What is the logic of this complaint? Why was Peirce, the radical synechist, so concerned here about the proper delineation of the *boundaries* between individual selves? Any answer to these questions must be grounded in Peirce's own suggestion, exceedingly vague and undeveloped, about how the Roycean metaphor might be repaired. "It will be necessary," he stipulated,

> to replace the idea of a map by that of a continuum of maps overlying one another. A map is a section of a projection of which the surface mapped is another section. The projection itself is a sheaf of lines which diverge from one point. Instead of saying that a Self is a map, a more adequate metaphor would call it a projection of the reality, of which projection any one idea of the Self is

a section. At any rate, it is plain that the map-metaphor requires deep emendation in order to answer the purposes of philosophy. (*CP* 8.125)

Note what even this partial emendation accomplishes. In the map metaphor, all of the maps converge at a single point. This point is a "degenerate Third," as Peirce explained in another context, "the representation of nothing but itself and to nothing but itself" (*CP* 5.71).[5] It is therefore the "precise analogue of pure self-consciousness," to be regarded as a "mere feeling that has a dark instinct of being a germ of thought." Now this is exactly the way that Peirce in his cosmological essays described the universal mind in its primordial state. But *this* point cannot represent that mind because, while it is *self-sufficient,* "it is not *all-sufficient,* that is, is not a complete representation but is only a point upon a continuous map" (*CP* 5.71). And so that metaphor must be replaced by another.

Peirce's map projection avoids at least this one difficulty. If the entire projection is a Self, then its point of self-consciousness is that from which all the lines of the projection diverge. Each section of that projection is a map, depicting a separate self with its own unique point of self-consciousness; for the maps are no longer perceived to be lying one *within* another, all of them containing and converging at a single point. Rather, the projection is "a continuum of maps overlying one another" (*CP* 8.125). So there will be a continuum of selves, but the boundaries of each self will be clearly delineated.

A few guesses can be formulated at this point about what Peirce *might* have intended to accomplish with his map-projection model. These must remain as hypotheses since his brief remarks supply very little evidence that can be utilized in order to test them. At the same time, Peirce's often terse analyses of religious topics have been shown throughout this study to be connected intimately with his treatment of other matters. Perhaps this is one such instance of Peirce's providing for a given problem the sketch of a solution, only to develop some of the details of that sketch elsewhere.

Consider first the fact that in Royce's picture the aggregate of all the selves is portrayed as being of the same *dimensionality* as each of its constituents. But on Peirce's account, the relationship between the Absolute Self and any one of its ideas, a subsidiary self, is that of the entire projection to one of its sections. So while the whole is continuous, each of its parts can be shown to be determinate in certain respects; each is, in fact, different in kind from the embracing whole, and less "real." It hardly seems misleading to link this sort of talk with Peirce's topological discussions and with his invention of the Gamma graphs.[6] Recall that these latter consist of a book of sheets, each sheet representing the determination of a more general universe of possibilities. So too each finite self is a determinate idea, a specific thought-sign within some greater mind, likewise represented as a two-dimensional section of the three-dimensional projection. In any event, the "book" metaphor is really a very old one; and for Benjamin Peirce's "book of nature," as for Charles's "great poem," a divine authorship is presumed.

Here is further evidence, albeit quite inconclusive, that the Absolute Mind ought to be distinguished from God in some sense.[7] From Peirce's perspective, the reality projected is not the mere aggregate of all selves but their creative source. It is a point of pure self-consciousness, the Absolute First, a dark "germ of thought" that will develop into a cosmic argument, fleshed out in "living realities." It need not be conceived as representing the whole of God's reality but rather a single creative act that occurs in the divine mind, an act the implications of which gradually unfold in time. Even the language of creation, on this interpretation of Peirce's metaphor, would be consistent with some of his other utterances. For the divine agape, Peirce had argued in 1893, *projects* its "creations into independency" (*CP* 6.288).

This projected reality in its entirety, this Absolute Mind, is the embodiment of a divine purpose. It *represents* that purpose by developing under its law-like influence, crudely similar to the way that a map-projection is generated through the application of certain rules, in accordance with certain mathematical principles.[8] Like a Mercator chart, the created universe forms a rather distorted image of the divine idea that it maps. It is nonetheless a genuine symbol of the divine, with iconic and indexical features. That is to say, at the same time that it performs its representative function by virtue of the law that governs its development, this universal mind also embodies a *quality* of purposefulness, of reasonableness, and is an index of that purpose, having been *caused* by it, having been projected, through a divine act of volition, into being.

This universe is, moreover, a general symbol, a vast argument, that consists in a living inferential metaboly of symbols. In fact, "all this universe is perfused with signs, if it is not composed exclusively of signs" (*CP* 5.448, note 1). Each map, as the section of a continuous projection, is the interpretation of another map, and is itself interpreted in a third (see *CP* 5.77). So Peirce's metaphor exemplifies his own theory of the nature of signs as triadic. For he defined a sign as "anything which determines something else (its interpretant) to refer to an object to which it itself refers" (*CP* 2.303).

The sense in which a sign "determines" its interpretants ought to be clarified here. As Peirce uses the word in this context it is to be distinguished from the sort of mechanical or efficient causation invoked by the necessitarians. That which is indefinite is rendered less so when it is determined, that is, when it is rendered *determinate* with respect to some character or set of characters. (See *W* 2:155–58.) This process of determination generates outcomes of a certain sort; no *specific* outcome is necessitated. So the word "determination" signifies a causal relation that is a good deal "gentler" than the word itself seems typically to connote.

In this instance, the universe is a symbol of God's purpose that determines its interpretants as also signifying that purpose. Since a person is nothing more than a symbol, this process of determination can take the form of a communication event occurring between minds in dialogue. Indeed, all semiosis is dialogue on Peirce's account. This is true even of an individual's thinking, which takes shape as a conversation between a past and future self, always mediated through a present thought-sign.[9] The life of an individual thus will be a "train of thought," a continuous stream of symbols that is representative of the purposes embodied in that life. For "the identity of a man consists in the *consistency* of what he does and thinks, and consistency is the intellectual character of a thing; that is, is its expressing something" (*CP* 5.315). In summary, a person as symbol is general, and represents some general purpose by virtue of the habits that he or she possesses.

What is true of individual thoughts and of human individuals is equally true of anything that properly can be called a self; it will be a significant reality, standing in certain relations to other selves that both determine its meaning and acquire meaning from it. These, like all real relations, are *continuous*. So the great power of a sign consists in the fact that it establishes a certain continuity between its object and its interpretant. It brings them into relation. It places them in conversation. God's "poem" achieves just such an effect, bringing its interpreters into an active communion with the divine mind. What they then come to "mean" is in conformity with its purposes (the essence of freedom). For whatever is real is the law of something less real; and to be in conformity with a law is to signify that law.[10] Consequently, the Deity works its cosmic effects through signs, and a sign is, essentially, "a thing which is the representative, or deputy, of another thing for the purpose of affecting mind" (*MS* 142:3).

Now "the highest kind of symbol is one which signifies a growth ... of thought, and it is of that alone that a moving representation is possible" (*CP* 4.9). Peirce's most serious attempt to provide such a "moving picture" of semiosis was recorded in his elaboration of the system of existential graphs. Perhaps this is another problem with Royce's account. His infinite, ordered series of maps is too static a picture of reality. Peirce's universe, on the other hand, is projected into and unfolds in space and time, becoming more determinate as this great argument approaches its conclusion. "The object is the antecedent, the interpretant the consequent of the sign" (*MS* 318:18v), in this case, the Absolute First and Second, God the Creator and God completely revealed. The function of any sign is to convey to some interpreting agent an idea that springs from a source that Peirce called the "Graphist-Mind" (see *MS* 280). Suppose, in this instance, that the Graphist-Mind is of a divine nature. Peirce himself invited this sort of analysis, since he suggested (again, in *MS* 280) that it should be possible to develop a "good religious argument" by analyzing semiosis in terms of his notions of Graphist-mind and interpreter-mind. Now, on Peirce's account, the actual being of anything must consist in the "Graphist's assent" to it. But this is not being-in-stasis, since any idea that this Mind thinks will necessarily evolve, as a series of inferences or arguments, in obedience to the law of mind, the gentle law of love. It remains to determine whether or not the Neglected argument is, indeed, the "good religious argument" that Peirce envisioned in this manuscript, to discern its relation to his general theory of signification.

One final aspect of Peirce's semiotic ought to be reviewed at this point. The effect of any sign upon a mind that it determines was described by Peirce in terms of the production of interpretants within that mind. Notice three significant facts about this process. First, interpretation is essentially a process of inference. Second, there ought to be some correspondence between the vagueness of a given sign and that of the interpretant-sign that it determines. And third, Peirce distinguished three different types of interpretants: *emotional, energetic,* and *logical* (see *CP* 5.470ff.). That is, a sign may produce in its interpreter certain feelings or move that interpreter to act in a specific way (as when one responds instantaneously to a command). These feelings and actions can constitute the meaning of a sign, and they will mediate any general conception that one might form of what a sign means. Such a conception will be the logical interpretant of that sign; but it itself is a thought-sign subject to further interpretation. So the *final logical interpretant* must consist, rather, in the entire set of habits, habits of feeling, conduct, and thought, that a sign will produce in some mind or "quasi-mind" (*CP* 5.491).

Why is this brief discussion of interpretants, of their nature and varieties, especially significant within the present context? Precisely because it will be suggested below that Peirce's Neglected Argument is both an exercise in sign-interpretation and a commentary on that process. Much more could be said here about Peirce's semiotic,[11] then, that might be relevant to the task of understanding his argument for God's reality. But it no longer seems appropriate to delay the direct examination of that important article.[12]

II

What does it mean to affirm that God is real? Peirce began his inquiry by analyzing the key terms in such a claim. "God," he explained, "is the definable proper name signifying *Ens necessarium*; in my belief Really creator of all three

Universes of Experience" (*CP* 6.452). Here Peirce invoked his doctrine of categories; so the three "universes," exhaustive of reality and comprising the objects of all possible experience, consist in, first, the realm of ideal qualities or pure possibility, second, brute actuality or existence, and third, real generality or law (see *CP* 6.455). God is their creator, but it is inappropriate to conclude, as a consequence, that God "exists." To do so would be to reduce the Deity to the category of Secondness, for Peirce, the realm of brute reaction-events, devoid of generality and thus of intelligibility. (Remember that, from his point of view, it is inadequate to say, even about a physical object enduring in time, simply that it exists; since it endures, it is a continuity of reactions and its nature must be law-like.) Rather, God is "real," invoking here what Peirce perceived to be Duns Scotus's notion of a *reality* as that which is what it is independently of what any mind or finite collection of minds might conceive it to be (*CP* 6.453, 496).

Peirce did not in this context say anything more precise about the divine nature and attributes. Indeed, he suggested elsewhere that more readily definable metaphysical terms are to be eschewed for reasons that have been outlined above, their relevance to this argument assessed below. In this regard, it is important to note that Peirce's argument for the reality of God is exactly that, the description of an "argument" rather than the development of an "argumentation." "An 'Argument' is any process of thought reasonably tend-ing to produce a definite belief. An 'Argumentation' is an Argument proceed-ing upon definitely formulated premises" (*CP* 6.456).

Just as the concept of God is invariably vague, the argument for the reality of such a being resists precise formulation. The philosophical commentary on this "process of thought" ought to be distinguished, as supplementary argumen-tation, from the natural and informal line of reasoning that actually produces belief in God. Now there were a number of factors that motivated Peirce to draw this distinction, not the least of which was his concern that rational belief in God be recognized as universally accessible. For,

> If God really be, and be benign, then, in view of the generally conceded truth that religion, were it but proved, would be a good outweighing all others, we should naturally expect that there would be some Argument for His Reality that should be obvious to all minds, high and low alike, that should earnestly strive to find the truth of the matter; and further, that this Argument should present its conclusion, not as a proposition of metaphysical theology, but in a form directly applicable to the conduct of life, and full of nutrition for man's highest growth. (*CP* 6.457)

This natural expectation is fulfilled by the "Humble Argument." "Its per-suasiveness is no less than extraordinary; while it is not unknown to anybody"

(*CP* 6.457). Nonetheless, Peirce contended, it has been strangely neglected by theologians, who, in their attempts to supply rational support for the belief in God, have ignored the very process of reasoning that typically generates such a belief. It is this process or form of reasoning that Peirce labeled as "Musement" and described as "Pure Play"; "it involves no purpose save that of casting aside all serious purpose" (*CP* 6.458).[13] Governed by no rules other than the "law of liberty," the Muser proceeds not with the goal of "becoming convinced of the truth of religion" but simply to contemplate "some wonder in one of the Universes, or some connection between two of the three" (*CP* 6.458). This was essential from Peirce's point of view; that "religious meditation be allowed to grow up spontaneously out of Pure Play without any breach of continuity" (*CP* 6.458). He supplied a general prescription for the potential Muser.

> The dawn and the gloaming most invite one to Musement; but I have found no watch of the nychthemeron that has not its own advantages for the pursuit. It begins passively enough with drinking in the impression of some nook in one of the three Universes. But impression soon passes into attentive observation, observation into musing, musing into a lively give and take of communion between self and self. If one's observations and reflections are allowed to specialize themselves too much, the Play will be converted into scientific study; and that cannot be pursued in odd half hours. (*CP* 6.459)

So, he continued,

> Enter your skiff of Musement, push off into the lake of thought, and leave the breath of heaven to swell your sail. With your eyes open, awake to what is about or within you, and open conversation with yourself; for such is all meditation. (*CP* 6.461)

Peirce's reference to the "lively give and take of communion between self and self" (*CP* 6.459) most probably ought to be interpreted in the light of his description of meditation as a dialogue or conversation with oneself. That reference is not altogether unambiguous, however, and Peirce also seemed to be suggesting here that this contemplative activity will serve to initiate communion with a greater Self. For it is in the Pure Play of Musement, he explained, that

> the idea of God's reality will be sure sooner or later to be found an attractive fancy, which the Muser will develop in various ways. The more he ponders it, the more it will find repose in every part of his mind, for its beauty, for its supplying an ideal of life, and for its thoroughly satisfying explanation of his whole threefold environment. (*CP* 6.456)

The Muser will recognize upon carefully considering the idea of God that it represents the summum bonum, the three-fold esthetic, ethical, and logical ideal that, for Peirce, constituted the ultimate object of inquiry in the normative sciences. It is this ideal quality that will recommend the idea, as a highly plausible *hypothesis*, for subsequent investigation. Yet Peirce made it clear that the actual belief in God will not, in most cases, be contingent upon the outcome of such an investigation. The idea of God will suggest itself as being so attractive and so plausible that the Muser

> will come to be stirred to the depths of his nature by the beauty of the idea and by its august practicality, even to the point of earnestly loving and adoring his strictly hypothetical God, and to that of desiring above all things to shape the whole conduct of life and all the springs of action into conformity with that hypothesis. (*CP* 6.467)

To shape the "whole conduct" of one's life in conformity with a proposition, Peirce argued, is precisely to *believe* that proposition, since, on his account, all beliefs are nothing other than habits of inference and of action. If it seems odd for Peirce to speak in this context about loving and adoring a "hypothetical God," it should be noted that he regarded all perceptual judgments as being hypothetical inferences; that is, to perceive anything at all involves, however unconscious, automatic, or indubitable it may be, the formation of a hypothesis. Labeling the God who is revealed in the process of Musement as strictly hypothetical need not conflict, then, with those claims made about the power of the experience of such a reality. The hypothetical status of an idea reflects the stage of inquiry at which it is being considered, and does not necessarily tell one anything about its power or plausibility at that stage. But these comments anticipate Peirce's own subsequent analysis of the Humble Argument. Before turning to that analysis, some models for the concept of Musement should be considered.

Review the basic tenets of Peirce's objective idealism. All of reality is of the nature of living mind. Against the background of such a principle, he attempted to develop a cosmology that would account both for the variety of phenomena in the universe and for the growth of ideas as objective habits or laws of nature. He speculated that the origin of both elements, variety and growth, is to be located in a primordial state of pure Firstness, of spontaneous feeling "sporting here and there in pure arbitrariness" (*CP* 6.33). Regarded objectively, such feelings constitute ideal qualities, possibilities, some of which are actualized, react with one another, and eventually form continua of qualities. But the element of chance or spontaneity remains, breaking up old habits, serving as a catalyst and a stimulant for the development of new laws of behavior. And so while such laws "grow" out of the chance "sporting" of qualities, their reign is never absolute, nor are the variety of phenomena in the cosmos brought, under the influence of law, to a state of perfect regularity and order.

There is no doubt that Peirce really did conceive of the universe as an Absolute Mind. Insofar as it is a mind characterized by spontaneous feeling, it is a sporting consciousness, indeed, a mind at play.[14] Here, Peirce generalized the Darwinian principle of fortuitous variation and gave it a much wider application. With bold and broad strokes he painted the sort of cosmic picture that has been briefly described here: the Absolute Mind muses, forms hypotheses, performs inductions, and so thinks the laws of nature.

In certain respects, then, the Muser in Peirce's Humble Argument actually imitates a cosmological phenomenon. Furthermore, Peirce prescribed as the ideal subject matter for meditation the very phenomenon that is being imitated. It is in pondering the variety and growth in the three Universes that questions about their relationship and origin will be raised. It is within this context that the idea of God will inevitably suggest itself. Indeed, the Muser will be in direct communion with the Absolute Mind, since Peirce insisted that all of reality is continuous. In fact, communication can only occur as the result of the continuous connection between ideas (recall *CP* 6.158–163); that is why religious meditation must spring from Musement with "no breach of continuity."

There is a logic, one can conclude, underlying this imitative practice. In the first place, the logic of human discovery parallels the divine logic of creation; the difference is that, in the case of the latter, whatever God thinks is *real*, in Peirce's Scotist sense.[15] But the process by means of which new ideas arise, either in the human or in the divine mind, is essentially a process of abductive inference. Moreover, human thinking is shaped by the ideas of objective mind; these ideas are final causes achieving their effects by virtue of their attractiveness as ideals, their great beauty. In order to have that sort of effect, however, they must be visible to the contemplative intellect; they must be perceived as embodied in the divine poem, exemplified in the actual growth of reasonableness.[16] Now this, exactly, is the rationale for the kind of meditative exercise that Peirce was describing here. The proper subject matter of Musement, as well as its playful form, seems to be crucial to its success. And to be successful in Musement is to be truly free, since, on the account supplied by Peirce, freedom is precisely that quality possessed by persons whose ideas and habits have been formed in communion with the mind of God.[17]

To a degree, contemplation of the three universes or fundamental categories of experience is nothing different from what Peirce understood to be the task of *phenomenology* (or *phaneroscopy*).[18] Consequently, his reflections on that topic also may have influenced his thinking about Musement. The analogy is not a perfect one, since phenomenology is a scientific discipline with specific objectives, none of which involve the formation of hypotheses about the reality-status of appearances. Nevertheless, both the phenomenologist and the Muser are concerned with the whole of experience, with "the collective total of all that is in any sense present to the mind" (*CP* 1.284). So, too, both struggle to develop a certain ideal attitude toward the object of contemplation, suspending conventional beliefs and biases in order to become fully open to the deliverances of experience. Consider Peirce's statement of the desideratum in phenomenology.

> The student's great effort is not to be influenced by any tradition, any authority, any reasons for supposing that such and such ought to be the facts, or any fancies of any kind, and to confine himself to honest, single-minded observation of appearances. (*CP* 1.287)

This is not the Cartesian project of attempting to doubt what in fact one holds to be true, but rather the "distancing" of such beliefs, the adopting of a "playful" attitude towards them, even more so in Musement where, unlike in phenomenological reflection, "fancies" or "castle-building" are to be encouraged (*CP* 6.458). If phenomenology is properly conceived as a science, Musement at least shares its basic scientific spirit and can easily be "converted" into a more rigorous study (*CP* 6.459).

While Peirce's phenomenology and evolutionary cosmology do shed some light on the concept of Musement, he himself reported that it was a notion borrowed from Schiller's esthetics, and that it was intended to convey nothing other than what the latter designated as the *Spieltrieb* (*PW* 77). A detailed comparison of Peirce and Schiller on this issue is not possible here, but four brief observations suggest that such a comparison might be highly instructive, while underscoring the features of Schiller's work that were most likely to have attracted Peirce.

1) Note first that the concept of a "play impulse" was formulated by Schiller within the context of a discussion of esthetics and of the nature of the beautiful.[19] For Peirce, esthetics grounds ethics and logic as the most fundamental of the normative sciences; its object is to describe the summum bonum, that which is admirable in itself. Now it is clear that the summum bonum has religious connotations for Peirce and, at several points in the Neglected Argument, he stressed the fact that the idea of God is distinguished by its great beauty (*CP* 6.465, 467, 487). Furthermore, the beauty of the idea is a quality that both inspires the immediate belief and love of the Muser and recommends it as a hypothesis for scientific consideration.

2) Schiller contended that the contemplation of the beautiful is morally edifying, "since it is only out of the aesthetic . . . state that the moral can develop."[20] Peirce, too, at least in one sense, located the final upshot of

Musement in the realm of the ethical. The most enduring and significant effects of the God-hypothesis derive from its "influence over the whole conduct of life" (*CP* 6.490). No belief is genuine unless it constitutes a real habit of action, and the end-result of Musement has already been described as a state of belief.

3) The purposelessness and disinterestedness that characterize Schiller's *Spieltrieb* render it analogous to the ideal scientific attitude. Only the Muser, who has cast aside all specific interests and purposes, can be said to be "inquiring in scientific singleness of heart" (*CP* 6.458). Peirce's commentary on the Humble Argument made it clear that that process of reasoning need not be but certainly can be identified as a legitimate stage in a scientific inquiry.

4) As such, it is the abductive phase of inquiry, that is to say, the process of hypothesis formation and selection. It is most interesting to speculate in this regard how Schiller's analysis of the play impulse might have shaped, perhaps quite subtly, Peirce's own development of the logic of abduction. Even Schiller's language resembles that of Peirce. Of the two conflicting impulses that are harmonized in play, one furnishes "cases" (*Falle*), the other gives "laws" (*Gesetze*).[21] Similarly, abduction, for Peirce, was a mode of inference whereby particular instances or "cases" are recognized as being governed by a specific law or "rule."[22] Inquiry originates in a form of cognitive play, a playing with the observed facts, with various rearrangements of them, and with the candidate hypotheses that might render them intelligible (see *CP* 6.488).

These remarks anticipate the plot of the next chapter in Peirce's story. His article actually embodies a "nest" of three arguments, only the first of which concludes that God is real. This playful meditation upon the idea of God constitutes a "reasonable argument" because it produces a "truly Religious belief" in God's "Reality" and "nearness" (*CP* 6.486). Why, then, did Peirce choose to supplement it with additional argumentation? Clearly, he regarded this sort of commentary as being in a sense superfluous, lacking the "religious vitality" of the Humble Argument and serving only as an "apology," a "vindicatory description" of it (*CP* 6.487). Nonetheless, for the individual who has never seriously engaged in Musement, these comments function as an invitation, a recommendation for that particular exercise. Furthermore, having been committed for most of his life to the scientific method as the only ultimately valid procedure for fixing belief, Peirce was predisposed to illustrate some relationship between the Humble Argument and systematic scientific inquiry.

Now Peirce was not rigorously consistent in specifying what he intended to include under the rubric of the "Neglected Argument." He sometimes indicated that this label should be applied to the Humble Argument proper (*CP* 6.483–84); elsewhere, he explained that he used the designation loosely for all three in his nest of arguments, but that more precisely it refers to the second of these (*CP* 6.487). This last account seems most accurate, since Peirce did contend that it was specifically the theologians who have been guilty of neglect; and what they have repeatedly neglected to do is carefully to *describe* the Humble Argument and to *defend* its reasonableness and force (*CP* 6.484, 487). This would involve showing that the argument, "if sufficiently developed, will convince any normal man" (*CP* 6.484), precisely because "a latent tendency toward belief in God is a fundamental ingredient of the soul" and "the natural precipitate of meditation upon the origin of the Three Universes" (*CP* 6.487). Such is the burden of the theological argumentation that focused the second phase of Peirce's discussion.

It is a significant burden and Peirce's claim is quite remarkable, especially in light of his own admission that "there is very little established fact" that can be enlisted in support of it. But note immediately that it is not a claim about the reality of God. Rather, it is a contention about the *naturalness*, the *instinctiveness* of the hypothesis concerning God's reality. That Peirce chose to explicate the Humble Argument in exactly this way is a fact of some importance; for example, it suggests that any interpretation of his essay that represents it as embodying a version of the argument from design is a misconstrual.[23] Peirce never affirmed that the order, purpose, and design manifest in the universe supply an adequate evidential basis for the logical inference (inductive or analogical) that God is real. Instead, such realities serve to focus the contemplative activity of Musement. Peirce's emphasis was on the inevitability with which the God-hypothesis will tend to arise in the midst of such activity, on the special type of human instinctiveness that displays itself in this process. Indeed, there is good reason to suspect that the Humble Argument is Peirce's own highly idiosyncratic version of the *ontological* proof. In addition to his revealing definition of God as *Ens necessarium*, Peirce actually admitted to defending that proof in a certain form.[24] He explained in a 1905 letter to William James that

> the esthetic ideal, that which we *all* love and adore, the altogether admirable, has *as ideal*, necessarily a mode of being to be called living. . . . Now the ideal is not a finite existent. Moreover, the human mind and the human heart have a filiation to God. (*CP* 8.262)

The great beauty of the summum bonum, its power over the mind that contemplates it, compels the affirmation of its reality. It is a general idea that finds its own vehicles, gets itself thought; that idea is personal, its influence gentle but nonetheless irresistible. As Peirce explained in another draft of the same correspondence,

> It is impossible to think that the ideal of our hearts is merely existent or limited

> another way, and it is impossible for a person who puts metaphysical definitions aside to think that the object of one's love is not living. The idea is a vague one, but it is only the more irresistible for that. (*MS* L224)

Despite the enormous differences between Peirce and Anselm, they both agreed that careful meditation on the idea of God will lead inevitably to the conclusion that such a being must be real ("living"). But for Peirce this process of reasoning resisted translation into clearly defined metaphysical terms. The God whose being is affirmed is understood only vaguely; moreover, this vagueness is mitigated at the great expense of the indubitability of the idea (see *CP* 6.499). To render any vague proposition more precise is to problematize it, to specify the predictions that can be derived from it, thus making it vulnerable to falsification. This sort of precision, of course, is a legitimate goal of rational inquiry, and it surely ought to be pursued. To falsify a specific formulation of some general hypothesis, however, is not to reject the hypothesis itself but only that precise explication of it; the vague instinctive hypothesis is, as such, indubitable.[25] Furthermore, one ought not to seek greater precision in one's discourse than a given subject matter will allow. It would be possible to speak with perfect precision only about a reality that was completely determinate in every respect. Since, for Peirce, the divine mind is a continuum of the highest level of generality, its symbol will be extraordinarily vague; so it is unreasonable to expect that the vagueness of religious utterances, of the interpretants of that symbol, can be drastically reduced.[26]

Now it seems to be the case that these remarks about vagueness relieve Peirce's argument of some of its burden. It is, after all, not a specific, clearly articulated idea of God that he claimed will inevitably suggest itself in the process of Musement; rather, it is a vague hypothesis about a necessary being who is both the creator of the universes and the ideal that ought to govern all human thought and action. The "playful" reasoning about such a being is continuous with the love and adoration that it inspires. Recall that, for Peirce, "emotion *is* vague, incomprehensible thought," and "that is why the highest truths can only be felt" (*MS* 891). That is also why the feeling-responses to the idea of God are integral to Musement and not merely its side-effect.

It should be noted, in addition, that Peirce was not guilty here of some form of special pleading for his religious claims. The argumentation about the instinctiveness of the God-hypothesis has been shown to be consistent with Peirce's contentions regarding the instinctive, common-sense beliefs that ground all scientific inquiry. Such inquiry is the rendering precise of these vague notions, but the notions themselves are generated in abduction as hypotheses.

Consequently, Peirce's Neglected Argument needs to be read against the background supplied by his own numerous remarks about a human "guessing instinct," a capacity that he explained as the natural product of evolution.[27] Once again, this is an extremely fallible instinct, far more often wrong than right, but right just frequently enough to account for the remarkable success with which scientists, in such a short period of time, have proceeded to unlock the secrets of nature. Other species clearly demonstrate instinctive capacities; on what grounds should humanity be excepted from the general rule?

> Animals of all races rise far above the general level of their intelligence in those performances that are their proper function, such as flying and nest-building for ordinary birds; and what is man's proper function if it be not to embody general ideas in art-creations, in utilities, and above all in theoretical cognition? To give the lie to his own consciousness of divining the reasons of phenomena would be as silly in a man as it would be in a fledgling bird to refuse to trust its wings and leave the nest. . . . *If we knew* that the impulse to prefer one hypothesis to another really were analogous to the instincts of birds and wasps, it would be foolish not to give it play, within the bounds of reason; especially since we must entertain some hypothesis, or else forego all further knowledge than that which we have already gained by that very means. (*CP* 6.476)

Galileo's reflections on *il lume naturale* were cited by Peirce as being compatible with and supportive of his own point of view on this issue. He confessed to having long misconstrued the former's defense of the criterion of simplicity in hypothesis selection as an appeal to *logical* simplicity; rather, Peirce now recognized that the simpler hypothesis is the one that is "the more facile and natural, the one that instinct suggests" (*CP* 6.477). Having evolved under the influence of nature, human beings have become adapted to the task of understanding their environment. Translated again into the terms of Peirce's objective idealism, this becomes an argument about the continuous connection between ideas, about Mind shaping minds.

The strength of Peirce's claims about Musement seems to be contingent, then, upon (1) the level of vagueness that he intended to ascribe to the idea of God that arises in this process, and (2) the general coherence and plausibility of his philosophy of science, especially his perspective on the instinctual basis of scientific knowledge. Unfortunately, the "sketch" that Peirce supplied here embodies no clear answer to the question about (1). And the careful and thorough assessment of Peirce's views about the logic of science is a huge task that lies beyond the scope of the present discussion. Nevertheless, this second argument in his "nest" does flow directly and comfortably into the third. There, at least, a few additional remarks about the general nature of scientific inquiry will lend some clarity to Peirce's overall exposition.

The preceding analysis has already anticipated Peirce's final series of moves. The Humble Argument concluded that God is real. The neglected defense of that argument was fashioned around the claim that this conclusion is instinctive, the "natural precipitate" of Musement. Now Peirce made explicit that which had already emerged as obvious. Musement is a form of abductive reasoning, the appropriate initial stage of any scientific inquiry. Abduction always involves observation, the imaginative manipulation of observed facts, and the formulation of explanatory hypotheses (*CP* 6.488). Such hypotheses, subsequently, can be explicated deductively and their validity must be tested inductively, but all inquiry receives its creative impetus from these preliminary abductive inferences. New or inventive ideas are already embodied in the hypothesis; deduction and induction merely serve to clarify and to confirm (or disconfirm) abductive insights.

If the second phase of Peirce's discussion involves the attempt to strengthen the conclusion about God's reality by underscoring its naturalness, this third phase is designed to link the argument for that conclusion with a general logic of inquiry (see *CP* 6.491). Religious knowing will be like scientific knowing and it will have a comparable validity if both are the end-results of the same rational process. In the case under scrutiny, however, that process seems to be short-circuited. In the first place, "So hard is it to doubt God's reality, when the Idea has sprung from Musements, that there is great danger that the investigation will stop at this first stage, owing to the indifference of the Muser to any further proof of it" (*CP* 6.488).

This in itself is no indictment of the hypothesis but rather a very strong claim about its plausibility. More troublesome is a second observation that, owing to its obscurity or vagueness, it is virtually impossible to deduce the testable implications of the hypothesis (*CP* 6.489). How could the behavior of such a divine being be predicted with enough specificity to enable one to subject the claim about its reality to experiment, to checking procedures? Peirce suggested that this "peculiarity" of the God-hypothesis is counteracted by another, "which consists in its commanding influence over the whole conduct of life of its believers" (*CP* 6.490). Here he invoked the basic principle of his pragmaticism: the meaning of a conception will consist in the set of habits that it engenders, in the manner in which it determines human cognition and behavior. But it is still unclear, even assuming that the hypothesis somehow can be explicated, precisely how the inductive phase of inquiry is to be initiated, how evidence is to be gathered for the claim about God.

Peirce could have responded to this sort of challenge, had he filled in the details of his sketch, in a number of ways. First, despite the enormous conceptual and practical difficulties, as well as the crudeness of our present state of knowledge, it is the ongoing task of philosophy to attempt to explicate the God-hypothesis and it is the goal of a truly scientific cosmology to gather evidence that can be brought to bear on that notion. Surely there are analogous examples in science of theories that, given our actual skills and expertise, cannot be immediately subjected to decisive verification or falsification.[28] Second, since the meaning of the idea of God is revealed in human conduct, a test of the reality of that being might consist in a long-range assessment of the fruitfulness, the success of behavior that conforms to this hypothesis as an ideal. If God is real then behaving as if God were real ought to be efficacious. But this is an obscure enough proposal and, ultimately, the test that Peirce would be proposing here would involve the gathering of data ranging over the entire scope of human history. Still, it is a proposal that Peirce might have taken seriously, since he was less concerned with the present epistemological status of any individual than with what the unlimited community of inquirers would be able to determine as the truth in the long run.

A more practical possibility might suggest itself were one to shift one's gaze to the heart of Peirce's discussion, to the innermost core of his nest of arguments. That is to say, Musement itself constitutes a kind of *experiment*. Peirce carefully prescribed the ideal set of conditions under which such an experiment should be conducted, and then invited the reader to test the normality of his (Peirce's) thinking and perceptions. Some evidence that this is very much what Peirce had in mind appears in an unpublished version of the Neglected Argument (*MS* 843:70). There he suggested that among the most powerful and visible effects of the God-hypothesis are those wrought upon the Muser in the very process of meditation, effects "produced by searching out and by finding the hypothesis itself." This experiment bears positive results if the Muser is brought to feel and to "see" what Peirce claims can and should be felt and seen under these circumstances. In fact, the very skills that one needs in order to discern the reality and nearness of God are acquired in or at least sharpened by Musement. And so "every person skilled in Musement will see that the doctrine of the Ens necessarium has a pragmaticist meaning . . . . So far as it has such meaning, it is verifiable" (*MS* 844).

These remarks invoke, once again, a semiotic context for the Humble Argument; it is with a brief discussion of that context that this chapter concludes.

III

Abduction is, on Peirce's account, the primary logic of sign-interpretation. To interpret the meaning of X is to supply an explanation for X, to form a certain kind of hypothesis about it. In fact, it is only through abduction, Peirce contended, "that the significant character of anything is suggested" (*MS* 318:20v). Given the enormous amount of time and energy that he expended in the process of attempting both to formulate a general semiotic and to explicate the logic of abduction, one would suspect that the depth and significance of his contribution in these areas have yet to be fully assessed. What insights might such an assessment yield for understanding Peirce's religious thought? One way to begin to answer this question is by taking a closer look at the role that beliefs play, on Peirce's account, in hypothetical inferences.

Generally speaking, beliefs about the typical features of a certain kind of thing will function as habits, predisposing an individual who observes this configuration of features to infer hypothetically that the observed X is of that kind.[29] Beliefs, both singly and in combination, serve in this fashion as the guiding rules of abductive reasoning. They are models or laws that are utilized, consciously or unconsciously, in the classification or explanation of specific cases. Consider Peirce's characterization of this habit-function.

> Habit is that specialization of the law of mind whereby a general idea gains the power of exciting reactions. But in order that the general idea should attain all its functionality, it is necessary, also, that it should become suggestible by sensations. That is accomplished by a psychical process having the form of a hypothetic inference. (*CP* 6.145)

How, more precisely, does such a general idea become "suggestible by sensations"?

> The mode of suggestion by which, in abduction, the facts suggest the hypothesis is by *resemblance*—the resemblance of the facts to the consequences of the hypothesis. (*CP* 7.218)

> Hypothesis substitutes, for a complicated tangle of predicates attached to one subject, a single conception. (*CP* 2.643)

It is this resemblance between the observed configuration of facts and the pattern of expectations generated by a given belief or system of beliefs that is the source of abductive insight. When, in some instances, this resemblance is not readily apparent, it becomes necessary "playfully" to manipulate or rearrange the observed data; at the same time, the various implications of hypotheses must be alternatively suppressed and emphasized in order to test their explanatory power. Musement greatly accentuates this playful aspect of abduction; indeed, it is playful enough to allow a latent belief-habit to exert its creative influence. On the other hand, hypothetical inferences can be immediate and unconscious, as well as indubitable. This is the case when something is simply perceived to be this or that sort of thing. It has already been noted that perceptual judgments are, for Peirce, instances of abduction (see *CP* 5.181ff.); that is, all experience is interpreted experience. Whether it is simply a matter of perceiving X as Y or of concluding after a careful and deliberate process of reasoning that X is of the Y-sort, the mode of inference is essentially the same.

At least three important features of Peirce's account need to be underscored at this point. Notice, first, that our complex inferences about the nature and meaning of specific phenomena employ as their basic premises certain perceptual judgments. And these judgments embody predicates that represent iconically, or by resemblance, the qualities of things in the world;[30] such qualities are themselves isolated, and made to form the objects of thought by means of a certain process of abstraction. Yet those things have the qualities that they do as a result of Nature's own inferences; they are determined as such in the conclusions of the arguments of an objective Mind (recall *CP* 5.119). So the perception, the cognition of meaning is a process governed by the law of mind, the law of the association of ideas. It represents an encounter between minds and is of the nature of a communication event.

In the second place, abduction is not always simply a matter of classification whereby observed phenomena are explained by being located in familiar, well-defined categories. Frequently, new categories and classifications will have to be created in the process of reasoning itself, ideas connected, disconnected, and rearranged in very much the same way that the data must be continuously played with and reorganized. If successful, a strong hypothesis will emerge out of this process. That hypothesis may function to identify some X, but not in the sense that X is now recognized as a Y, Y being the kind of thing that one was already quite familiar with. One's idea of that *kind* of thing is itself generated in the course of abduction, as an explanatory rule of thought.

Since Peirce regarded feelings as being vague thoughts, they might very well be perceived as partially constituting a vague hypothesis. For example, the love of God, as a habit of feeling that arises in response to the reality encountered, might form part of the "explanation" of that reality. That is to say, this love could function to organize, to unify, to interpret a "complicated tangle" of feelings. And this love, like the vague ideas that form the God-hypothesis, could enable the Muser to see the three universes in a new way, as it is often the case that a phenomenon can only be perceived clearly "in the light of the hypothesis" (*CP* 6.469). This is the third important feature of Peirce's account: just as he intended to connect the Humble Argument with a general logic of inquiry, the latter itself is directly linked to the logic of perception. To interpret the meaning of a sign can involve either a very extended process of reasoning or a simple matter of recognition, of "seeing" it; both are instances of abduction. Now Peirce seemed to be suggesting that as the effects of Musement accumulate, the "nearness" and "beauty" of the divine reality become more readily perceptible. In this case, meditative thinking facilitates or clarifies perception.

> Just as a long acquaintance with a man of great character may deeply influence one's whole manner of conduct, so that a glance at his portrait may make a difference, just as almost living with Dr. Johnson enabled poor Boswell to write an immortal book and a really sublime book, just as long study of the works of Aristotle may make him an acquaintance, so if contemplation and study of the physico-psychical universe can imbue a man with principles of conduct analogous to the influence of a great man's works or conversation, then that analogue of a mind is . . . God. (*CP* 6.502)

> Where would such an idea, say as that of God, come from, if not from direct experience? . . . Open your eyes—and your heart, which is also a perceptive organ—and you see him. (*CP* 6.493)

This is Peirce's formula, the encounter or acquaintance with a mind through the mediation of its ideas, its works, its signs. If the world is indeed God's "argument," God's "great poem," then this formula becomes the basic principle of a theological semiotic; although "we cannot think any thought of God's, we can catch a fragment of His thought as it were" (*CP* 6.502). In this regard, "Gautama Boodha, Confucius, Socrates" are all cited by Peirce as having been practiced in the contemplation of the physico-psychical universe (*CP* 6.503); on this account, they were master semioticians.

What is peculiar about such a possibility? For Peirce, perception is sign-interpretation, a matter of "reading" the phenomena encountered in any given situation as embodying a certain kind of information, of construing them as the signifiers of a certain kind of reality. The case of religious perception and of the knowledge that it yields does not differ in principle from instances of ordinary perception. It is peculiar only in the sense that the knowledge acquired is extremely vague and its power over the "whole conduct of life" quite extraordinary. But for Peirce religious knowledge is not the result of idiosyncratic inferential processes that, because they are unscientific, generate problematic conclusions. If religious knowledge is problematic it must be in a way that all human knowledge is problematic and fallible;[31] and the Muser will be as unlikely to doubt what she knows as the ordinary perceiver will the existence of his neighbor or friend. This may seem, of course, like a preposterous claim. Peirce argues that its seeming so, however, is a consequence of the fact that those perceptual skills (beliefs, habits of perception) that are adapted for the purpose of recognizing ordinary persons or objects are well-developed, while for most individuals the skills required for religious "seeing" have atrophied.

> Seldom do we pass a single hour of our waking lives away from the companionship of men (including books); and even the thoughts of that solitary hour are filled with ideas that have grown in society. Prayer, on the other hand, occupies but little of our time . . . . Consequently, religious ideas never come to form the

warp and woof of our mental constitution, as do social ideas. They are easily
doubted, and are open to various reasons for doubt, which reasons may all be
comprehended as one, namely, that the religious phenomenon is sporadic, not
incessant. (*CP* 6.437)

How should one interpret the reference to prayer in the passage quoted
above? What, for Peirce, is the nature and purpose of prayer? His opinion
about this matter seems to have remained remarkably stable throughout his
life. In a notebook entry (*MS* 891) dated as early as 1859, one discovers what
appears to be not a commentary but an actual prayer written by Peirce. He
entreated the Deity to help him to regard his "innate ideas" as being "objectively
valid," precisely because, one would assume, such ideas make knowledge of and
communication with God possible. In the same notebook a year later (April 1,
1860), Peirce recorded his private reflections on "solitude," describing it as a
"drawing nigh with the personality in nature, and that is, in a humble sense, a
walking with God." Then Peirce publicly articulated a similar point of view in
1863, in his Cambridge High School Reunion lecture.

> A man looks upon nature, sees its sublimity and beauty and his spirit gradually
> rises to the idea of God. He does not see the Divinity, nor does nature prove to
> him the existence of that Being, but it does excite his mind and imagination until
> the idea becomes rooted in his heart. (*W* 1:108–109)

This is, of course, very much the same sort of claim that Peirce advanced
thirty-five years later in his Neglected Argument, except that he seemed by then
to have concluded that it *is* possible directly to experience or "see the Divinity."
Consider, then, some additional remarks about prayer. In 1866, in the last of
his Lowell lectures, Peirce supplied what for him is a rather extended treatment
of the topic. He made a distinction between "spiritual and mechanical prayer"
and then illustrated that distinction in the following manner.

> Suppose a child to get up on its father's knee and ask to be loved. That would
> be an instinctive motion connected with an emotion and would certainly find a
> response in the father's breast. Suppose, again, that a child were to come and
> make a long harangue to its father, requesting that he would not neglect his
> paternal duties but would exercise a proper superintendence over its discipline
> and education, would see that its masters were proper persons, and in particular
> were to take it away from a certain school which the father must already know
> perfectly well to be an unfit place. (*W* 1:503)

So, too, prayer may represent either an "instinctive motion connected with
an emotion" or a mechanical series of petitions, a "long harangue." The first
kind of prayer, Peirce concluded, would "no doubt find its interpretant in the
divine symbol, being an emotion full of truth" (*W* 1:503). But the efficacy of

the second kind of prayer needs to be submitted to "methodical examination," although one would not expect it to get a "respectful hearing."

These remarks are interesting for a number of reasons. In the first place, spiritual prayer is described as being instinctive, and the embodiment of an "emotion full of truth." So, too, Musement has been portrayed in this chapter as a practice designed to "give play" to a certain natural instinct; moreover, the feeling responses that are constitutive of Musement form part of the interpretation of the divine symbol, roughly parallel to Peirce's suggestion here that it is in such a symbol that these emotions find their meaning. Peirce also strenuously recommended in this lecture and elsewhere that the objective efficacy of "mechanical" prayer be tested experimentally. But the claim has already been advanced above that Musement itself is a kind of experiment, a testing of the naturalness of the God-idea and of its typical effects. Of course, the Muser is hardly engaged in what Peirce called mechanical prayer. Rather, it is the instinctive movement of the soul to God, the first type of prayer, that seems to be closely analogous to Musement.

Finally, in 1906, forty years after this Lowell lecture (of November 1866) was written and two years before the publication of the Neglected Argument, Peirce again observed that

> We, one and all of us, have an instinct to pray; and this fact constitutes an invitation from God to pray. And in fact there is found to be not only *soulagement* in prayer, but great spiritual good and moral strength. I do not see why prayer may not be efficacious, or if not the prayer exactly, the state of mind of which the prayer is nothing more than an expression, namely the soul's consciousness of its relation to God, which is nothing more than precisely the pragmatistic meaning of God. (*CP* 6.516)

It hardly seems misleading to regard this "state of mind" as the one appropriate for Musement, with the single difference that Musement commences as a free meditation on the universe and only gradually flowers into prayer. Through prayer, certain habits of thought, feeling, and conduct are formed, so that one might suppose that these habits are what the symbol of God means, its final logical interpretant. Only the meaning of this symbol is too complex, too vast, to be embodied in the life of a single individual, so that one must appeal to the notion of an unlimited *community* of interpreters, destined to discover and to embody the meaning of this divine poem only in the indefinite long run. Still, individuals can succeed in catching a "fragment" of God's thought.

On the other hand, when prayer is or becomes, at best, a "sporadic" exercise, those habits are never formed or, if already formed, gradually dissolve, so that a semiotic breakdown occurs, one is blinded to the divine reality, and religious ideas are "easily doubted" (*CP*6.437). That is to say, a certain kind of religiously significant interpretive activity becomes impossible. In such an instance, the individual may still have a genuine faith in God, according to Peirce, without recognizing it as such;[32] but the cognitive and perceptual skills essential for such recognition are not likely to be developed.

So Musement liberates a "latent tendency" to believe in God, to perceive God as real, a natural capacity that has become dull from lack of use. What role of theological significance, then, can the subsequent stages of inquiry play in a process that, at its earliest phase, already results in a religiously satisfying belief? Perhaps, by analogy, it is the same sort of role that literary criticism plays vis à vis the immediate encounter with the artwork. (In fact, Peirce's own metaphor—God's "great poem"—supports such an analogy.) This second-order critical reflection and explication, this "argumentation," generally lacks the spontaneous power of the reading experience itself. It can facilitate a better understanding of the dynamics of such reading, however, perhaps motivating the critic to pursue and to cultivate that kind of experience. Moreover, careful, rigorous "study" can serve to reinforce or strengthen those perceptions that also result from a more playful reading (*CP* 6.502). The theological clarification and defense of the God-hypothesis does have a certain value, then, so long as it does not supplant living religious experience.[33]

This emphasis on the importance of experience in Peirce's philosophy of religion, justified by his own claim that God must be "directly experienced," is potentially confusing. After all, it has been argued that, on Peirce's later account of the logic of inquiry, experience is not to be regarded as the source of new ideas but serves only an "editorial" function, "pruning" down the knowledge that is acquired otherwise. How, then, can it form the basis for one's knowledge of God? The answer to this question is enormously complex, but perhaps a few remarks will suffice in this context.[34]

For Peirce, experience presents us with the *objects* but not with the meanings or *interpretants* of signs (see *MS* 322:11). To grasp the meaning of a sign is to have an abductive insight for which experience supplies only the occasion. But it is easy here to fall victim to an equivocation. If by "experience" one means only "that which is given in experience," the shock or Secondness of experience (as Peirce sometimes described it), then such experience remains "mute" apart from the creative input of the human intellect. What Peirce most often meant by "experience" or "perception," however, is that entire, complex semiotic event ("semiosis"), the linking of object and meaning via the mediation of a sign. In this sense, it is true to say that God can be directly perceived in Musement, and yet that Musement is itself a form of inference, of abduction. Because, in this sense, all knowledge comes to us by observation, part of it forced upon us from without from Nature's mind and part of it coming from the depths of that inward aspect of mind, which we egotistically call *ours*; though in truth it is we who float upon its surface and belong to it more than it belongs to us. Nor can we affirm that the inwardly seen mind is altogether independent of the outward mind which is its Creator. (*CP* 7.558)

Indeed, whether as the *object* of this universal symbol or as the *source* of our insight in interpreting its meaning correctly, God is ultimately responsible for our religious knowledge. We know that which we truly know precisely because the human mind and heart have "a filiation to God."

If Peirce's theological semiotic is grounded in experience, indeed, rooted in prayerful communion with God, its final upshot must be located in the realm of praxis, in belief-habits that shape human conduct as they do perceptions. Peirce regarded the developing and strengthening of habits as a matter of induction, in this case, a matter of consistency and reasonableness in behavior, of the *practice* of virtue, of conduct repeatedly shaped and conformed to an ideal. Even as habits inform human behavior, that behavior itself represents the further explication of such ideals, as well as the experimental testing of their validity. And one of the qualities that recommends the God-hypothesis for consideration in the first place, along with its great beauty and explanatory power, is its very suitability as an ideal for life.

Praxis should not be conceived so narrowly here, however, as to exclude the activity, the practice of Musement itself. How else, for example, is the habit of love to be nourished and deepened, if not as a result of the continuous or "incessant" acquaintance with the beloved. The birth of love itself, the first glimpse of it, the "falling in love" as it were, may constitute an abductive insight, the sudden recognition in a configuration of perceptions of that which is precious and lovable, like the sudden esthetic delight in that which is perceived to be beautiful. But this experience can recur even when the habit of love is firmly entrenched, like falling in love again with a person already well-loved, or having an insight that one has had before, a sharpening of one's vision; so that Musement itself is not an activity designed simply for the religious novice, but for the constant renewal of religious feelings and perceptions.

VI

THEOSEMIOTIC

I

Very late in his life, Peirce began to formulate some notes for a book about religion, tentatively entitled "A Logical Critique of Essential Articles of Religious Faith."[1] Recorded just three years after the publication of his "Neglected Argument" and only three short years before his death, these programmatic remarks are illuminating in several respects. They indicate first of all that Peirce himself had some vague intention of filling in the details of his argument for God's reality, of actually supplying the text for that "table of contents." In addition, they present further evidence for the claim that religious questions exercised Peirce's thinking throughout his philosophical career. Most important, these jottings outline a general strategy for the philosopher of religion, one that appeals to "a theory of the nature of thinking" (*CP* 6.491) in order to identify the logic of specific religious beliefs.

Peirce never wrote that book, but he did develop a rather impressive theory of thinking; in fact, most of his writings can be construed as contributions to a general logic of inquiry. Embedded there is a story of no small theological significance, one that tells of the religious ideas that shaped Peirce's reflections on a wide variety of topics, one that displays resources of considerable value for the contemporary student of religion. Review briefly, then, the main plot of that story.

Even in his early writings, Peirce tended to distinguish abduction, as a third, separate mode of inference, from deductive and inductive reasoning. His meditations on the Aristotelian syllogism seem most directly to have inspired this distinction. In *Barbara*, one deductively infers a *Result* from some *Rule* (the major premise) and a *Case* under that Rule (the minor premise) (*CP* 2.710). Induction reverses this process, moving "from Case and Result to Rule," so that it consists in "the formation of a habit or general conception" (*CP* 2.712). Finally, abduction or "Hypothesis" combines the information embodied in such a conception with the knowledge of specific Results in order to ascertain Cases, that is, in order to judge that *this* Result is a Case under *that* Rule. In the simplest sort of example, if "*all* Stanford professors are brilliant" and one observes that "Jane is brilliant," one might try to account for the latter fact by conjecturing that it could be the case that "Jane is a Stanford professor."

Two consequences follow immediately from this type of analysis. First of all, hypothetical inferences are typically quite fallible, their conclusions uncertain. (Jane might, after all, be a member of the faculty at Berkeley, a hypothesis that may just as readily accommodate the data.) Secondly, abduction is dependent upon induction, in the sense that the rules by which it operates must be formulated inductively. This fails to be true only when those general habits of thought are instinctive or "congenital" rather than acquired (see *CP* 2.711). Even these vague instincts might be grounded ultimately in some induction performed in the past by others, since Peirce, following Lamarck, allowed for the inheritance of acquired characteristics.

This second observation, about the relationship between induction and abduction, is potentially misleading. Peirce's initial interest in these modes of inference represented nothing more than a desire to provide an exhaustive account of the various *forms* of argument; only gradually did he become preoccupied with their significance as connected aspects of a general *process* of inquiry. By 1908, however, it is the latter perspective that dominated Peirce's thinking, the Neglected Argument now portraying abduction, deduction, and induction as distinctive but interdependent "stages" of inquiry. At the same time, this new perspective embodied a different understanding of the relations between the three, consequently, an altered perception of the roles played by both instinct and experience in the acquisition of knowledge. All knowledge, Peirce now argued, came originally from conjecture, only to be pruned down by experience. No inductive examination of specific Cases and Results, then, no mere collecting of the data of experience can produce a general rule of thought. Rather, such rules represent abductive insights, hypotheses that experience can only serve to confirm or disconfirm.

What factors precipitated this shift in perspective? Undoubtedly Peirce's investigation of the problem of the continuum was pre-eminent among them, resulting in the conclusion that genuine continuity cannot consist in a collection of discrete units, no matter how infinitely great their multitude. Recall that generality was a specific form of continuity for Peirce. He was compelled, then, to admit that a general principle or habit of thought is always underdetermined by the inductive evidence that supports it. Here is the key to Peirce's "fallibilism," the epistemological "flip-side" to his synechistic metaphysics, his extreme scholastic realism.

Similarly, Peirce's evolutionism helped to shape the plot of his story about the nature of human thinking. The attractiveness of certain ideas to the instinctive intellect rather than the exigencies of actual experience is the fundamental stimulus of thought, much as final causation, the gentle influence of ideal ends, came to be of primary significance in Peirce's theory of evolution, usurping the role played by efficient causation and the principle of natural selection in other accounts.[2] Instinctive guesses are the ultimate source of human knowledge, and the human mind is vaguely predisposed to guess correctly about the real nature of things. Consequently, this instinct represents a natural skill, remarkable but nonetheless quite fallible, so that it needs always to be exercised critically.

The upshot of these changes is a "theory of the nature of thinking" that proved to be quite congenial to Peirce's religious world-view. After all, the divine mind was for him a vast continuum within which all other realities are embedded as its determinations or singularities, sub-continua of a lower dimensionality. Its cosmic thoughts are the laws of nature and they comprise the proper object of scientific inquiry. No experience is adequate to the determination of these laws, but they can be instinctively gleaned by human minds whose habits of thought and feeling have been gradually formed under their influence. Likewise, Peirce's evolutionism was the articulation, he contended, of insights first recorded in the Gospel of John. The final causes that effect the development of the universe represent Love's teleology, a selfless, cherishing Love that Peirce, like the author of the fourth gospel, identified with the very being of the Deity. The musing intellect is gently drawn to the truth about nature by the beauty of God's purposes, themselves embodied in natural facts. Such facts are to be perceived, barring any blindness to their real character, as the *representation* of those divine intentions.

This is the essence of a *theosemiotic*. The universe is God's great poem, a living inferential metaboly of symbols. Fragments of its meaning are accessible to the human intellect, most especially to a genuine community of inquirers devoted to discovering that meaning and governed by the principles of a valid scientific method. These will be the basic principles of logic, of abductive conjecture, deductive explication, and inductive testing. So Peirce's theory of inquiry supplies the rubric for what is, in essence, a complex theological method. That method commences with an act of interpretation, a reading of the signs that are presented in human experience, proceeds with the exploration and clarification of that interpretation, and then with its utilization as a rule for living, a habit of action. Once again, these signs are presented in human experience, but their *meaning* is not empirically determined. Rather, the human mind must "guess" at their meaning, a process facilitated by its own instinctive capabilities, and one that only eventuates in the crucible, the "test" of lived experience, of actual practice. Nor should this be regarded exclusively as the model for a purely natural theology. The pattern of abduction-deduction-induction is paradigmatic for all of human inquiry. And all sorts of beliefs, acquired beliefs as well as natural or instinctive ones, can function as habits of thought and feeling, as habits of interpretation, ultimately, as habits of conduct.

These remarks begin to suggest certain implications of Peirce's philosophical perspective, religiously meaningful implications that he was never able to pursue systematically. But his very latest writings indicate that he would have liked to pursue them, so that it seems appropriate to conclude the present study by briefly assessing the significance of what he did in fact accomplish and its relevance to contemporary discussions about religion and religious ideas.

II

One would hardly want, in this sort of a commentary on Peirce's writings, to leave the impression that his religious thought is unproblematic. Even the reader who is predisposed to find Peirce's perspective a congenial one is likely to be distanced, at least initially, by the strangeness of his articulation of it. Despite being so thoroughly grounded in the philosophical tradition, steeped in the history of philosophy, Peirce was in many ways an idiosyncratic thinker. He created new categories for his own philosophical enterprise, transformed the meanings of old labels that he applied to himself (for example, "scholastic realist"), and was uncomfortable with the labels that others were eager to apply to him (for example, James's "pragmatism"). All of these observations help to explain the fact that Peirce, despite his continuously growing influence at present, was never the founder of some school of thought. None of them, however, is intended to suggest that it is impossible to subject his work to a critical examination.

That sort of evaluation represents an enormous undertaking, an ongoing task, the execution of which this study is surely not designed to accomplish. With special regard to Peirce's philosophy of religion, however, several lines of critical analysis at least can be outlined here, even if not carried to some definite conclusion.

In the first place, the extent to which Peirce's semiotic can be divorced from his synechistic metaphysics needs to be determined. It is certainly true that semiotic has provided the creative stimulus for many contemporary developments in philosophy and literary theory. Indeed, Peirce is generally regarded, along with de Saussure, as being one of the founding fathers of modern semiotic. His classification of signs and description of the sign function have been most influential. But his objective idealism and synechism have not tended to be incorporated into this modern work. They have not, in any important way, shaped the contemporary perspective on semiotic; rather, they often seem to be regarded as the vestiges of a nineteenth century post-Kantian idealism that most philosophers today would regard as archaic. Peirce, in so many ways an exciting innovator and prophet, was in this respect, it would seem to some critics, clearly a child of his times.

That Peirce's thinking and concerns display many characteristics that were quite typical of his immediate historical and cultural milieu is not to be denied. Nor is it to be denied that his semiotic can, to a great extent, be lifted from its metaphysical underpinnings and employed for various contemporary purposes. In doing so, however, it must be admitted that this theory loses a good deal of its original power. For Peirce's own claims were really quite extraordinary in precisely this sense: he was interested not only in the fact that a sign brings its object and its interpretant into relation, but also in the fact (for him) that all such relations are really *continuous*. Universal semiosis is the mechanics, the dynamics of objective mind. In religious terms, then, it is the means by which God relates to and communicates with lesser minds. Moreover, given the fact of continuity, in one sense, semiotic is always already theosemiotic. If all of reality is continuous, then everything is potentially a sign of God's presence.

Now Peirce never really established the superiority of such a general point of view over the alternatives in the philosophy of religion. His quick disposal of a more complex dualism of mind and matter, by appealing to Ockham's razor, is a move that might certainly be regarded with suspicion. Nor will his claim that the basic principles of Newtonian physics must fail to account for the phenomenon of consciousness, of spontaneous feeling, be very compelling for contemporary philosophers who employ an entirely different set of scientific premises. Finally, Peirce's topological considerations, so essential to the development of his synechistic world view, are largely grounded in the relatively weak conceptual resources supplied by Johann Listing.

This is not to suggest that a more adequate defense of the Peircean position could not be constructed. The contention that all of reality is mind is not so "spooky" as it might seem at first blush, especially when one considers that Peirce was willing to label his doctrine materialistic so long as that label be understood properly. The discoveries and theories of modern physics, on the whole, have not proven to be uncongenial to Peirce's general outlook. In particular, modern field theory might be employed creatively in support of his synechism;[3] it is curious that Peirce himself, having lived long enough to witness some of the most exciting developments in this area, was not more inclined to appropriate them. Likewise, the emergence of nonstandard analysis in analytical geometry, with its revival of the infinitesimal as a conceptual tool for analysis, represents something of a movement back to the Peircean perspective.[4] Finally, topology has evolved far beyond the state in which Listing and Peirce left it.

These comments will not suffice to establish that the synechistic hypothesis is verifiable, much less true. They do indicate, however, that the sort of program that Peirce outlined for a truly scientific metaphysics might be one that can be pursued; and the final intelligibility of many of his religious claims could only be determined once some significant progress has been made in that direction. For this study has revealed that Peirce's conception of God, as well as of God's relationship to the world, was largely fashioned out of materials that he drew from mathematics and the sciences.

At the same time, it would be mistaken to suppose that Peirce's religious claims are meaningless unless one assumes the ultimate validity of that metaphysical framework within which they are embedded. Other criteria are available for the task of evaluating his religious thought. Some of these are purely theological. For example, Peirce's "solution" to the problem of evil seems to suggest either that he was a process thinker whose Deity was constrained by the logic of a certain temporal development or that Peirce failed to be sensitive enough to the reality of suffering as something that *individuals* experience, to the reality of evil as a force that can be purely destructive of harmonious relations, a purely irrational force. If the former is concluded, the classical theist will judge Peirce's position to be problematic; but it has been argued above that a careful reading of Peirce does not warrant that conclusion anyway. The latter interpretation, however, is not likely to make his treatment of this topic an attractive one from any theological perspective.

Other criticisms of Peirce might be formulated, on grounds neither purely philosophical nor theological. Consider again his critical common-sensism in general, the Neglected Argument in particular. He seemed to presume as instinctive in humans certain beliefs and attitudes that a contemporary sociologist of knowledge would be likely to regard as culturally and historically quite specific. What he took to be common-sensical notions about the laws of "mechanics" and "psychics" might not seem so to someone living in a time or culture not as clearly shaped by the perspective of modern western science. A Taoist might see things quite differently, or an ancient Egyptian. Most pertinent to the present discussion is the extent to which specific *religious* ideas can be labeled "instinctive." The God encountered in Musement, it is true, is only vaguely described by Peirce, but still sounds suspiciously like the personal creator God of Jews and Christians. This sort of conception of the divine reality might confuse, again, the Taoist, certainly the Therevada Buddhist.

But exactly how significant a complaint is this? One would expect Peirce, as a nineteenth-century thinker, to be somewhat naive in this respect, just as one should not be too surprised by the sort of post-Darwinian evolutionary optimism that colored his treatment of the problem of evil. After all, the sociology of knowledge and the history of religions are disciplines that have matured only in the twentieth century; in large measure, their significant impact is a quite recent phenomenon. Peirce was, in fact, relatively sophisticated on this score, more sensitive than many of his contemporaries to the extent to which our thinking and perceptions are shaped by our prejudices, our acquired beliefs and habits. Moreover, he was a thoroughgoing fallibilist, not dogmatic about his claims, but open to having his own feelings and conceptions subjected to further testing; indeed, it has been argued above that the invitation to Musement should be interpreted as the invitation to perform just such an experiment.

This sort of negative critique of Peirce's religious thought, then, is likely to yield predictable results and, to that extent, to be of less than compelling interest. His metaphysics was clearly a work-in-progress, still plagued by difficulties for which he had no solution. He was, to be sure, bound in certain inevitable ways by the Zeitgeist. And he was formally trained neither as a theologian or a historian of religion. Despite all this, he thought deeply and with insight about religious questions; if he supplied no ready list of answers, at least he posed them creatively and from his own unique and illuminating perspective. There is no distinctively "Peircean" agenda for the philosophy of religion. But what might it mean to pursue this discipline within the general framework of a "theosemiotic"?

III

It would mean, most significantly, that the problem of religious knowledge is to be conceived primarily as a problem of sign-interpretation. Here, none of Peirce's religious assumptions need be invoked. The scientist's vague confidence in the reasonableness of phenomena need not represent, as he suggested, an implicit faith in God. The world may not be, in truth, God's great poem. But to the extent that religious claims of that or any other sort are made, to the extent that they represent claims to know certain religious facts, they will be claims grounded in experience, either contemporary experience or that of the founders of a tradition of belief. And they will be thus grounded in Peirce's peculiar sense that some experience or set of observations occasioned the abductive insight into their truth, while further experience confirmed such a belief about their status. This will be a matter of "divining" the meaning of certain signs and continuously testing the implications of acting on the belief that one's interpretation is correct. The signs must be given in experience even if their meaning is not so generated. There is no purely a priori, deductive path to religious knowledge.

What are the consequences of this sort of perspective for the philosophy of religion? It illumines, one might suggest, the true nature of religious reasoning, of theological argumentation. It exposes the logic of religious belief by appealing to a general "theory of the nature of thinking." That is to say, it supplies the framework of intelligibility for a claim that, in its more recently articulated versions, has received considerable attention from philosophers. For example, in an article that has achieved the status of a modern classic in the philosophy of religion, John Wisdom describes a mode of reasoning that is neither simply deductive nor inductive in a straightforward sense. It involves "a presenting and representing of those features of the case which *severally cooperate* in favor of the conclusion." In such an argument "the reasons are like the legs of a chair, not the links of a chain."[5] (Compare Peirce's own metaphor for reasoning as a "cable" woven out of various "fibers" rather than a "chain" with "links," in *CP* 5.265.) Nor is it a matter here of gathering new evidence or testing expectations experimentally; rather, as Wisdom explains it, the argument employs and is sustained by the special logic of interpretation.[6]

It would not be extraordinarily difficult to demonstrate that this sort of logic is what Peirce analyzed and designated as abduction. Abductive inference is precisely the mode of thought that consists in the formation and contemplation of hypotheses. As such, it involves the arrangement and rearrangement of observed facts so that they correspond to the implications of a given hypothesis, and it is, essentially, the logic of sign-interpretation. Moreover, for both Peirce and Wisdom, it is this type of thinking that facilitates religious experience and grounds religious claims to know; as a form of argument, it is designed to help others also to see things the way that one sees them.[7]

What is the potential significance then, besides his having anticipated this more recent discussion, of Peirce's philosophical perspective? The following sketch is intended only as a partial answer to that question, more precisely as a list of those features of Peirce's thought that might prove to be important stimuli for future research, for the development of a theosemiotic.

In the first place, his extensive *classification of signs*, a task that Peirce pursued with a peerless rigor and enthusiasm, provides an important part of the background for what he had to say about interpretation. If instances of religious seeing, of religious knowing, are in fact instances of sign-interpretation, then one's understanding of those phenomena ought to be enriched considerably by a detailed account of the various kinds of signs that might be distinguished, the sort of information that each conveys, their mode of representation. In the present study, this topic was barely touched upon, only one of Peirce's many sub-classifications (icon-index-symbol) analyzed in a very cursory fashion. Likewise, his account of the variety of interpretant-signs was briefly invoked here but its importance should not be underestimated. Philosophers need to attend to the implications of Peirce's claim that the meaning of a religious symbol can be embodied in feelings and actions as well as in conceptions, that these all can be said legitimately to form part of its *interpretation*.[8] On this account, religious behavior and religiously meaningful experiences are more than data requiring interpretation; they themselves have an irreducible hermeneutic function. They themselves form part of the continuous stream of semiosis that renders the idea of God more determinate.

In similar fashion, one hardly knows how to begin to estimate the importance of Peirce's remarks about the *vagueness of signs*. If the construal of his position in the chapters above is correct, then for Peirce God is a real continuum actually dimensionless, perfectly free and indeterminate, the primordial No-thing. Thus, religious utterances would have to be infinitely vague in order to be truly accurate; in fact, our conventional philosophical talk about the Deity has as its proper object that more determinate reality, God's living symbol, perhaps a "Deity relatively to us."[9] Even so, such talk is mostly "wild gabbling" to the extent that Peirce seemed occasionally to prefer silence on these matters.

Now does this sort of perspective represent some insight comparable to that of the mystics, a negative theology, or is it mere obscurantism? Here Peirce truly could have been more helpful to his readers. Yet surely there is some rationale underlying Peirce's claim that religious language is vague of necessity, that it is misleading or issues in falsehood when excessively precise, and that predicate-signs attached with clear meaning to other subjects can be applied to God only vaguely. His logic of vagueness was a genuinely pioneering effort foreshadowing the kind of work that is now being done in the analysis of fuzzy sets and systems.[10] Furthermore, if such vague symbols are the models most appropriately employed for the representation of a real indeterminacy, then a better understanding of the special logic of their usage seems crucial to the development of a general theory of religious language. For example, seemingly paradoxical utterances about the Deity might be explained in terms of their vagueness, by appealing to a logic that defines the "vague . . . as that to which the principle of contradiction does not apply" (*CP* 5.505).

Consider, also, what Peirce had to say about *habits of interpretation*, the role played by beliefs in inference and experience. As a system, they constitute the "starting-place" of thought, the rules that govern our reasoning, the gentle forces that shape our perceptions. If his account is even roughly correct, then surely it must inform any explanation of how religious knowledge is generated, how religious experiences acquire the meanings that they have.[11] In his own philosophy of religion, Peirce emphasized, perhaps to excess, the importance of natural beliefs. Clearly, however, culturally induced beliefs will have the same sort of habit-function, will play the same normative role in cognition and perception. What are the dynamics, then, underlying the formation and dissolution of belief-habits? Certainly Peirce himself moved far beyond the simple account that he originally presented in "The Fixation of Belief." One need not accept even his later formulations, however, in order to appreciate the importance of the question that he raised.

It is much too simple, of course, to contend that the failure to recognize a certain X as Y entails the *absence* of some relevant belief or habit of interpretation (whether that absence is explained as the dissolution of or the failure to form such a habit). One might be vaguely predisposed to construe X as being a particular sort of thing but at the same time be blinded to its character because of the influence of some more powerful or lively habit of perception. That is to say, in a conflict of beliefs, the more vivid belief might trump its vague counterpart. This is not to deny that it is equally possible for a given belief, despite its vagueness, to operate as a law regulating the influence of other habits of a lesser generality.

Perhaps this line of inquiry can be given a slightly sharper focus. Peirce admitted that there are those who are unable to perceive the reality of God. This inability *might* be attributed to a powerful conviction, however formed, that there is no such reality, a conviction that will habitually determine the quality of one's experiences. But Peirce also seemed to suggest that this blindness is a rather common phenomenon, that even among those who claim to be *believers* in God there is evidence of this failure to experience God's "reality" and "nearness." Now if Peirce's argument is correct, such a phenomenon can be analyzed in semiotic terms.[12] For it will represent a failure to process a certain kind of information, to interpret the meaning of certain signs, and the appropriate capacity for doing so consists in the possession of a religious skill, a habit of interpretation. Of course, from an atheistic perspective, this would not be a worthwhile "skill" to possess because it would generate false interpretations. Nevertheless, the atheist's argument with the theist would still unfold within this semiotic context; it would be an argument *about* the correct interpretation of signs.

It seems that Peirce intended *Musement* to be not only a kind of experiment, then, a test *for* the instinctiveness of the God-hypothesis and *of* its effects on one who contemplates that idea, but also a form of therapy, designed to facilitate religious perceptions. For Peirce, ideally, Musement evolves into religious meditation, becomes a type of prayer, filling the heart and mind of the Muser with the love of God. The more "incessant" such a practice, the more imbued does that individual become with the sense of God's presence. Obviously there are a number of important presuppositions underlying this argument, in fact, theological presuppositions about the reality of God and the naturalness of belief in God. Yet it is only the Muser, Peirce contended, who is in a position to evaluate or test those presuppositions.

Peirce's description of Musement, by his own admission, is indebted to a particular conception of esthetic play. One should not be surprised to discover in his account, then, certain insights into the relation between religion and esthetics, resources for construing the religious significance of art.[13] Every artwork is, in a sense, an invitation to "Musement" in which the Muser is given license, within the environment created by the work, to playfully entertain various notions and feelings, to test the implications of various hypotheses. This is a playing that is gently, artfully shaped by the substance, form, and context of that specific work of art, rather than, as in Peirce's Neglected Argument, by the nature of reality as a whole. So there may indeed be some "rules" for playing (other than the one "law of liberty") stipulated by the artist; the player may be directed to engage in the exploration of a certain complex of beliefs, perhaps religious beliefs, acquired as well as seemingly instinctive beliefs.

Peirce's account was designed to illustrate the manner in which this sort of cognitive play generates new ideas and insights. Ideally, such playfulness will prove to be therapeutic in the religiously significant sense specified above. That is to say, the logic of esthetic experience is essentially abductive; so if a given artwork facilitates or stimulates the hypothetical consideration of religious ideas, this sort of localized Musement may also flower into religious meditation, become a "*preparatio* for prayer."[14]

Now Peirce considered abduction not in isolation but as an integral part of a *general theory of inquiry*. Herein lies a great deal of the power of his account. If interpretant-signs are formed in the process of abduction, then deduction is concerned with the mitigation of their vagueness, induction with the testing of their adequacy. For the purposes of this discussion, it makes the most sense to unpack these claims, albeit quite briefly, by linking them to the description of a theological method that was presented in the first section of this chapter.

That method will begin, necessarily, with the making of certain interpretive judgments. These need not be restricted to perceptual judgments (although Peirce's Neglected Argument *is* preoccupied with how the universes of experience will acquire a certain significance in Musement). Judgments about the meanings of sacred texts, about the significance of historical events, about the morality of certain actions, are all likewise abductive in form. It would be reasonable, on Peircean premises, to assume that such judgments will be informed by a whole system of living beliefs, powerful habits of interpretation, the legacy of both nature and nurture. These consist of a wide range of cultural beliefs, linguistic habits, acquired or innate modes of thought. The philosopher of religion will want first of all, then, to expose as fully as possible these implicit belief-habits. They function as the rules shaping religious discourse, as the leading principles for religious inferences. The more open and creative one's religious musing, the more frequently such principles themselves will become the objects of contemplation.

Interpretations must be elaborated, their implications clarified and explored. In a sense, this deductive process is already involved in the first stage of inquiry; upon entertaining a hypothesis, one will want to infer immediately at least some of the more significant consequences of holding it to be true. This process of explication will continue, however, even after some hypothesis has been embraced, has acquired the status of a living belief, and is already shaping one's conduct and perceptions. The logical analysis of a belief reduces its vagueness, specifies its determinate implications, for example, the precise bearing it ought to have on our experiences, and how, in particular instances, it will function as a habit of action. This is the sense, it seems, in which one would have to understand all *a priori* deductive proofs of God's existence within a Peircean scheme. They cannot succeed as proofs. Yet they might be regarded as valuable "explications" of the God-hypothesis, clarifications of its meaning. So that *if* a particular hypothesis about God is true, then God is necessary being, or the first uncaused cause, etc. That is why, in the Neglected Argument, the idea of God is of an *Ens necessarium*, but that idea has a hypothetical status nevertheless.

Perhaps the most interesting implication of Peirce's logic of inquiry for theological reflection, given the contemporary theological mind-set, is the importance, in his account, that must be attached to praxis and to the role of the community. Both themes have emerged at earlier points in this story. For Peirce, the God-hypothesis, indeed, any interpretive judgment, will be both explicated and tested in practice, pragmatically, in terms of its effects on human conduct. This conduct will be at least partially motivated or inspired by the beauty of specific religious ideas, and actions themselves will be deemed morally appropriate only if they display a positive esthetic quality, a certain fittingness. Moreover, religious ideas must be rejected, whatever their apparent intrinsic beauty and reasonableness, if they fail to promote genuinely reasonable behavior, if they cannot be effectively embodied in conduct. So praxis will have a certain critical purchase on reflection; at the same time, meditative practices *are* practices, the immediate effects of contemplating an idea forming part of the pragmaticistic meaning of that very conception.

To put it succinctly, religious meditation, theological inquiry, and moral practice need to be perceived as continuous. Likewise, a certain logical continuity ought to link one's philosophical and systematic theology with one's practical, political, and moral judgments. This was not an explicit concern for Peirce himself, of course, since he regarded all theologizing as anathema. But his disdain for that enterprise as it was commonly practiced was largely a function of its utter illogicality, as he saw it, its deviance from the methods of sound reasoning, its lack of animus for the truth.

That truth, for Peirce, is what the unlimited community of inquirers will discover to be the case in the long run. Even in the short run inquiry is best conceived as a communal activity, whether its purpose be considered as having a religious or a purely secular significance.[15] So theological reflection, ideally, will be an activity pursued by individuals who are attentive to the opinions of others, both past and present, individuals who are responsive to and empowered by the gentle force of reasonable ideals. At the same time, communities need not be characterized by any particular degree of homogeneity; they constitute systems rather than classes of individuals, individuals bound by relations that transcend the mere sameness of thought and belief.

On the one hand, Peirce's argument implies that there is an "ethic of interpretation"; logic is after all a normative discipline, so that there must be correct and incorrect ways of thinking theologically. On the other hand, every sign has an infinite number of interpretants for Peirce, so that no rigid notion of consensus should be invoked to effect a radical delimiting of the field of possible religious meanings. Moreover, within the context of theosemiotic, individuals *are* signs, communication between them consisting of reciprocal acts of interpretation. Here one might envision religious dialogue as a kind of living intertextuality, persons and communities, their sacred texts and traditions, each the living embodiment of meaning, each the fragment of some more complex system of meaning.

All of the remarks above are intended themselves to be nothing more than fragmentary suggestions of how Peirce's vision might be pursued in the realm of religious studies. Peirce's own ideas about religion, no matter how incomplete *they* may appear to be, are continuous with what he thought and wrote about in detail on other topics. That is the conclusion of this study. Now a good idea, for Peirce, is one that will eventually get itself thought. As long as his ideas are "living," they will persist in exerting their gentle influence, proving to be continuous as well with the reflections of others who are eager to explore his insights.

NOTES

Introduction

1. See the "Editorial Note" supplied by Hartshorne and Weiss on page v of *CP* 6.

2. One interesting exception here is Josiah Royce, who, in *The Problem of Christianity* (New York: The Macmillan Co., 1913), a work published during Peirce's lifetime, drew heavily on the latter's semiotic for the purpose of developing his own religious philosophy.

3. For a brief review of the secondary literature dealing with Peirce's philosophy of religion, consult the remarks in the bibliography attached to this study.

4. The word "theology" had extraordinarily negative connotations for Peirce, representing for him the sort of vicious, narrow-minded, and politically charged discourse that was all too typical of the theological debates between Calvinists and Unitarians in the nineteenth century. Hardly a genuine form of inquiry, it was simply a set of strategies designed to reinforce beliefs already assumed to be true at the outset (see *CP* 6.3). This sort of theologizing is as frequently encountered on the contemporary scene as it was in Peirce's day. Still, there is a species of argument and analysis often classified under the rubric "philosophical theology" that, it seems to me, not only would be more congenial to Peirce but in fact is actually exemplified in some of his writings. Many of the medieval thinkers whom Peirce so greatly admired were philosophical theologians in this sense, so that I feel it is legitimate to attach to his work a label that he himself would have disdained.

At the same time, I make no rigid, technical distinction here between "philosophical theology" and the "philosophy of religion." As the latter appears in the title of this study, it is intended simply to suggest that this work represents an investigation of Peirce's philosophical thinking about a variety of religious topics.

5. This is the language that Peirce used to distinguish the operation of final from efficient causation. See *CP* 1.220.

I. Scientific Theism

1. Benjamin Peirce, *Ideality in the Physical Sciences* (Boston: Little, Brown & Co., 1881), p. 54.

2. Ibid., pp. 18–19.

3. Ibid., p. 21.

4. Ibid., p. 36.

5. For a sketch of this theory within the context of a discussion of the impact of the elder Peirce on Charles's religious thought, see M. G. Murphey's *The Development of Peirce's Philosophy* (Cambridge: Harvard University Press, 1961), pp. 13–15.

6. On the nebular theory, see Benjamin Peirce, pp. 51ff. For an extended commentary, consult R. L. Numbers, *Creation by Natural Law: Laplace's Nebular Hypothesis in American Thought* (Seattle: University of Washington Press, 1977).

7. Benjamin Peirce, pp. 56–57.

8. Ibid.; see, for example, p. 186ff.

9. Ibid., p. 56.

10. Consult Andrew Dickson White's classic study of this issue and this period, *A History of the Warfare of Science with Theology* (London: D. Appleton & Co., 1896), as well

as Peirce's commentary on that work in *MS* 1331 and *MS* 1404, and his published review of it in *The American Historical Review* 2 (1896): 107–113.

11. For a brief discussion of the religious impact of Darwin's theory, see E. Flower's and M. G. Murphey's *A History of Philosophy in America* (New York: G. P. Putnam's Sons, 1977), vol. 2, chapter 9, especially p. 525ff. Peirce seemed at a very early point in his intellectual development to have abandoned any type of faith grounded in a literal reading of scripture or based on the scriptural evidence for miracles, and there is no indication that he was preoccupied with the arguments of the German critics. Indeed, Peirce seemed to have been somewhat unfamiliar with the writings of the German biblical scholars (see *CP* 6.513), and he conflated their general mode of argument with that of Hume (see also *HP* 2:707). He *did* regard the Humean critique of miracles to be problematic. (See section III of this chapter.) On the proofs of the existence of God, he appeared, at least, to have approved of Hume's rejection of the argument from design (*CP* 6.419–27), so that any interpretation of Peirce's Neglected Argument that construes it as a "version" of the former must specify the crucial difference between his and other versions.

12. See the discussion in section II of chapter three below.

13. Peirce did seem at times to drive a wedge between science and theology (*CP* 6.3), even to have opposed the "spirit" of science to that of religion (*CP* 6.426). But he was quite ambivalent on this issue, as the comments already cited about the religious significance of science would suggest. Peirce had two basic concerns here: (1) that the narrow-mindedness and mean-spiritedness characteristic of so much of theology not be allowed to infect the scientific enterprise, and (2) that genuine "religion" not be confused with any purely intellectual activity, with either theology or the philosophy of religion (see *CP* 8.125). He was not objecting to such activities in principle, but only as practiced by those who fail to recognize that any knowledge of God must be grounded in or "related to" actual experience (*CP* 6.492–93).

On the moral-religious dimension of scientific inquiry, see also Peirce's interesting review of Arabella B. Buckley's *The Moral Teachings of Science*, published on June 2, 1892, in *N* 1:155.

14. Murphey, *Development*, p. 15; and D. Orange, *Peirce's Conception of God: A Developmental Study*, Institute for Studies in Pragmaticism (Bloomington: Indiana University Press, 1984), pp. 1, 45–46.

15. On Peirce's concept of truth, consult N. Rescher's analysis in *Peirce's Philosophy of Science* (Notre Dame: University of Notre Dame Press, 1978), pp. 19ff. Also refer to R. Almeder, *The Philosophy of Charles S. Peirce: A Critical Introduction* (Totowa: Rowman & Littlefield, 1980), pp. 62ff. Almeder argues, quite convincingly, that Peirce did *not* insist that the truth as the final opinion of the community of inquirers is approached as a limit, but rather that the probability that the final answer is true approaches 1 as a limit; see *CP* 5.565 and *CP* 8.226.

16. See Murphey in *Development*, pp. 56ff.

17. I do address the relationship between Peirce and Duns Scotus more directly in "Habits and Essences," *Transactions of the Charles Peirce Society* 20 (1984): 147–67. Sections of that article are incorporated here.

18. Peirce was an accomplished historian of science whose claim that the fundamental presuppositions of scientific inquiry must be at heart realistic was in large measure a consequence of his historical studies. In this regard, see the rich collection of material in C. Eisele's *HP*.

19. The basic similarity between the perspective and agenda of Abbot and that of Peirce is revealed in the following passage:

Scientific Theism is more than a philosophy: it is a religion, it is a gospel, it is the Faith of the Future, founded on knowledge rather than on blind belief, —a faith in which head and heart will be no more arrayed against each other in irreconcilable feud, as the world beholds them now, but will kneel in worship side by side at the same altar, dedicated, not to the "Unknown God," still less to the "Unknowable God," but to the KNOWN GOD whose revealing prophet is SCIENCE.

Abbot, *Scientific Theism* (Boston: Little, Brown & Co., 1885), pp. 217–18.

20. Ibid., p. 25.

21. Ibid., p. 27.

22. Ibid., p. 28.

23. Ibid., pp. 41–42.

24. Peirce pioneered in the study of the logic of relatives and wrote extensively on this topic. Perhaps the best brief introduction to Peirce's thinking about "relatives" is his article bearing that title in the second volume of J. M. Baldwin's *Dictionary of Philosophy and Psychology* (New York: The Macmillan Co., 1902), pp. 447–50.

25. See J. Boler's excellent analysis in his *Charles Peirce and Scholastic Realism* (Seattle: University of Washington Press, 1963), pp. 73–78.

26. J. Owens, "Common Nature: A Point of Comparison between Thomistic and Scotistic Metaphysics," *Mediaeval Studies* XIX (1957): 7–8.

27. Boler, p. 77.

28. See N. Goodman on the notion of projection in *Fact, Fiction, and Forecast* (London: The Athlone Press, 1954).

29. For Peirce, a reality is that which is what it is, independently of what any mind or finite collection of minds may conceive it to be. He indicated his indebtedness to Duns Scotus for this concept in a variety of places, for example, *CP* 4.28, 6.495, 8.319.

30. Once again, I recognize that Peirce might be uncomfortable with this use of the word "theological." (See my introduction, note 4.) In this study, I use the word vaguely, not to specify some particular set of doctrines but only to identify Peirce's religious thought, his "thinking about God."

31. Murphey observed this fact in *Development*, p. 396.

32. This critique appears in a number of manuscripts; see, for example, *MS* 318:66ff. See also Peirce's letter to William James, *CP* 8.262.

33. I am indebted here to Murphey's interpretation of Peirce on individuals; see *Development*, pp. 398–99, and his chapter on Peirce in Flower and Murphey, *History of Philosophy*, pp. 613–14.

34. One early example is the interpretation of P. Weiss in his "Charles S. Peirce, Philosopher," in *Perspectives on Peirce*, ed. R. Bernstein (New Haven: Yale University Press, 1965), p. 134.

35. These arguments are unpacked in the discussion of Peirce's synechism in chapter two.

36. For example, Boler, *Peirce and Scholastic Realism*, pp. 160ff.

37. Consult Boler's "Peirce, Ockham and Scholastic Realism," *The Monist* 63 (1980): 296ff.

38. I discuss this relationship between final and formal causality in "Habits and Essences," p. 160.

39. See Duns Scotus on final causality as the "cause of causes" in his *Treatise on God as First Principle*, ed. A. Wolter (Chicago: Franciscan Herald Press, 1966), section 2.11. See also Wolter's commentary, especially his correlation of final causality with the view that the world is God's "work of art," pp. 179ff.

40. Murphey in *Development*, pp. 43–45, and in *History of Philosophy*, p. 571. This early Kantian position may have been mediated to the young Peirce via the writings of Henry Mansel, especially the latter's *Limits of Religious Thought* (London: John Murray, 1867), a work that Peirce criticized, but knew quite well. See his own essay of the same title in

W 1:37–42. See also Orange's excellent commentary on the Mansel-Peirce relation in *Peirce's Conception of God,* pp. 7–12.

41. In the eighth of his Lowell Lectures of 1903, *MS* 475, Peirce indicated the significance of Boole's work for him on this issue. I am grateful to Kenneth Ketner for his observation that the entire Boole family may have influenced Peirce's thinking about religion as well as logic. (See the latter's review in 1905 of Mary E. Boole's *The Preparation of the Child for Science,* in *N* 3.) In addition, my colleague, Steven Goldman, has underscored for me the important continuity between William Whewell and Peirce on the topic of abduction. Whewell's writings on logic and the history of logic were clearly held in high esteem by Peirce. (See, for example, *CP* 2.761.)

42. Boler has briefly discussed the relationship between abstraction and abduction in Peirce's thought; *Charles Peirce and Scholastic Realism,* pp. 78ff.

43. Peirce's article actually embodies a "nest" of three arguments, only the first of which concludes that God is real. This is the "Humble Argument," consisting in Musement, the form of meditative thinking that Peirce prescribed.

44. "The Laws of Nature and Hume's Argument against Miracles," published in the *Selected Writings* (here, *SW*), ed. P. Wiener (New York: Dover Publications, 1958), p. 294. (My references here are to the essay as it appears in Wiener's edition. That edition is more accessible to the general reader than the microfilm edition of Peirce's *MS*; moreover, Wiener supplies, in addition to the final draft of that essay, the relevant Peirce-Langley correspondence with some insightful commentary. But the reader may also want to consult the manuscript drafts of this text, *MS* 869–73, as well as the material in *CP* 6.522–46.)

45. Peirce, *SW*, p. 284 (letter of April 20, 1901).

46. Ibid., *SW*, p. 286 (letter of June 1, 1901).

47. See Wiener's introductory remarks in *SW*, pp. 275–79.

48. Peirce, *SW*, p. 294.

49. Ibid., *SW*, p. 309.

50. Ibid., *SW*, p. 309.

51. Ibid., *SW*, p. 310.

52. Aquinas seems to occupy an ambiguous position in Peirce's argument. In *CP* 6.537 and *CP* 6.541, he clearly identified Aquinas as the originator of the definition of a miracle as a violation of a law of nature. Elsewhere (e.g., *CP* 6.511) he grouped Aquinas with Augustine and Bishop Butler as a thinker who rejected the notion that God ever interferes with the "cursus naturae." Indeed, Peirce's interpretation of Aquinas on this issue seems to be correct. Aquinas did supply such a definition (see *Summa Theologica,* Q. 110, Art. 4, Reply Obj. 2); but he also posited a hierarchical plurality of natural "orders," so that while "He is not subject to the order of secondary causes," God cannot do anything against that "order of things depending on the first cause" (see *ST*, Q. 105, Art. 6).

53. Peirce, *SW*, p. 294; see also p. 319, and *CP* 6.92 and 6.101.

54. Peirce, *SW*, p. 300. Peirce directly attributed this notion of law as "energizing reasonableness" to Aristotle and the scholastics.

55. A more detailed account of the nature of abduction appears in sections II and III of chapter five, within the context of an interpretation of Peirce's concept of Musement.

56. Peirce, *SW*, p. 316.

57. Ibid., *SW*, p. 320.

58. Peirce was sometimes ambiguous in his use of the word "experience"; his own conception of the nature of experience clearly differed considerably from that of the classical British empiricists. As a result, his negative claims about the epistemological significance of experience may seem inconsistent with what he said in other places. There is no real inconsistency, however, and such claims apply only to the sort of narrow

empiricism that he rejected. For Peirce, any discovery, all new knowledge, is the result of abductive inference; but our very perceptual judgments are hypothetical in form. So there is no meaningful "experience" at all apart from or prior to this inferential, interpretive activity. (See the discussions in chapters five and six below, as well as Peirce's own comments in *CP* 5.611–13.)

59. Peirce, *SW*, pp. 300–301, note 45.

II. The Absolute Mind

1. The manner in which Peirce, in fact, did anticipate some of the principles of modern quantum mechanics was noted very early on; see C. J. Keyser, "A Glance at Some of the Ideas of Charles Sanders Peirce," *Scripta Mathematica* III (1935): 22–23.

2. Indeed, B. Kuklick has argued that even contemporary philosophers such as Quine and Goodman share some basic perspectives with the earlier idealists; see his *Josiah Royce* (Indianapolis: Hackett Publishing Co., 1985), pp. 4–5. Compare M. G. Murphey's article, "Kant's Children: The Cambridge Platonists," in the *Transactions of the Charles S. Peirce Society* 4 (1968): 3–33.

3. Consult Kuklick's *Josiah Royce*, esp. pp. 132ff. and 214ff., for a discussion of Peirce's influence on Royce. With special regard to Peirce's impact on the latter's philosophy of religion, particularly *The Problem of Christianity*, see F. Oppenheim's work on *Royce's Mature Philosophy of Religion* (Notre Dame: University of Notre Dame Press, 1987). (Peirce's attitudes towards some of Royce's ideas are considered in sections II and III of this chapter.)

4. For an extended treatment of Peirce's conception of personality, refer to S. M. Harrison's "Man's Glassy Essence: An Attempt to Construct a Theory of Person Based on the Writings of Charles Sanders Peirce." Dissertation, Fordham University, 1971.

5. M. G. Murphey, *The Development of Peirce's Philosophy* (Cambridge: Harvard University Press, 1961); see pp. 405–407, where Murphey argues that the principle of continuity was the key to a philosophical system that Peirce was never able to complete.

6. J. B. Dauben insightfully contrasts Peirce's approach to the problem of the continuum via his logical studies with the more purely mathematical concerns of Cantor and Dedekind; refer to his "Peirce's Place in Mathematics" in *Historia Mathematica* 9 (1982): 311–25.

7. In addition to Dauben's analysis of Peirce on the mathematics of the continuum, cited in note 6 above, I am indebted here to two other important commentaries: Murphey's ground-breaking work in his *Development*, especially part III, and V. G. Potter's and P. Shields's article "Peirce's Definitions of Continuity," *Transactions of the Charles S. Peirce Society* 13 (1977): 20–34. The latter supplies a useful account of the various stages of development of Peirce's thinking about this topic.

Perhaps the most accessible collection of Peirce's own mathematical musings on the continuum theme is located in *NEM*, especially volume 3, section 2 ("Multitude and Continuity").

8. Peirce's definition and explication of the notion of "multitude" appears, among other places, in *CP* 3.626–31.

9. Cantor had made the discovery at an earlier point in time, but Peirce seems to have arrived at the same conclusion independently (see *CP* 4.204).

10. Peirce admitted to having fallen into the same error as Kant regarding the interpretation of this definition; see *CP* 6.168.

11. Refer to Peirce on infinitesimals in *CP* 3.563–70. Benjamin Peirce defended the infinitesimal calculus, as did most of the other leading mathematicians of his day, until it was quickly replaced by the theory of limits late in the nineteenth century. Charles clung stubbornly to that approach, however, which put him in the distinct minority. (A fact that he was well aware of, but unmoved by: see his response to Royce's comment

in *CP* 3.565.) In certain respects, Peirce was actually ahead of his time, as he anticipated the nonstandard analysis of Abraham Robinson and others. But unlike Peirce, Robinson clearly never believed in the "reality" of infinitesimals; see his *Selected Papers*, volume 2: *Nonstandard Analysis and Philosophy*, ed. W. A. J. Luxemburg and S. Korner (New Haven: Yale University Press, 1979), e.g., pp. 542ff.

12. Listing is something of an obscure figure in the history of mathematics. His impact on Peirce's thinking was considerable, however. Murphey supplies an extended and insightful analysis of both Listing's topology and Peirce's appropriation of it in *Development*, especially in chapter ten.

13. On topical singularities, refer to Peirce's analysis in *NEM* 2:497–99.

14. The relationship between Peirce's synechism and his existential graphs has been neatly underscored by J. J. Zeman in his article "Peirce's Graphs: The Continuity Interpretation," *The Transactions of the Charles S. Peirce Society* 4 (1968): 144–54. For a thorough treatment of Peirce's graphs, consult D. Roberts's *The Existential Graphs of Charles S. Peirce* (The Hague: Mouton, 1973).

15. Peirce described, in an unpublished manuscript, the cosmological process that corresponds to the drawing of the line on the blackboard.

> The ultimate antecedent is a *zero* without extension; the ultimate consequent is a vast manifold. Hence the continuum of possible quality in N dimensions must be in a sequence starting from a point and expanding to a final limit of $N-1$ dimensions. Logic radiates like light. (*MS* 942:3)

16. This fact has some interesting implications for Peirce's theory of communication (see *CP* 6.159), and consequently for his theory of religious knowledge.

17. In sketching the basic details of Peirce's synechistic metaphysics and cosmology, I am especially indebted to the interpretations of M. G. Murphey, in chapters 16–18 of *Development*; in his chapter on Peirce in volume 2 of *A History of Philosophy in America* (New York: G. P. Putnam's Sons, 1977) pp. 608–20; and in his article "On Peirce's Metaphysics" in *The Transactions of the Charles S. Peirce Society* 1 (1968): 12–25.

18. D. Orange offers some very helpful comparisons of Peirce and Royce in her *Peirce's Conception of God*, Institute for Studies in Pragmaticism (Bloomington: Indiana University Press, 1984), pp. 32–35 and 58–63.

19. It seems clear that Royce, especially in his later writings, was indeed attentive to the volitional aspect of the divine mind. My only interest here is in Peirce's perspective on these thinkers: he *did* want to criticize Royce's Deity, like Hegel's, as being one who thinks but does not will, at least not in any creative or effective sense. (The characterization of Hegel may not be particularly accurate either.)

20. Peirce's definition of pantheism is quoted by Orange, page 38. See her commentary on this divine transcendence/immanence issue, pp. 38 and 91–92.

21. Orange, pp. 52ff., makes just this sort of analogy; but then she comes to the rather odd conclusion that Peirce considered God and Nature to be "metaphysically identifiable" realities (pp. 64–65). See my discussion in section III of this chapter.

22. The term "panentheism" is used here only in the broadest possible sense, and not to designate a specific doctrine associated with a particular thinker or group of thinkers. Decades ago, Charles Hartshorne noted Peirce's panentheistic tendencies, regretting only that he "falls short" of embracing the dipolar God of contemporary process philosophy, clinging instead to a more classical theism. See Hartshorne's "A Critique of Peirce's Idea of God" in *The Philosophical Review* 50 (1941): 516–23; also, consult Hartshorne and W. L. Reese in *Philosophers Speak of God* (Chicago: The University of Chicago Press, 1953), pp. 268–69. But in arguing that these classical elements are inconsistent with elements in Peirce's own system, Hartshorne does not appear to have

assessed carefully enough what Peirce had to say about continua and their singularities, about the logic of vagueness, or about the *semiotic* relationship between God and the universe. See my discussion of these issues in the present chapter and in chapter five. Moreover, whatever tensions may exist in Peirce's religious thought, I am convinced that he would have considered Hartshorne's process deity, like the finite God of William James, to be a completely unsatisfactory "solution." (Refer to Peirce's confession of his theism and critique of James's finite God in a letter to James dated July 22, 1905, in *MS* L224.)

23. As such, panentheism ought to be regarded as a form of theism. Indeed, Karl Rahner and Herbert Vorgrimler, in their *Dictionary of Theology* (New York: Crossroad, 1981), pp. 359–60, judge at least some versions of this perspective to be perfectly compatible with orthodox Christian thought. They identify panentheism as nothing other than the embodiment of "a demand that ontology undertake thinking out much more profoundly and much more accurately the relation which exists between absolute and finite being."

24. I borrow the metaphysical notion of "levels of reality" from James Ross, who has creatively developed it in various places, most prominently in his *Philosophical Theology* (Bobbs-Merrill, 1969), pp. 250–72.

25. See the analysis in my "Habits and Essences," *The Transactions of the Charles S. Peirce Society* 20 (1984): 161–63.

26. J. Boler compares Peirce's Absolute with Hegel's "concrete universal" in *Charles Peirce and Scholastic Realism* (Seattle: University of Washington Press, 1963), pp. 142, 149, and 164.

27. L. Wittgenstein, *Philosophical Investigations*, ed. G. E. M. Anscombe (New York: Macmillan Publishing Co., 1953), part 2, pp. x-xi.

28. J. E. Smith noted this tension in Peirce's thought decades ago in his "Religion and Theology in Peirce" in *Studies in the Philosophy of Charles Sanders Peirce*, ed. P. Wiener and F. H. Young (Cambridge: Harvard University Press, 1952), pp. 251–67. (See also my own brief comments in chapter one, note 13.)

29. V. Potter provides an excellent review and analysis of the elements of both anthropomorphism and vagueness in Peirce's theism in his article "Vaguely Like a Man: The Theism of Charles S. Peirce" in *God Knowable and Unknowable*, ed. R. J. Roth (New York: Fordham University Press, 1973).

30. In "Charles Sanders Peirce's Logic of Vagueness" (Dissertation, University of Illinois, 1969), J. E. Brock supplies a comprehensive and sophisticated account of Peirce's thought on this topic.

31. See the discussion in chapters four and five below, as well as *CP* 5.370ff., on the relation between belief and doubt.

32. This line of interpretation is developed in my discussion of Peirce's cosmological writings, a discussion located in the initial section of chapter three.

33. Orange, pp. 64–65. Here the author seems to be suggesting that God and the universe or "Nature" are identical realities for Peirce, although elsewhere she applauds him for balancing the notions of divine transcendence and immanence.

34. See *CP* 5.119; Peirce also remarked, in *MS* 280, that a "good religious argument" might be developed out of his analysis of "signification" and of the roles played in it by the "Graphist-mind" and the "interpreter-mind." (This suggestion, as well as the semiotic aspect of Peirce's anthropomorphism, will be pursued in chapter five.)

35. J. Royce, *The World and the Individual*, First Series, (New York: Dover Publications, 1959), pp. 473ff.

36. See ibid., p. 505, where indeed he is willing to grant the "infinite divisibility" but not the continuity of the map.

III. Evolutionary Love

1. A. Cayley, "A Sixth Memoir upon Quantics," *Collected Mathematical Papers* (Cambridge: The University Press, 1889–97), vol. 2, p. 592.

2. See the commentary of E. T. Bell in *The Development of Mathematics* (New York: McGraw-Hill, 1945), pp. 352–53 and 442ff.; also, Bertrand Russell's *An Essay on the Foundations of Geometry* (New York: Dover Publications, 1956), pp. 29–30.

3. Consult M. Kline, *Mathematical Thought from Ancient to Modern Times* (New York: Oxford University Press, 1972), pp. 909–913, for a compact description of Klein's program as well as an explanation of his nomenclature.

4. D. Pedoe, *An Introduction to Projective Geometry* (New York: The Macmillan Co., 1963), pp. 14–17; and J. W. Young, *Projective Geometry* (Chicago: Open Court Publishing Co., 1930), chapter VI.

5. Kline, *Mathematical Thought*, p. 913.

6. Refer also to *CP* 6.82, where Peirce, after having reviewed the alternatives, argued that real space is hyperbolic in nature.

7. This universe, Peirce noted, is not identical with the *physical* universe, which the theologians held to be finite.

8. See the relevant passage in the biblical book, *The Revelation to John*, chapter 1, verse 8; also, compare Peirce's definition of religion in *CP* 6.429 where the Absolute is identified as the "Alpha" and "Omega."

9. In *MS* 861:3, Peirce contends that God is "Omniscient," "Omnipotent," and "Impeccable," and that the Deity is more properly conceived, in Fiske's terms, as being "remote" rather than "immanent."

10. For the notion of "continuous creation" as well as for his "solution" to the problem of evil, Peirce was most likely indebted to the argument of Henry James, Sr., in his *Substance and Shadow* (Boston: Ticknor and Fields, 1863); see *N* 2:209, 210; *CP* 6.287.

11. Hartshorne perceives these difficulties to be the necessary consequence of one's embracing classical theism rather than a panentheistic process theism. He criticizes Peirce on this score as one who came so close to seeing the truth of the matter but resisted it. Refer, again, to his "A Critique of Peirce's Idea of God."

12. What I take to be Peirce's argument here resembles Paul Tillich's perspective when the latter contends that "God is a symbol of God"; Tillich insists that one distinguish between that which is experienced as "ultimate" and any concept that one might form of such a reality. See his *Dynamics of Faith* (New York: Harper & Row, 1957), pp. 45ff.

13. Compare Peirce's approval (*CP* 6.396), in 1878, of Vacherot's description of God as the Supreme Ideal with his fervent confession to William James, some 30 years later, that God as Ideal is not only real, but necessarily so (*MS* L224).

14. Examine Peirce's discussion in *CP* 6.508–509. God's very thought is creative, and to talk about other "possible worlds" that have not also been created is to imply some limitation on the divine omnipotence.

15. Indeed, in another unpublished manuscript, 942, Peirce actually proceeded to correlate the essential ingredients of his own cosmological story with elements in the opening passage of *Genesis*. Regarding the Babylonian philosopher from whom "the first chapter of Genesis was cribbed," Peirce observes that:

> It is remarkable that though subconsciously yet he has perceived the need of every element which was needed for the first day. His *tohu wabohu*, *terra inanis et vacua* is the indeterminate germinal Nothing. His *Spiritus Dei ferebatur super aquas* is consciousness. His *Lux* is the world of quality. His *fiat lux* is an arbitrary reaction. His *divisit lucem a tenebris* is the recognition of the necessary duality.

His *vidit Deus lucem quod esset bona* is the waking consciousness. Finally, his *factumque est vespere at mane, dies unus* is the emergence of time.

16. See Vincent G. Potter's commentary in the last chapter of his book, *Charles S. Peirce on Norms and Ideals* (Amherst: University of Massachusetts Press, 1967), pp. 197–98.

17. But such a conception of the absolute as a divine nothingness would have considerable precedent in the history of western religious thought. See L. Kolakowski's fascinating meditations on this topic in *Metaphysical Horror* (Oxford: Basil Blackwell, 1988).

18. For an interesting commentary on Peirce's cosmological writings, including an evaluation of his conception of primordial "nothingness," consult P. Turley's *Peirce's Cosmology* (New York: Philosophical Library, 1977).

19. I am referring to the order of the present discussion and to the logical order of Peirce's cosmological notions. In terms of actual chronology, the essay on "Evolutionary Love" was published in 1893, five years *before* the reflections on "objective logic" (*CP* 6.189–237) were recorded.

20. Peirce talked, in *CP* 6.297, about work that was published in a variety of disciplines between 1846 and 1859. Of course, Darwin had already formulated his theory of evolution more than a decade before he published, but Peirce was not likely to have been aware of this fact.

21. It is not to be supposed that this sort of argument was developed by Peirce for the very first time in the *Monist* series. In *CP* 6.270, he himself referred the reader to his discussion, published a quarter of a century earlier, in the article on the "Consequences of Four Incapacities" (see especially *CP* 5.313ff.). Indeed, as early as 1866, in his eleventh Lowell Lecture, Peirce advanced a semiotic conception of persons; see *W* 1:490–504.

22. See Henry James Sr.'s *Substance and Shadow*, especially chapters II, IV, and XXII.

23. Since Peirce insisted that God cannot be "one of a genus," it seems odd to complain that he failed to apply systematically his system of categories to the Deity: see Hartshorne and Reese in *Philosophers Speak of God* (Chicago: The University of Chicago Press, 1953), p. 268. This is precisely the sort of move that he was reluctant to make, since he understood God to be not confined by but the *Creator of* all three Universes of experience. And so, despite the temptations recorded here, one should be hesitant to identify Peirce's God with his category of Thirdness, unless such a claim is carefully qualified. Orange seems to succumb to this temptation at times in her study of *Peirce's Conception of God*.

24. Given his familiarity with and positive evaluation of Duns Scotus's philosophy, it is reasonable to assume that Peirce was influenced by the latter's voluntarism, that this influence strengthened his conviction that Secondness is an irreducible category of experience, and that the act of creation is essentially a matter of divine volition. For a lucid interpretation of Duns Scotus on this issue, see the account of B. Bonansea in "Duns Scotus' Voluntarism," *Studies in Philosophy and the History of Philosophy*, vol. 3, ed. J. K. Ryan and B. Bonansea (Washington, D.C.: The Catholic University of America Press, 1965), pp. 83–121.

25. See my discussion in "Habits and Essences," *The Transactions of the Charles S. Peirce Society* 20 (1984): 158–63.

26. I am indebted to Kenneth Ketner for information concerning the availability in the nineteenth century of eastern texts in translation. For example, Paul Carus, whose relationship with Peirce as an editor and correspondent was a significant one, published in 1894 a collection of Buddhist materials entitled *The Gospel of the Buddha.* Ketner evaluates the eastern influences on Peirce's thought as being a good deal more

important than I suggest that they are in the present account. See his essay "The Importance of Religion for Peirce" in *Gedankenzeichen*, ed. R. Claussen and R. Daube-Schackat (Stauffenburg verlag, 1988). Consult also D. Bishop, "Peirce and Eastern Thought" in *Proceedings of the C. S. Peirce Bicentennial International Congress*, ed. K. Ketner et al., Graduate Studies 23 (Lubbock: Texas Tech University Press, 1981), pp. 265–70.

27. I am not suggesting here that Peirce selected and adopted moral and religious ideas simply because they fit neatly into a world-view already presupposed. This is the sort of "nominalistic" procedure that Peirce so consistently contrasted with genuine inquiry. Nevertheless, his thinking is, to a remarkable degree, all of a piece. The organic, architectonic quality of his philosophy, alluded to in the introduction above, is manifested in the complex set of interrelationships that one discovers when exploring his mathematical, metaphysical, ethical, and religious conceptions.

28. Consider Emerson's notion of "compensation," as presented in the material collected in *The Early Lectures of Ralph Waldo Emerson*, ed. R. Spiller and W. Williams (Cambridge: Harvard University Press, 1972), pp. 114–15 and 145–50. Royce's theodicy is developed in a number of places; for example, see "The Problem of Job," included in *The Philosophy of Josiah Royce*, ed. J. K. Roth (New York: Thomas Y. Crowell Co., 1971), pp. 85–106. Also consider Royce's most mature work in the philosophy of religion, *The Problem of Christianity* (New York: The Macmillan Co., 1913). Finally, refer to Teilhard de Chardin's "Some Remarks on the Place and Part of Evil in a World in Evolution," appearing as the appendix to *The Phenomenon of Man*, tr. Bernard Wall (New York: Harper & Row, 1965), pp. 311–13. Teilhard, a later, twentieth-century thinker, shared a number of Peirce's scientific and theological interests and concerns.

29. Peirce argued that the divine love must embrace its opposite, the hateful or that which is "defect" of love. Compare Simone Weil's claim that God creates from "the greatest possible distance," that God's love is infinite because it overcomes this "infinite distance" between the Deity and that which is most "wretched" in creation. See her *Waiting for God*, tr. E. Craufurd (New York: G. Putnam's Sons, 1951), pp. 123ff.

30. See Murphey, *Development*, pp. 351ff.

31. Orange, in *Peirce's Conception of God*, pp. 89–90, defends Peirce's theodicy, identifying him as a "process" thinker.

32. Even Hartshorne admits this about Peirce, while regretting that it is so. See again his "A Critique of Peirce's Idea of God."

33. This sort of argument, invoking certain claims about the relation between different "reality levels," is once again a crude summary of the extended analysis of the problem of evil that J. F. Ross supplies in his *Philosophical Theology* (Indianapolis: Bobbs-Merrill Co., 1969) pp. 250–52.

IV. Habits and Values

1. Of course, in large measure, William James was responsible for the way in which Peirce's work was perceived by its earliest interpreters, James having identified Peirce as one of the founders of pragmatism in his 1898 Berkeley lecture on "Philosophical Conceptions and Practical Results." For some discussion of the historical implications of this event, refer to M. Fisch's essay, "American Pragmatism before and after 1898" (first published in 1977), included in the collection entitled *Peirce, Semeiotic, and Pragmatism*, ed. K. Ketner and C. Kloesel (Bloomington: Indiana University Press, 1986), pp. 283–304.

2. Even "The Order of Nature" (*CP* 6.395–427), which does address certain religious issues, can hardly be said to represent Peirce's maturest, most well-developed perspective on religion. Here he did little more of positive value than resist the claim "that science can at present disprove religion" (*CP* 6.426).

3. See Peirce's reference to this definition in *CP* 5.12. Consult also Max Fisch's

classic account of Bain's influence on the American philosophers, including Peirce, in his essay "Alexander Bain and the Genealogy of Pragmatism" (originally published in 1954) in *Peirce, Semeiotic, and Pragmatism,* pp. 79–109.

4. These remarks are taken from Peirce's essay on "Some Consequences of Four Incapacities" which appeared in the *Journal of Speculative Philosophy* in 1868, some nine years before the publication of "The Fixation of Belief." (Such remarks anticipate quite remarkably what Hans-Georg Gadamer had to say nearly a century later about how our "prejudices" constitute the conditions, the "horizon" of our understanding, in *Truth and Method* [New York: Continuum Publishing Co., 1975], especially pp. 245ff.)

5. On the nature of and distinction between formal and material leading principles, see *CP* 2.588–89.

6. Refer to the discussion in section II of chapter one above.

7. This is, essentially, the claim embodied in Peirce's Neglected Argument (see especially *CP* 6.482). Also compare Peirce's comment in a letter to Lady Welby that all true "men of science," whether they recognize it or not, have a genuine "Faith in God"; in *PW* 75, from a letter of December 23, 1908.

8. The comparison with Quine's perspective, evoked by this phrase, seems fully appropriate, but I certainly am not the first to remark about it; consult H. Wennerberg, *The Pragmatism of C. S. Peirce* (Uppsala: Almquist & Wiksells, 1962), p. 114.

9. The sets of comments quoted above both appear in twentieth-century writings. *CP* 2.148 is from a section of the unfinished "Minute Logic," dating to 1902; *CP* 5.417 is from the essay "What Pragmatism Is," published in *The Monist* in 1905.

10. B. Peirce, *Ideality in the Physical Sciences* (Boston: Little, Brown & Co., 1881), pp. 56–57.

11. For a sophisticated general account of Peirce's attempt to delineate the logic of scientific inquiry, consult R. Tursman's *Peirce's Theory of Scientific Discovery* (Bloomington: Indiana University Press, 1987).

12. Peirce never used this term, it appears, until after the turn of the century; see Justus Buchler's commentary in *Charles Peirce's Empiricism* (New York: Octagon Books, 1980), pp. 1ff.

13. Peirce was uncomfortable with, perhaps even a bit irritated by, the task that had been assigned to him for these lectures of 1898 on "vitally important topics." Here more than elsewhere he tended to exaggerate the distinction between instinct and reason, criticizing the latter in unusually harsh tones while narrowly circumscribing its power and function. See *CP* 1.662, as well as the commentary of John E. Smith in *Purpose and Thought: The Meaning of Pragmatism* (New Haven: Yale University Press, 1978), p. 167 and note 15.

14. William James's *Principles of Psychology* (New York: Dover, 1890) probably ought to be considered an important influence here, as a work that shaped or at least exercised Peirce's thinking about instinct, mental association, and the habit-function. See his review in *The Nation,* reprinted in *N* 1:107–110.

15. Of course, what I label here as "mature" others might want to evaluate more negatively; for example, examine T. Goudge's critique of Peirce's "transcendentalism" in *The Thought of C. S. Peirce* (New York: Dover Publications, 1969). Consider also D. Savan's argued rejection of Goudge's "two-Peirce" thesis in "The Unity of Peirce's Thought" published in *Pragmatism and Purpose: Essays Presented to Thomas A. Goudge* (Toronto: University of Toronto Press, 1981), pp. 3–14.

16. Murphey's account of this shift in Peirce's perspective on the nature and dynamics of inquiry appears in *Development,* pp. 356ff., and in Flower and Murphey, *A History of Philosophy in America* (New York: G. P. Putnam's Sons, 1977), pp. 615ff.

17. Of course, since the future is *really continuous* with the past on Peirce's account, ideal ends, operating as final causes, can and do shape human conduct and character in the present. Furthermore, natural selection is inadequate rather than simply false

as an explanatory principle. The divine agape "cannot have a contrary"; agapism embraces other, "degenerate" modes of evolution (*CP* 6.302ff.); final and efficient causation are interdependent. So it is conceivable that this adaptation "for eternal life" might somehow be a naturally selective process, that is, represent a "survival of the fittest," while still constituting a response to God's creative and cherishing love.

18. Recall Peirce's critique of Hume's empiricism; see section III of chapter one above.

19. Flower and Murphey, *A History of Philosophy in America*, p. 616.

20. At times, Peirce hesitated to classify esthetics as one of the normative sciences, since "a thing is beautiful or ugly irrespective of any purpose to be so" (*CP* 1.575). Consult V. Potter's analysis of Peirce on this issue in his *Charles S. Peirce on Norms and Ideals* (Amherst: University of Massachusetts Press, 1967), especially pp. 20 and 34ff. Potter distinguishes several senses in which Peirce used the word "esthetics," only one of which is limited to the "doctrine of the beautiful."

21. Refer to the commentary in the final section of chapter one above.

22. See my commentary in chapter three above and in "Habits and Essences," *The Transactions of the Charles S. Peirce Society* 20 (1984): especially pp. 157–62.

23. Consider Potter's interpretation in *Norms and Ideals*, pp. 31–32.

24. Compare Peirce's conception of beauty with that of Emerson in his essay on *Nature*, ed. J. Blau (Indianapolis: Bobbs-Merrill, 1948), pp. 8–13. Here too one encounters a coherentist perspective: "Nothing is quite beautiful alone, nothing but is beautiful in the whole" (p. 13).

25. Peirce designated 1855, at the tender age of sixteen, as the date of his first encounter with Schiller's esthetic letters. On the relationship between Schiller's *Spieltrieb* and Peirce's concept of Musement, see my discussion in the next chapter. For Peirce's own very early (1857) meditation on Schiller and the idea of the beautiful, see his "The Sense of Beauty Never Furthered the Performance of a Single Act of Duty" in *W* 1:10–12.

26. Peirce often observed that the normative sciences are characterized by a certain dualism: true/false; good/bad; beautiful/ugly. But he also suggested that in the case of esthetics this dualism is least pronounced. If one could perceive the world through the "eyes of God," one might see that everything ought to be pronounced beautiful and good (review *MS* 283:43).

27. Once again, Peirce's indebtedness to Schiller will be explored in somewhat greater detail in chapter five below.

28. See Potter's commentary in *Norms and Ideals*, pp. 50ff.

29. These types of claims generate a picture of the "self" that resembles the general perspective on the individual ego developed in eastern systems of thought, especially in Hinduism; but it is difficult to identify clearly any direct causal influence on Peirce's thinking about this topic. Did he make any sort of careful study of these eastern philosophical and religious materials or was his knowledge of them thoroughly second-hand, mediated by the thought and writings of Emerson, the Booles, and others? There is little evidence to suggest the former; but the latter hypothesis may overstate the case.

30. Peirce's discussion of this topic frequently took the form of a running commentary on a nineteenth-century work entitled *Phantasms of the Living*, in which the authors evaluated positively the direct evidence for spiritualism, telepathy, and other related psychic phenomena. (See *CP* 6.549; *MS* 884).

V. Musement

1. See James's *Pragmatism*, ed. B. Kuklick (Indianapolis: Hackett Publishing Co., 1981; originally published by Longmans Green in 1907), p. 7.

2. The significance or logical depth of a sign must be abstracted from it. As Peirce explained, "when we speak of the depth, or signification, of a sign we are resorting to hypostatic abstraction, the process whereby we regard a thought as a thing, make an interpretant sign the object of a sign" (*CP* 5.448, note 1). This line of thinking developed out of Peirce's study of scholastic logic. Its relationship to his theory of abduction has already been noted in chapter one above; its relevance to understanding the Neglected Argument will be explored in the last section of the present chapter.

3. I should, perhaps, explain my use of "theological semiotic" (or "theosemiotic") in this book. It is my contention that Peirce's Neglected Argument is an exercise in semiotic, in sign-interpretation; this is not an interpretation of just any sign, however, but of God's "argument," God's "great poem," a universal symbol that has a specifically religious significance. Moreover, I propose in the following, concluding chapter that Peirce's semiotic might be brought to bear on the task of developing a contemporary theological method. So the term seems appropriate to me, and my use of the word "theological" is consistent with its ancient, medieval, and modern usages, even if, for Peirce, that word had an excessively narrow and negative connotation (see introduction note 4 above).

4. *N* 3:83. See my initial discussion of the Roycean metaphor in chapter two, section III above.

5. Here in the third of his 1903 "Lectures on Pragmatism" Peirce was describing his system of categories, linking his notion of the various forms of Thirdness to his trichotomy of icon-index-symbol. Icons represent the most degenerate Thirdness, and Peirce selected Royce's map metaphor as an illustration for this claim. In a humorous aside, he correlated this discussion of "pure self-consciousness" with God-talk, and Royce himself clearly understood the metaphor to have a religious significance.

6. See Carolyn Eisele's article on Peirce's map-projections, where she links that topic to his discussion of existential graphs: "Charles S. Peirce and the Problem of Map-Projection," in *Proceedings of the American Philosophical Society* 107 (1963). Of course, Gamma represents only the final third of Peirce's system of graphs (Alpha and Beta were substantially completed by Peirce), and the entire system is grounded in topology. Consult *MS* 482, as well as K. Ketner's illuminating commentary in "Peirce's Most Lucid and Interesting Paper: An Introduction to Cenopythagoreanism," *International Philosophical Quarterly* XXVI (1986): 375–92.

7. This semiotic approach to the problem of God may bear some relation to Peirce's Trinitarian beliefs. Max Fisch has described Peirce's movement (at least partially under the influence of his first wife) away from the Unitarianism of his youth and towards his confirmation as an Episcopalian in 1862 (see Fisch's Introduction to *W* 1:xxx-xxxii). In 1866, in his last Lowell Lecture (*W* 1:502–503), Peirce identified the Creator of the world as an "infinite symbol," its interpretant and ground being identical with it. He then correlated this scheme with the doctrine of the Trinity: "The interpretant is evidently the Divine *Logos* or word . . . the *Son of God.* The *ground*, being that partaking of which is requisite to any communication with the Symbol, corresponds in its function to the *Holy Spirit.*" Now the notion of the "ground" of signification figures less prominently in Peirce's mature thinking. Still, Fisch observes that even in 1907 Peirce continues to show traces of this Trinitarianism when he argues that "A Sign mediates between its *Object* and its *Meaning* . . . Object the father, sign the mother of meaning" (*W* 1:xxxii). Fisch adds that in this scheme the interpretant would be the "Son." And such a picture very roughly corresponds to the account that I have supplied, in which the "World Spirit" is the living symbol of God, its final interpretant, God completely revealed (Christ as Omega?). But Peirce never even attempted to develop this Trinitarian argument in any clear and systematic fashion.

8. Consult Peirce's own work on the problem of map-projection, in *NEM* 3:503–504 and 710–21.

9. See *CP* 4.6, 5.283ff., 5.313ff., 6.338, and *MS* 200:E76f., for the development of this argument that all thinking is dialogical in form.

10. Such a law, of course, is a habit of objective mind. On Peirce's account, a sign is the "consciousness of a habit." Any instance of a sign is to be understood as the determination of a "quasi-mind" effected by means of the "direct action of a habit of that quasi-mind" (*MS* 339:271r).

11. For a brief, systematic, and penetrating interpretation of Peirce's semiotic, refer to T. L. Short, "Semeiosis and Intentionality," *Transactions of the Charles S. Peirce Society* XVII (1981): 197–223.

12. The analysis of the Neglected Argument that follows here represents a revised, expanded version of my article that first appeared in the *Journal of Religion* 67 (1987): 493–509, entitled "Peirce's Theological Semiotic."

13. In some unpublished versions of the Neglected Argument, the word "Musement" does not appear. At times this form of thinking is described simply as "contemplation" or "meditation." Occasionally he used "reverie," but in the published article he rejected that term because it implies a certain "vacancy and dreaminess" (see *CP* 6.458); and he understood Musement to be a playful but *vigorous* exercise. He also contrasted his notion with any talk about "games," which are governed by strict rules and lack the spontaneity of "pure play" (see *MS* 843:013ff.). Finally, although Peirce seemed to use the word "Musement" here for the first time, the idea itself had already been developed. For example, in an earlier unpublished essay, he stated that "there is an attitude of spirit that is separated only by a swordblade from fun, and yet is in full harmony with all that is spiritual and even hungers for that which is devotional" (*MS* 280:23).

14. Three years before the appearance of the Neglected Argument, in some unpublished remarks, Peirce described the creation of the world as the "exercize of the World Spirit's Spieltrieb," done for no ulterior aim, but for "mere amusement," like the performance of a symphony (*MS* 283:102–103).

15. See, for example, *CP* 6.508. Notice that, at this point in my discussion, God-talk and talk about the Absolute Mind have been more or less conflated. I think the distinction between the two realities is a significant one, and I have worried it at great length in the analysis above. But Peirce himself never systematically pressed the distinction, nor, since the Absolute Mind is God's real symbol and, perhaps, "a Deity relatively to us," is it crucial for the purposes of all discussions that they be so distinguished.

16. This is why, in certain respects, Peirce's painting metaphor is less felicitous than his poem metaphor. For the former conveys too static an image, while the images and ideas in a poem, like the plot of a novel, unfold for their reader in time. Refer to the discussion in chapter three above, and recall Peirce's comments in *NEM* 4:140.

17. Indeed, on Peirce's account, the law of liberty that the Muser is encouraged to obey *is* in fact the law of mind, the law of agape. To obey that law is to be open and responsive to the ideality of the universe, to those gentle forces that work to shape the growth of mind.

18. Peirce came to prefer the word "phaneroscopy" to "phenomenology" (see, for example, *CP* 1.284ff.), and his reflections on the fundamental categories of experience were pursued independently of Husserl's phenomenological investigations, despite a few basic similarities between them. See W. Rosensohn's *The Phenomenology of Charles S. Peirce: From the Doctrine of Categories to Phaneroscopy* (Amsterdam: Gruner, 1974).

19. F. Schiller, *On the Aesthetic Education of Man*, ed. and tr. E. M. Wilkinson & L. A. Willoughby (Oxford: Oxford University Press, 1982).

20. Ibid., p. 165.

21. Ibid., p. 81.

22. Consult, for example, *CP* 2.146, 2.708ff., 2.776, 6.145, and 8.218ff.

23. Orange seems to imply that this essay represents "a species of the design argu-

ment" (*Peirce's Conception of God*, Institute for Studies in Pragmaticism [Bloomington: Indiana University Press, 1984], p. 91), although she does distinguish the Humble from the Neglected Argument, the latter being said to constitute a version of the ontological proof. In fact, however, the logic of Musement itself represents Peirce's own peculiar esthetic version of that proof, the Neglected Argument only serving as a commentary on that process of reasoning. See Peirce's rejection of the argument from design, *CP* 6.419ff.

24. This is not Anselm's version of the proof, which Peirce clearly rejected (see *MS* 890), but rather that of the nineteenth-century British writer William Johnson Fox (see *CP* 8.262). The student of Peirce's religious thought will find Fox's argument for the necessary reality of religious ideals to be quite interesting; consult his work *On the Religious Ideas* (London, 1849). And for a more modern version of this argument, see Simone Weil's "experimental ontological proof" in *Simone Weil: An Anthology*, ed. S. Miles (New York: Weidenfeld & Nicolson, 1986), p. 240. Weil argued that no purely "imaginary perfection" could affect us in the way that the idea of perfection does when we contemplate it.

25. The sense of "indubitable" here should, once again, be specified. (See chapter two, page 58 above.) Peirce affirmed of such vague, commonsense beliefs that they cannot be genuinely doubted as a matter of contingent fact (in contrast to "paper" doubt). This is not to say that such instinctive notions represent logically necessary truths or that they will *never* be doubted.

26. See *CP* 6.190–99. Peirce did speculate about whether or not the Deity determines itself, makes itself more "precise," *in time* (*CP* 6.466). But this more determinate reality would have to be the living symbol of God, the Absolute Mind (recall the discussion in chapter two, section III).

27. Compare Quine's hypothesis about an innate "spacing" capacity, necessary for successful inductions, and for him, also, the product of evolution. See "Natural Kinds," in *Ontological Relativity and Other Essays* (New York: Columbia University Press, 1969), pp. 122ff.

28. Peirce did at least attempt to supply a pragmaticistic explication of the God-hypothesis (see, e.g., *CP* 6.490); and I argue immediately below that Musement itself is a kind of experimental testing of the hypothesis. But Peirce rejected positivistic criteria of meaning and he was never what one would regard as a "strong verificationist." He only demanded that a hypothesis have some discernible implications, that it be testable at least in principle (if not immediately, then in the long run), and he resisted conceiving of such implications in the narrowest of empirical terms.

29. Recall the discussion in chapter one above of how ideas in the mind *habitualiter* can shape cognition. This topic was pursued again in the first part of chapter four.

30. See Peirce's discussion of contemplation in *CP* 7.555ff. He suggested there that in the uncontrolled "play" of thought, certain "interesting combinations" of thought-feelings will occur. Contemplation focuses our attention on these so that we may consider "the interesting bearings of what may lie hidden in the icon, so as to cause the subjective intensity of it to increase."

31. And Peirce meant, quite literally, that *all* human knowledge is fallible, including mathematical knowledge, which he argued is the result of experimentation with iconic signs, imaginary diagrams (*NEM* 2:12).

32. This, once again, was Peirce's contention in his letter to Lady Welby (December 23, 1908), where he defined "faith" so as to include "*that belief which the believer does not himself recognize*" (*PW* 75).

33. John E. Smith has explored carefully the relationship between experience and reflection in Peirce's Neglected Argument; see his "The Tension between Direct Experience and Argument in Religion," *Religious Studies* 17 (1983): 487–97.

34. Refer also to the brief discussion in chapter one above, section III, and note 58.

VI. Theosemiotic

1. See *MS* 846–56. Most of these jottings can be dated to the year 1911.

2. Note, however, that efficient causes are still crucial to Peirce's explanatory scheme, and that natural selection is a principle that continues to have some limited significance for him.

3. I owe this insight, vaguely articulated as it is here, to Murray Murphey. For a superb general history of field theories in physics, see Mary B. Hesse's *Forces and Fields* (London: Thomas Nelson and Sons, 1961).

4. See chapter two, note 11 above.

5. John Wisdom, "Gods," reprinted in *Religious Language and the Problem of Religious Knowledge*, ed. R. Santoni (Bloomington: Indiana University Press, 1968), p. 303.

6. Refer also to Wisdom's essay "The Logic of God," in *Paradox and Discovery* (New York: Philosophical Library, 1966).

7. Wisdom is pursuing the special religious implications of a more general inquiry initiated by Wittgenstein with his talk about aspect-seeing in *Philosophical Investigations*, ed. G. E. M. Anscombe (New York: Macmillan Publishing Co., 1968), especially pp. 193ff. Consult also John Hick's discussion of "levels of significance" in *Faith and Knowledge* (Ithaca: Cornell University Press, 1957).

8. Compare Wittgenstein's argument that there is a way of "grasping a rule" that is "exhibited" in one's actually "obeying the rule." *Philosophical Investigations*, #201. Unlike Wittgenstein, Peirce would be willing to call such behavior an "interpretation" of the rule.

9. This sort of talk is not absolutely without parallel in modern theology. Consider Paul Tillich's insistence that "'God' is a symbol of God" in his *Dynamics of Faith* (New York: Harper, 1958); and Karl Rahner's portrayal of the *Logos* as God's "real symbol," so that God, immutable in himself, can be said nonetheless to change in his "other." See *A Rahner Reader*, ed. G. McCool (New York: Seabury, 1975), pp. 120ff. and pp. 145ff.

10. For an outstanding bibliography of the literature on fuzzy sets and systems, consult Abraham Kandel, *Fuzzy Techniques in Pattern Recognition* (New York: John Wiley & Sons, 1982), pp. 209–353.

Consult also Mihai Nadin's essay "The Logic of Vagueness and the Category of Synechism" in *The Monist* 63 (1980): 351–63. Nadin evaluates Peirce's contributions from the perspective of contemporary fuzzy logic.

11. For a contemporary psychological examination of the role that habits and hypotheses play in thinking and perception see Jerome Bruner, *Beyond the Information Given*, ed. J. M. Anglin (New York: Norton Publishing Co., 1973). Compare with this account Peirce's own remarks on hypotheses as cognitive "skills," in *CP* 6.145.

12. This is the sort of analysis that I have attempted in my essay on "Boredom and the Religious Imagination," *Journal of the American Academy of Religion* LIII (1985): 75–91.

13. I draw on such Peircean resources in order to assess the possible religious significance of verbal art, in "Art, Religion and Musement," *Journal of Aesthetics and Art Criticism* XLII (1984): 427–37.

14. I borrow the phrase from N. A. Scott, Jr., who in his essay "Poetry and Prayer" develops an account of the possible relation between religion and art, the logic of which could be explicated in the Peircean terms supplied here. Scott's essay was first published in *Thought* XLI (1966).

15. This communal aspect of Peirce's semiotic was the feature that most recommended that theory to Josiah Royce, as he employed it in *The Problem of Christianity* (New York: The Macmillan Co., 1913). For entirely different reasons, Karl-Otto Apel has chosen also to focus, in his own study of Peirce, on the significance of the latter's theory of communication, his attention to the social contexts of interpretation. See Apel's *Charles S. Peirce: From Pragmatism to Pragmaticism*, tr. J. Krois (Amherst: University of Massachusetts Press, 1981).

BIBLIOGRAPHY

Bibliographical Notes

The body of secondary literature on Peirce is both vast and rapidly expanding. Yet, since Peirce is still not widely perceived to be a religious thinker of great stature, a rather small percentage of that material is devoted specifically to the religious dimension of his thought. Apart from dissertations, this material consists of a single monograph (Orange, 1984), roughly two dozen articles, and selected chapters in general studies of Peirce's philosophy. It is impossible for me to review all of those works here, nor do I attempt to consider any of them in detail. These notes serve merely to earmark selected items in the bibliography below for special consideration.

Josiah Royce was the first philosopher to apply Peirce's notions in any systematic way to the development of a religious argument (Royce, 1913). Peirce's logical deliberations, his analysis of signs as triadic, and his emphasis on the communal aspect of inquiry were all resources that Royce employed in his philosophical treatment of Christianity. Nearly three decades later, Charles Hartshorne (1941) initiated the task of assessing Peirce's religious outlook as a whole, rather than employing certain aspects of it piecemeal, in a constructive endeavor. Yet Hartshorne's own constructive philosophical theology seems most definitely to supply the background for his critique of Peirce. The latter is applauded for anticipating twentieth-century process theology, but taken to task for failing to embrace fully a process perspective. Now this hardly seems to be the most advantageous standpoint from which to assess Peirce's religious metaphysics. For reasons explored in my account of Peirce in this book, I would contend that he was a theist of a more traditional sort, that he clearly rejected any notion of God as finite, as less than omnipotent, or as subject to time. (See especially chapter two, note 22 above.)

Similarly, Thomas A. Goudge's generally insightful account of Peirce's religious ideas in chapter ten of his book *The Thought of C. S. Peirce* (1950) is infected by his now famous "two Peirce" thesis: in his religious writings, Goudge contends, Peirce's "transcendentalism" is most readily apparent, this being "the least cogent aspect of his work" (p. 7). In contrast, I have tried to demonstrate throughout this study that what Peirce had to say about religion is remarkably continuous with what he wrote about mathematical, logical, and scientific topics.

Perhaps the best work dealing explicitly with Peirce's philosophy of religion has been done by John E. Smith and Vincent G. Potter, S. J. Among the former's numerous articles, see his early classic "Religion and Theology in Peirce" (1952). More recently, see chapter six of Smith's *Purpose and Thought* (1978) and his essay "The Tension between Direct Experience and Argument in Religion" (1983). Potter is the author of two excellent studies in this vein: "Vaguely Like a Man: The Theism of Charles S. Peirce" (1973) and "Peirce's Argument for God's Reality: A Pragmatist's View" (1976).

The only book-length study of Peirce's religious thought to date is Donna M. Orange's monograph *Peirce's Conception of God* (1984). This work is especially useful not only because it traces the *development* of Peirce's religious thought but also because Orange locates and identifies most of the relevant primary materials, many of them still only available in manuscript form. Nonetheless, this study is significantly limited in scope. Orange focuses her attention on Peirce's conception of God, never intending to supply a full explication of other religious ideas (Peirce on miracles, immortality, community, etc.); and she never treats the Neglected Argument in any detail. Moreover, as I have indicated above (chapter two, notes 21 and 33; chapter three, notes 23 and 31; chapter five, note 23), I differ with Orange on some points of interpretation; that is, I am reluctant to label Peirce as a process theist, to identify his Deity, unless carefully qualified, with the category of Thirdness, or to consider even the initial stages of the Neglected Argument as a form of the argument from design. (See my 1986 review of Orange in *The New Scholasticism.*)

Numerous article-length treatments of Peirce's Neglected Argument have been published and are listed below (for example, Caspar, 1980, Clarke, 1974, 1977, and Rohatyn, 1982, in addition to Potter, 1976). Here, Clarke and Potter offer the most rigorous and insightful accounts, although Clarke, like Orange, wants to link the Neglected Argument with various historical formulations of the argument from design. By his own admission, however, this requires radically revising the logic of those traditional arguments so that they will be perceived as being essentially abductive in form.

Several recent essays supply general sketches of Peirce's religious thought, such as those authored by Ketner (1988) and Pfeifer (1981). Ketner presents a neat characterization of Peirce's theory of religion, organized around twelve basic notions. I would want to quarrel only with the last two items on this list; here, it seems to me, Ketner overemphasizes the eastern/Buddhist character of Peirce's perspective.

Finally, several contemporary philosophers of religion have begun, like Royce early in this century, to develop and apply creatively some of Peirce's ideas. Robert C. Neville's religious metaphysics and cosmological speculations (1968, 1980, 1982) are well-informed by Peirce's thought. In an entirely different vein, Wayne Proudfoot (1985) has appropriated features of Peirce's early theory of inquiry (1860s and 70s) in order to analyze theories and descriptions of religious experience. Most recently, Peter Ochs (1985, 1988) has formulated an interesting critique of Peirce's religious views from the perspective of Jewish thought and tradition; despite his reservations about Peirce, Ochs regards the latter's pragmatism as providing an important stimulus for contemporary theological endeavors.

Many other works, not all of them devoted to Peirce, are relevant to the present study. Titles of the most significant among these are provided in the following list of references.

References

Abbot, F. E. *Scientific Theism.* Boston: Little, Brown & Co., 1885.

Alexander, G. "The Hypothesized God of C. S. Peirce and William James." *Journal of Religion* 67 (1987): 304–21.

Almeder, R.F. *The Philosophy of Charles S. Peirce: a Critical Introduction.* Totowa: Rowman & Littlefield, 1980.

Anderson, Douglas R. *Creativity and the Philosophy of C. S. Peirce.* Dordrecht: Martinus Hijhoff, 1987.

Apel, K.-O. *Charles Sanders Peirce: From Pragmatism to Pragmaticism,* tr. Krois. Amherst: University of Massachusetts Press, 1981.

Bell, E.T. *The Development of Mathematics.* New York: McGraw-Hill, 1945.

Bishop, D. "Peirce and Eastern Thought." *Proceedings of the C. S. Peirce Bicentennial International Congress.* Graduate Studies 23. Ed. K. Ketner et al. Lubbock: Texas Tech University Press, 1981. Pp. 265–70.

Boler, J. F. *Charles Peirce and Scholastic Realism.* Seattle: University of Washington Press, 1963.

_____ . "Peirce, Ockham and Scholastic Realism." *The Monist* 63 (1980): 290–303.

Boehner, P. *Medieval Logic.* Chicago: University of Chicago Press, 1952.

Bonansea, B. "Duns Scotus' Voluntarism." In *Studies in Philosophy and the History of Philosophy,* volume three. Ed. J. Ryan and B. Bonansea. Washington, D.C.: The Catholic University of America Press, 1965. Pp.83–121.

Britton, K. "Introduction to the Metaphysics and Theology of C. S. Peirce." *Ethics* XLIX (1938–39): 435–65.

Brock, J. E. "Charles Sanders Peirce's Logic of Vagueness." Dissertation, University of Illinois, 1969.

Bruner, J. *Beyond the Information Given.* Ed. J. Anglin. New York: Norton, 1973.

Buchler, J. *Charles Peirce's Empiricism.* New York: Harcourt & Brace, 1939.

Caspar, R. "The *Neglected Argument* Revisited: From C. S. Peirce to Peter Berger." *The Thomist* 44 (1980): 94–116.

Cayley, A. "A Sixth Memoir upon Quantics." In *Collected Mathematical Papers,* volume 2. Cambridge: Cambridge University Press, 1889.

Clarke, B. "The Argument from Design: A Piece of Abductive Reasoning." *International Journal for Philosophy of Religion* 5 (1974): 65–78.

_____ . "Peirce's Neglected Argument." *Transactions of the Charles S. Peirce Society* 13 (1977): 277–87.

Darwin, C. *The Origin of Species.* New York: Penguin, 1968 (originally published in 1859).

Dauben, J. "Peirce's Place in Mathematics." *Historia Mathematica* 9 (1982): 311–25.

Davis, W. *Peirce's Epistemology.* The Hague: Martinus Nijhoff, 1972.

DeMarco, J. P. "God, Religion and Community in the Philosophy of C. S. Peirce." *Modern Schoolman* 49 (1972): 331–47.

Duns Scotus, J. *Philosophical Writings.* Ed. and tr. A. Wolter. New York: Bobbs-Merrill, 1962.

_____ . *A Treatise on God as First Principle.* Ed. A. Wolter. Chicago: Franciscan Herald Press, 1966.

_____ . *God and Creatures: The Quodlibetal Questions.* Ed. A. Wolter. Princeton: Princeton University Press, 1975.

Eisele, C. *Studies in the Scientific and Mathematical Philosophy of Charles S. Peirce.* The Hague: Mouton, 1979.

Emerson, R. W. *The Early Lectures of Ralph Waldo Emerson.* Ed. R. Spiller and W. Williams. Cambridge: Harvard University Press, 1972.

_____ . *Nature.* Ed. J. Blau. Indianapolis: Bobbs-Merrill, 1948.

Esposito, J. *Evolutionary Metaphysics: The Development of Peirce's Theory of Categories.* Athens: Ohio University Press, 1980.

Feibleman, J. *An Introduction to the Philosophy of Charles S. Peirce.* New York: Harper, 1946.

Feuer, L. "God, Guilt and Logic: The Psychological Basis of the Ontological Argument." *Inquiry* 11 (1968): 257–81.

Fisch, M. *Peirce, Semeiotic and Pragmatism: Essays by Max Fisch.* Ed. K. Ketner and C. Kloesel. Bloomington: Indiana University Press, 1986.

Fitzgerald, J. *Peirce's Theory of Signs as a Foundation for Pragmatism.* The Hague: Mouton & Co., 1966.

Flower, E. and Murphey, M. G. *A History of Philosophy in America.* 2 volumes. New York: G. Putnam's Sons, 1977.

Fox, W. J. *On the Religious Ideas.* London, 1849.

Freeman, E. *The Categories of Charles S. Peirce.* Chicago: Open Court, 1934.

Gadamer, H. G. *Truth and Method.* New York: Continuum, 1975.

Gallie, W. B. *Peirce and Pragmatism.* New York: Dover Publications, 1966.

Goodman, N. *Fact, Fiction, and Forecast.* London: The Atlone Press, 1954.

Goudge, T. A. *The Thought of C. S. Peirce.* Toronto: University of Toronto Press, 1950.

Greenlee, D. *Peirce's Concept of Sign.* The Hague: Mouton & Co., 1973.

Haas, W. P. *The Conception of Law and the Unity of Peirce's Philosophy.* Notre Dame: University of Notre Dame Press, 1964.

Harrison, S. M. "Man's Glassy Essence: An Attempt to Construct a Theory of Person Based on the Writings of Charles Sanders Peirce." Dissertation, Fordham University, 1971.

_____ . "Charles S. Peirce: Reflections on Being a Man-Sign." *Proceedings of the American Catholic Philosophical Association* 53 (1979): 98–106.

Hartshorne, C. "A Critique of Peirce's Idea of God." *Philosophical Review* 50 (1941): 516–23.

_____ and Reese, W. *Philosophers Speak of God.* Chicago: University of Chicago Press, 1953.

Hausman, C. "Eros and Agape in Creative Evolution: A Peircean Insight." *Process Studies* 4 (1974): 11–25.

Hesse, M. *Forces and Fields.* London: Thomas Nelson and Sons, 1961.

Hegel, G. W. F. *The Phenomenology of Spirit.* Tr. A. V. Miller. Oxford: Oxford University Press, 1977.

Hick, J. *Faith and Knowledge.* Ithaca: Cornell University Press, 1957.

Hookway, C. *Peirce.* London: Routledge & Kegan Paul, 1985.

Hume, D. *Inquiry Concerning Human Understanding.* Ed. C. Hendel. Indianapolis: Bobbs-Merrill, 1955.

James, Sr., H. *Substance and Shadow.* Boston: Ticknor and Fields, 1863.

James, W. *The Principles of Psychology,* 2 volumes. New York: Dover, 1890.

Kant, I. *Critique of Pure Reason.* Tr. F. Max Muller. New York: Doubleday, 1966.

Kandel, A. *Fuzzy Techniques in Pattern Recognition.* New York: John Wiley & Sons, 1982.

Ketner, K. L. "Peirce's Most Interesting and Lucid Paper: An Introduction to Cenopythagoreanism." *International Philosophical Quarterly* XXVI (1986): 375–92.

_____ . "The Importance of Religion for Peirce." In *Gedankenzeichen.* Ed. R. Claussen and R. Daube-Schackat. Stauffenburg verlag, forthcoming, 1988.

Keyser, C. J. "A Glance at Some of the Ideas of Charles Sanders Peirce." *Scripta Mathematica* III (1935):11–37.

Kline, M. *Mathematical Thought from Ancient to Modern Times.* New York: Oxford University Press, 1972.

Kolakowski, L. *Metaphysical Horror.* Oxford: Basil Blackwell, 1988.

Krolikowski, W. P. "The Peircean Vir." In *Studies in the Philosophy of Charles Sanders Peirce,* second series. Ed. E. Moore and R. Robin. Amherst: University of Massachusetts Press, 1964. Pp. 257–70.

Kuklick, B. *The Rise of American Philosophy.* New Haven: Yale University Press, 1977.

_____ . *Josiah Royce.* Indianapolis: Hackett Publishing Co., 1985.

Mahowald, M. "Peirce's Concepts of God and Religion." *Transactions of the Charles S. Peirce Society* 12 (1976): 367–77.

Mansel, H. *The Limits of Religious Thought.* London: John Murray, 1859.

Martin, R. M. *Peirce's Logic of Relations and Other Studies.* Dordrecht: Foris Publications, 1980.

Moody, E. A. *Truth and Consequence in Medieval Logic.* Amsterdam: North Holland Publishing Co., 1953.

Moore, E. C. *American Pragmatism: Peirce, James and Dewey.* New York: Columbia University Press, 1961.

Murphey, M. G. *The Development of Peirce's Philosophy.* Cambridge: Harvard University Press, 1961.

_____ . "On Peirce's Metaphysics." *Transactions of the Charles S. Peirce Society* 1 (1965): 12–25.

_____ . "Kant's Children: The Cambridge Pragmatists." *Transactions of the Charles S. Peirce Society* 4 (1968): 3–33.

Nadin, M. "The Logic of Vagueness and the Category of Synechism." *The Monist* 63 (1980): 351–63.

Neville, R. C. *God the Creator.* Chicago: University of Chicago Press, 1968.

_____ . *Creativity and God.* New York: Seabury Press, 1980.

_____ . *The Tao and The Daimon.* Albany: State University of New York Press, 1982.

Numbers, R. L. *Creation by Natural Law: Laplace's Nebular Hypothesis in American Thought.* Seattle: University of Washington Press, 1977.

Ochs, P. "Torah, Language and Philosophy: A Jewish Critique." *International Journal for Philosophy of Religion* 18 (1985): 115–22.

_____ . "Charles Peirce's Unpragmatic Christianity: A Rabbinic Appraisal." *American Journal of Philosophy and Theology* 9 (1988): 41–73.

O'Connell, J. "C.S. Peirce and the Problem of God." *Philosophical Studies* 8 (1958): 24–45.

Oliver, W. D. "The Final Cause and Agapasm in Peirce's Philosophy." In *Studies in the Philosophy of Charles Sanders Peirce*, second series. Ed. E. Moore and R. Robin. Amherst: University of Massachusetts Press, 1964. pp. 289–303.

Oppenheim, F. *Royce's Mature Philosophy of Religion.* Notre Dame: University of Notre Dame Press, 1987.

Orange, D. "Peirce's Falsifiable Theism." *American Journal of Semiotics* 2 (1983): 121–27.

_____ . *Peirce's Conception of God: A Developmental Study.* Peirce Studies 2, Institute for Studies in Pragmaticism. Bloomington: Indiana University Press, 1984.

Owens, J. "Common Nature: a Point of Comparison between Thomistic and Scotistic Metaphysics." *Mediaeval Studies* XIX (1957): 1–14..

Pedoe, D. *An Introduction to Projective Geometry.* New York: Macmillan, 1973.

Peirce, B. *Ideality in the Physical Sciences.* Boston: Little, Brown & Co., 1881.

Pfeifer, D. "Peirce's Application of Semiotic to God." In *Studies in Peirce's Semiotic.* Peirce Studies 1. Ed. K. Ketner and J. Ransdell. Bloomington: Indiana University Press, 1979. Pp. 89–100.

_____ . "Charles Peirce's Contribution to Religious Thought." In *Proceedings of the C. S. Peirce Bicentennial International Congress*, Graduate Studies 23. Ed. K. Ketner et. al. Lubbock: Texas Tech University Press, 1981. Pp. 367–73.

Potter, V. G. *Charles S. Peirce on Norms and Ideals.* Amherst: University of Massachusetts Press, 1967.

_____ . "Vaguely Like a Man: The Theism of C. S. Peirce." In *God Knowable and Unknowable.* Ed. R. J. Roth. New York: Fordham University Press, 1973.

_____ . "C. S. Peirce's Argument for God's Reality: A Pragmatist's View." In *The Papin Festschrift: Essays in Honor of Joseph Papin.* Ed. J. Armenti. Villanova: Villanova University Press, 1976.

_____ . "Charles Sanders Peirce." In *American Philosophy.* Royal Institute of Philosophy Lecture Series 19. Ed. M. G. Singer. Cambridge: Cambridge University Press, 1985. Pp. 21–41.

_____ and Shields, P. "Peirce's Definitions of Continuity." *Transactions of the Charles S. Peirce Society* 13 (1977): 20–34.

Proudfoot, W. *Religious Experience.* Berkeley: University of California Press, 1985.

Quine, W. *Ontological Relativity and Other Essays.* New York: Columbia University Press, 1969.

Rahner, K. *A Rahner Reader.* Ed. G. McCool. New York: Seabury, 1975.

_____ and Vorgrimler, H. *Dictionary of Theology.* New York: Crossroad, 1981.

Raposa, M. L. "Habits and Essences." *Transactions of the Charles S. Peirce Society* 20 (1984): 147–67.

_____ . "Art, Religion and Musement." *Journal of Aesthetics and Art Criticism* XLII (1984): 427–37.

_____ . "Boredom and the Religious Imagination." *Journal of the American Academy of Religion* LIII (1985): 75–91.

_____ . Review of Orange's *Peirce's Conception of God*, in *The New Scholasticism* LX (1986): 235–38.

_____ . "Peirce's Theological Semiotic." *Journal of Religion* 67 (1987): 493–509.

Reilly, F. E. *Charles Peirce's Theory of Scientific Method.* New York: Fordham University Press, 1970.

Rescher, N. *Peirce's Philosophy of Science.* Notre Dame: University of Notre Dame Press, 1978.

Roberts, D. *The Existential Graphs of Charles S. Peirce.* The Hague: Mouton, 1973.

Robinson, A. *Selected Papers,* volume 2: *Nonstandard Analysis and Philosophy.* Ed. W. Luxemburg and S. Korner. New Haven: Yale University Press, 1979.

Rohatyn, D. "Resurrecting Peirce's 'Neglected Argument' for God." *Transactions of the Charles S. Peirce Society* 18 (1982): 66–74.

Rosensohn, W. *The Phenomenology of Charles S. Peirce.* Amsterdam: Gruner, 1974.

Ross, J. F. *Philosophical Theology.* New York: Bobbs-Merrill, 1969.

_____ . "Ways of Religious Knowing." In *The Challenge of Religion.* Ed. F. Ferre, J. Kockelmans, and J. E. Smith. New York: Seabury Press, 1982. Pp. 83–103.

Royce, J. *The World and the Individual,* first series. New York: Dover Publications, 1959.

_____ . *The Problem of Christianity,* 2 volumes. New York: The Macmillan Co., 1913.

Russell, B. *An Essay on the Foundations of Geometry.* New York: Dover Publications, 1956.

Schiller, F. *On the Aesthetic Education of Man.* Tr. E.M. Wilkinson and L.A. Willoughby. Oxford: Oxford University Press, 1967.

Short, T. L. "Semeiosis and Intentionality." *Transactions of the Charles S. Peirce Society* 17 (1981): 197–223.

Smith, J. C. "Peirce's Religious Metaphysics." *International Philosophical Quarterly* 19 (1979): 407–25.

Smith, J. E. *Royce's Social Infinite.* Liberal Arts Press, 1950.

_____ . "Religion and Theology in Peirce." In *Studies in the Philosophy of Charles Sanders Peirce,* first series. Ed. P. Wiener and F. Young. Cambridge: Harvard University Press, 1952. Pp. 251–67.

_____ . *Purpose and Thought.* New Haven: Yale University Press, 1978.

_____ . "The Tension between Direct Experience and Argument in Religion." *Religious Studies* 17 (1983): 487–97.

Skagestad, P. *The Road of Inquiry: Charles Peirce's Pragmatic Realism.* New York: Columbia University Press, 1981.

Swedenborg, E. *Divine Love and Wisdom.* Tr. J. C. Ager. New York: The Swedenborg Foundation, 1982.

Teilhard de Chardin, P. *The Phenomenon of Man.* Tr. B. Wall. New York: Harper and Row, 1965.

Thompson, M. *The Pragmatic Philosophy of C. S. Peirce.* Chicago: University of Chicago Press, 1953.

Tillich, P. *Dynamics of Faith.* New York: Harper Torchbook, 1958.

Trammel, R. L. "Religion, Instinct and Reason in the Thought of Charles S. Peirce." *Transactions of the Charles S. Peirce Society* 8 (1972): 3–25.

Turley, P. *Peirce's Cosmology.* New York: Philosophical Books, 1977.

Tursman, R. *Peirce's Theory of Scientific Discovery.* Peirce Studies 3. Bloomington: Indiana University Press, 1987.

Weil, S. *Waiting For God.* Tr. E. Craufurd. New York: G. Putnam's Sons, 1951.

_____ . *Simone Weil: An Anthology.* Ed. S. Miles. New York: Weidenfeld & Nicolson, 1986.

Weiss, P. "Charles S. Peirce, Philosopher." In *Perspectives on Peirce.* Ed. R. Bernstein. New Haven: Yale University Press, 1965. Pp. 120–40.

Wennerberg, H. *The Pragmatism of C. S. Peirce.* Lund: C. W. K. Gleerup, 1962.

White, A. D. *A History of the Warfare of Science with Theology.* London: D. Appleton & Co., 1913.

Wiener, P. *Evolution and the Founders of Pragmatism.* Cambridge: Harvard University Press, 1949.

_____ , ed. *Charles S. Peirce: Selected Writings.* New York: Dover Publications, 1958.

Wisdom, J. "Gods." Reprinted in *Religious Language and the Problem of Religious Knowledge.* Ed. R. Santoni. Bloomington: Indiana University Press, 1968. Pp. 295–314.

_____ . *Paradox and Discovery.* Oxford: Basil Blackwell, 1965.

Wittgenstein, L. *Philosophical Investigations.* Ed. and trans. G. E. M. Anscombe. New York: Macmillan, 1953.

Wolter, A. *The Transcendentals and Their Function in the Metaphysics of Duns Scotus.* St. Bonaventure, N.Y.: Franciscan Institute, 1946.

_____ . "An Oxford Dialogue on Language and Metaphysics." *Review of Metaphysics* 31 (1978): 615–48, and 32 (1978): 323–48.

Young, J. W. *Projective Geometry.* Chicago: Open Court Publishers, 1930.

Zeman, J. "Peirce's Graphs: The Continuity Interpretation." *Transactions of the Charles S. Peirce Society* 4 (1968): 144–54.

Index

Abbot, F. E.: comparison with Peirce, 17–19, 156–57

Abduction: 24–25, 32–33, 133, 134–37, 142–43, 149; and scholastic notion of abstraction, 24–25; Hume's misconception of, 26, 27, 32–33; and Musement 133, 134–37

Absolute: Mind, 32, 39–40, 45–62 *passim*, 65–68, 121, 127; distinguished from God, 54–62, 121, 168; in geometry, 63–65. *See also* God

Agapism. *See* Love

Anselm of Canterbury: 131, 169

Anthropomorphism: 56, 58–59, 100

Apel, Karl-Otto: 170

Aquinas, Thomas: 26, 30, 158

Aristotle: 17

Augustine: 30, 31, 158

Bain, Alexander: 94, 165

Belief: 94–101; as habit, 94–96, 135, 137, 145, 150–51, 152–53; unconscious, 96, 135

Book of nature: 66, 121, 168; in Benjamin Peirce's thought, 7

Boole, George: 24, 158

Buddhism: 84, 147, 163–64; the Buddha, 84, 137

Butler, Bishop: 30, 158

Cantor, Georg: 42–44, 159

Cayley, Arthur: 63–64

Christian Church: 11–13, 76–77; and the community of inquirers, 12–13, 98–99, 103–104; Peirce's relationship with, 11, 13, 167; narrowness of creeds, 10–11

Christianity: teachings of, 29, 30, 66, 73, 75, 84, 103, 112, 116. *See also* Christian Church

Common-Sensism. *See* Instinct

Confucius: 84, 137

Continuity: 18–19, 21–22, 33, 41–46, 48, 83, 88, 119, 120, 143, 146, 150, 159; genuine contrasted with pseudo-, 42–44; of the Absolute Mind, 48–54, 57; of time, 49. *See also* Synechism

Cosmology: Peirce's evolutionary, 9, 31–32, 65–87, 160, 162–63

Creation: Peirce's account of, 68–72, 79–80, 121

Darwin, Charles: influence on Peirce, 9–10, 72–74, 100, 163

Design, argument from: 130, 156, 169

Doubt: 58, 169; as stimulus to inquiry, 94–95, 100

Duns Scotus: 14–25 *passim*, 52, 156, 163; Scotistic realism, 16–21; concept of *haecceity*, 21–22; concept of reality, 20, 124, 127, 157; on final causality, 22–23, 157; on ideas in the mind *habitualiter*, 23–24, 96

Emerson, Ralph W.: 84, 87, 107, 166

Esthetics: 86, 92, 101, 102, 106–10, 117–18, 152, 166

Ethics: 101–106; Peirce's social ethic, 82–87

Evil: problem of, 77, 87–92, 109, 147, 164

Evolution: theories of, 9, 72–80

Existential graphs: 45, 46, 59–60, 120–121, 122–23, 167

Experience: Peirce's conception of, 33, 140, 144, 148, 158–59

Feeling: as vague thought, 57–58; as interpretant, 123, 136, 150

Final causation: 22–23, 80–81, 165–66

Firstness: 10, 102, 106

Fortuitous variation: 10, 73–74, 127

Fox, William Johnson: 169

Freedom: divine, 70; human, 114–16

Galileo Galilei: 132

God: Peirce's conception of, 3, 9, 13, 20–21, 23, 30, 40, 41, 48, 49–62 *passim*, 66–71, 123–34, 147, 160–61, 162, 163, 167, 168, 169; distinguished from the Absolute Mind, 54–62, 121, 168; as creator, 50, 66–71, 79–80; topological metaphor for, 51–52; divine transcendence and immanence, 50–52; as Nothingness, 70–71, 150, 163; and evil, 87–92; Royce's conception of, 119. *See also* Absolute Mind

Goodman, Nelson: 157, 159

Gospel of John: 25, 75, 78, 83, 89, 144

Habit: 18, 29, 31, 46, 54, 55, 69, 78–79, 93–116 *passim*, 123, 135, 137, 139, 150–51, 152–53, 168; scholastic influence on Peirce's notion of, 23–24

Haecceity. *See* Duns Scotus

Hartshorne, Charles: 160–61, 162, 163, 164, 171

Hegel, G. W. F.: 38, 47–48, 54 , 74–75, 114, 160, 161

Hume, David: critique of miracles, 9, 26–34, 156

Immortality: 41, 110–14; semiotic conception of, 114